Torn

Torn

Asian/white Life and the Intimacy of Violence

ANNA M. MONCADA STORTI

Duke University Press *Durham and London* 2026

Printed in the United States of America on acid-free paper ∞
Cover designed by A. Mattson Gallagher
Typeset in Warnock Pro by Westchester Publishing Services

Library of Congress Cataloging-in-Publication Data
Names: Storti, Anna M. Moncada, [date] author
Title: Torn : Asian/White life and the intimacy of violence / Anna M. Moncada Storti.
Other titles: Asian/White life and the intimacy of violence
Description: Durham : Duke University Press, 2026. | Includes bibliographical references and index.
Identifiers: LCCN 2025026864 (print)
LCCN 2025026865 (ebook)
ISBN 9781478032885 paperback
ISBN 9781478029441 hardcover
ISBN 9781478061632 ebook
Subjects: LCSH: Asian Americans—Social conditions | Critical race theory—United States | Multiracial people—United States | Asian diaspora | United States—Race relations—20th century
Classification: LCC E184.A75 S66 2026 (print) | LCC E184.A75 (ebook) | DDC 305.895/073—dc23/eng/20251113
LC record available at https://lccn.loc.gov/2025026864
LC ebook record available at https://lccn.loc.gov/2025026865

Cover art: Gina Osterloh, *Pressing Against Looking, Movement,* 2019. Archival pigment print, 34 × 43 in. Courtesy of the artist.

For my family

Contents

Preface

Never am I most in unison, most at one with the body and its meaning, than in moments of anticipation. In these moments, I am often by myself and away from home. On the street, on the trail, in transit. Sometimes there are people around, and even when there are not, I figure they could show up because they can always show up. What I anticipate is an encounter, usually an unwanted one. A comment, a touch, a prolonged stare. Anticipation has become my posture, a habit, and it takes many shapes. It can double as defense, a preparedness that stems from intuition, trauma, or anxiety. It can be a distraction. Hopeful. Like a routine, anticipation provides a certain level of comfort, less an ease than a bitter confidence, as if you were to suddenly slap yourself and see on your hand your own blood and the dead mosquito that sucked that blood and whose presence you accurately sensed. Even when I am wrong, when there is no pest, when there is nothing to worry about, I expect something to happen because it has happened enough times before. The past carries over. Anticipation is merely an aid for navigating the world, a way to brace myself for what has by now become an ordinary feature of life, and that is racial and sexual subjection, persistent reminders of what my body is to its beholder: worthy of remark, a source of confusion, a sign of desire.

Made ordinary, racial and sexual subjection remain foundational features of colonization, anti-Blackness, and imperialism. This is a book about enduring such violence, and I want you to know at the outset that I have skin in the game. Life experiences inform my research questions, and the scholarship I produce helps me contextualize those experiences. Here, at the beginning, I acknowledge my embeddedness in the work to clarify that while the work touches on individual lives including my own, it does so with the intent to trace connections, contending with what concerns us all, what I describe as the *intimacy of violence*. In these pages, you will come to see how imperial expansion ensues beyond national borders, extending into the psychic lives of empire's subjects. I will ask you to confront US empire as an ambiguous, obscure, and routine relation. We will set disparate cases alongside each other, widening the frame of empire while narrowing our focus on the tensions it engenders. Allow me to lead by example.

For as long as I can remember, strangers, even those I let become more, rarely let me forget the history I bring into the present. Misinterpreted as ancestry, this history seems to rest on visual markings like facial features and the color of my skin, a combination that incites inquiry and irritation. *Where are you from?* Let's get that out of the way. My mother is the first of her family to migrate to the United States. She arrived in California from Parañaque, Metro Manila in February 1986, just days before the demonstrations of the People Power Revolution took over the Philippines' capital city. She soon met my father, the grandson on his father's side of Italian immigrants from Lucca, Tuscany and Naples who settled in Chicago via Ellis Island in 1928 before moving to Southern California in 1952. On his mother's side, my father is a descendant of English and French settlers who made their home on a ranch in Bozeman, Montana.

Growing up, I came to expect the chatter and curiosity. *You're so fair. You have your mother's eyes. What are you?* A '90s kid, I was born and raised in Orange County (OC), California. I was never the only Asian in school, but I remember feeling both unseen and hypervisible because of the kind of Asian I was. Of course, no place is a monolith and the OC is no exception. Youth found me in Anaheim, Huntington Beach, Westminster, and Orange, each suburb lending a different perception of being. I felt most like my mother's daughter near the coast, our Filipino heritage unmistakable in scenes marked by white bodies, palm trees, and the Pacific. Traveling inland, I became more of my father's daughter, my freckled skin a confession.

I've spent the better part of my adult life making sense of why my body comes in contact with the world in the way it does. Too formulaic of an answer, ancestry never felt capacious enough to account for the body, its meaning and its doings. So, like others, I studied *because the knot in my chest will never otherwise be eased.*[1] *I read all I can for a clue.*[2] I learned that people retain remnants of a past that transcend their first breath. Like an echo, one may recall the presence of something given its reverberation, a clarity found through reemergence. These traces emerge in subtle and not-so-subtle enactments of daily living. No matter their form, the vestiges of history exist as historical record, material one may brush aside or attempt to chronicle and assemble into a repository. Sensation is evidence, bodies are time capsules, and lives are treasure troves—*the issue is to leave a record . . . a clue that will suddenly reveal the crucial fact of our connection.*[3] I began to piece together an archive of which I am included. It encapsulates a history of interracial and imperial desire, a history alluded to in queries about my background but most readily comes to surface when an interest in my race is contingent on my gender.

As a teenager, attempts to pinpoint my race were innocent unless they weren't, forcing me into a crash course on sexuality and power. Remarking on my *exotic* look, older men would invite me into their studios to photograph me, a predatory scheme. Rejected, their requests happened most when I worked at a frozen yogurt shop. *You can make more money modeling.* In my early twenties, I found myself back in the gym where I played varsity basketball. Sitting in the bleachers with my dad, I overheard whispers behind us as we watched my brother's team on the court. After the game, some kid's father went up to my dad, shook his hand, and patted him on the back, the way men do when they're congratulatory but jealous. *How did you score her?!* This was not the only time I have been mistaken for my father's partner or presumed straight for that matter. Even at the queer bars I frequented, in West Hollywood, Pomona, Long Beach, Santa Ana, and Upland, my kind of femininity seemed out of place.

When I moved to the East Coast for graduate school, I learned how to distinguish intrigue from affection, threat from good faith. In Washington, D.C., men have asked me point blank if I would be their *geisha girl* and *China doll.* At a Honda dealership in College Park, Maryland, the mechanic, upon finding out I was Filipina, made a proposition to me. Trained in Filipino martial arts, this white man with blue eyes wanted to coach me in the art of war, in its method of reaction and recovery. *The world is dangerous,* he said. I walked away as he went on about disarming an attacker. Some interactions seem flirtatious, unwarranted, while others naive even if blunt. In northeast D.C., at a park in Eckington, a group of middle schoolers wanted to play basketball with me and my friends. After a few possessions, one boy asked if I was in the WNBA, a question about my skill given my gender. He then asked if I ate cats, a question about my race. Elsewhere, like in Louisville, Kentucky, after I was hit by a moving vehicle, a police officer ran his fingers through my hair. Concussed and sitting on the pavement, I made eye contact as he spoke. *Your beautiful thick hair saved you.* Once in Durham, North Carolina, as I sat outside Ninth Street, I felt eyes on me. Still but buzzing, I searched for the pest. When I met the gaze of a middle-aged man standing across the street, he pointed at me and yelled, *You're hot for an Asian.*

Crude and suggestive comments, I've been told, will subside over time as I "age out" of desirability. I too have been told to be fortunate, that receiving attention is a compliment. I know, however, that these encounters have more to do with control than desire. I know also that racial subjection forces a reckoning with space and place. Outside the United States, in my ancestral homes, the sentiment rings clear. In Italy, I am Asian. In the Philippines, I am blessed. In a small hillside town in Tuscany, a woman exclaimed from her balcony, *Una China! Una China!*, alerting her family as I, the spectacle, walked along the road. In Quezon City, I see myself reflected most in billboards, the ones where light-skinned mestizas advertise American products. Before, such confrontations were shocking, sad, disorienting. Now they are the forecast, a prognosis, too likely to not foresee. What is familiar is what I anticipate and what I have begrudgingly come to accept.

When I cross paths with other Asian people with white heritage, a kinship occurs. In spite of our differences in ethnic makeup, it is gender and sexuality that determine not only how we navigate the world but also how we find affinity with one another. With cis women and queer and trans people, affirmation usually materializes in a look of recognition even if no words are spoken. Men, on the other hand, tend to initiate conversation. One time, at the Long Beach airport, as I was waiting to board a flight to Honolulu for the 2019 Annual Meeting of the American Studies Association, a veteran commented on *my beautiful hapa eyes*. We were in line for breakfast burritos. It was too early for this. Sensing my irritation, he reassured me that he wasn't being *fresh*, that he was married and hapa too. Sometimes I play along. I force a smile, engage, and deepen the encounter, manufacturing a sense of control. This was one of those times. I told him about my work and why I identify as mixed and not hapa, thinking this will put him in his place. He interrupted me, to no surprise, but then, to my surprise, he lifted his T-shirt, exposing war scars on a tattooed chest, scars he pointed to as he warned, *You die when you forget*. There was an arrogance in his voice, assuming yet urgent. I knew where he was coming from. Waiting to order, we diverged to small talk, which is to say, he asked where I was from. At the time, I lived in Vermont. He laughed. *Well, that's why you lost your color! It's nice, though. Makes your eyes pop*. Retreating from the depths, he could not help but comment on surface-level things, curtailing a bond with much deeper potential. He insisted I enjoy his military discount. I obliged. A year earlier, at Nellie's, a gay sports bar in D.C., a queer guy approached me. *Let me guess, your mom is the Asian one*. He was half-Asian too. I was in a good mood, so I asked him about himself. Growing up, he was made to feel insecure in his masculinity, bullied for what his race and sexuality did to his gender. Being mixed, he was told, was a sign of inferiority. *Our genes and bodies are weaker because we're mixed, you know.* When I told him about the concept of hybrid vigor, that some forms of racial mixture are viewed as superior or stronger, he was beside himself. *Stronger? Stronger? We are not stronger.*

Burdened by norms and expectation, racialized gender can be a site of pain, pleasure, and refusal. Susceptible to harassment, my Asian/white femininity affords a level of access precisely because my Asianness is whitened and my gender is femme. When this access configures my presence into a less threatening one or a more adept one, it is a privilege. When it manifests into hypersexualization or assumed subservience, it is not. Whiteness is an advantage no matter its form or dosage. Nevertheless, a proximity to whiteness and racial ambiguity can recast the Asianness of Asian/white life as defunct, less than. Palatability comes at a cost. Whereas this logic applies across all forms of Asian/white life, specific discriminations of objectification, emasculation, misgendering, and gender policing unveil nuances across feminine, masculine, androgynous, trans, cis, and nonbinary life. On the whole, we are desirable and/or despised. Adored and/or envied. Exceptional and/or criticized. We represent the sex act gone right and/or gone wrong. The uncertainty conveyed in the slash frames the variability of Asian/white life.

In the face of difference, there is one constant: a presence marked by the past and present of imperial encounter. Imperialism, by all means, sets off glaring and destructive reverberations, from intergenerational trauma and the assault on refugee life to the military's culpability in environmental disaster. Empire also resonates in subtleties. It is in the prying, innuendo, harassment, and erasure. Folded into the day-to-day, war and militarism linger in the shadows of Asian/white life if not already at the front and center, a material reality that once gave me pause but to which I am now adjusted. I expect intrusion. I expect violation. This could be read as submission. I see it more as the aftermath of a reckoning, the fruits of my labor—that is, as the findings of an investigation concerned with empire's quotidian life to which I am not immune.

I begin this book this way, with anecdotes, not to introduce myself or invite sympathy but to lay the cards on the table: Imperialism constitutes our present. It fuels battles for state power, armed insurrection, and the culture wars. It encourages silence, complicity, and violation, disciplining its subjects even those most anti-imperial. That we are engulfed by imperialism, subjected to empire's hard and soft forms, is an intellectual and political diagnosis, but it is also an embodied knowledge. For me, I sense it most in moments of anticipation, when the body becomes tight and weighted, tense and ready. For you, it could be more intense or less obvious. Although differently, we remain affected. This is my conclusion and our starting point.

Anticipation is one of countless strategies, no one more justified than the other, for contending with imperialism and its unwavering presence. Whether premeditated, inadvertent, or instinctual, these strategies are as much a method for survival as they are a sign that empire has left its mark on us. If we dare, these marks can become a means for critical inquiry, introspection, and coalition. They invite speculation and honest assessment. When and where does an empire surface? When is its violence most inconspicuous, most undeniable? Have we been trained to see the difference? My sense is that there is work to do. Questions need reframing, patterns await discovery. If you are to ask questions, ask me not where I am from, but if we are liable to an empire's extension. Ask me not what I am, but how we can be a source of its tempering. Until space is made to grapple with what underlies our present, that which not only binds us together but also distinguishes one life from another, we lose ourselves in the pieces.

Anna Storti
Durham, NC
November 2024

Acknowledgments

They say writing is a solitary process, and for me, there is truth and fiction to that saying. Now in book form, the ideas that live in these pages would not have found home here if not for my family and support network, as well as the training and long hours that took me away from them. What a gift it has been to discover the pleasures of thinking and writing. What a gift to have been nourished by the support of many. I only have deep gratitude for the process and the lives I have been fortunate enough to meet along the way.

I did not realize it back then, but I began laying the groundwork for this book in college, at Cal Poly Pomona, where I had the great fortune of studying ethnic and women's studies and the even greater fortune of having Anita Jain as a teacher. Through the highs and lows of undergrad, I worked various jobs and switched my major several times. By the time I found myself in Dr. Jain's classroom, I was a quiet but eager and newly politicized student, and she helped hone my passion, showing me how to read theory, ask the hard questions, and instill habits that still help me find a way when I am unsure. Thank you for everything, Anita. I simply would not be here if not for you. To my other professors, your generosity in the classroom and in office hours have become models for how I approach this work. You showed me what it meant to bear witness and listen, *really listen* to students. Thank you, Patricia de Freitas, Brian Foster, Terri Gomez, Toni Humber, Jocelyn Pacleb, and the McNair dream team of Wei Bidlack, Winny Dong, and Frank Torres.

As influenced as I remain by my college professors, now that I am one myself, I am just as moved by my advisees and students. For contributing to my work in profound ways, my thanks go to Hady Elrafei, Katherine Gan, Emily Ngo, Becca Schneid, Hanna Tawasha, Jaeyeon Yoo, Nichole Zhang, and Jess Blumenthal, who was the best research assistant, as well as the students in seminars on "Intimacies," "Race and Memory," "Race, Gender, and Sexuality," "New Directions in Asian American Studies," and "Asian American Feminisms."

Although writing was a predominately isolating experience, I felt extremely seen and supported as this book entered the editorial phase. I cannot express enough gratitude to the people who helped me reconceptualize and revise this book. First and foremost, I feel incredibly lucky to have worked with Courtney Berger, an editor as generous with her feedback as she is with her guidance, always insightful and full of care. My thanks to everyone at Duke University Press, especially Laura Jaramillo, Erika Jackson, and Ihsan Taylor for helping steward this book through production, and Elizabeth Ault and Ken Wissoker for their enthusiasm and generative conversations. I learned a great deal about the publishing process when I enrolled in one of Laura Portwood Stacer's Manuscript Works courses. Without question, this book is in its best form because of the affirming and constructive reports from two anonymous reviewers, as well as feedback and support from Ideas on Fire, particularly Catherine Fung, Rachel Fudge, and Cathy Hannabach.

When I arrived at Duke University in 2021, colleagues and students across campus welcomed me with open arms, during a pandemic no less. Although racialized grief and feminist rage seemed so routine during those years (and still), I go to work feeling inspired by many at my academic home, and for that I am grateful. I must first extend my deepest admiration to the student activists who long labored to establish Asian American studies at Duke, making my position possible. To my colleagues in the Gender, Sexuality, and Feminist Studies Department, I admire the depths of your intelligence and our commitment to March Madness; thank you, Rachel Gelfand, Frances Hasso, Lauren Henschel, Kimberly Lamm, Nikki Lane, Jennifer Nash, Gabriel Rosenberg, Nicki Washington, Kathi Weeks, and Ara Wilson. To my colleagues in the Asian American and Diaspora Studies Program, what a joy it has been to build with and learn from each and every one of you. Thank you, Calvin Cheung-Miaw, Eileen Chow, Jingqiu Guan, Aimee Kwon, Esther Kim Lee, Jecca Namakkal, Emily Rogers, Susan Thananopavarn, and Emily Wang. Duke has provided a vibrant intellectual community, and I am grateful to the many people who have offered their time, support, and kindness over the years, including Stanley Abe, Anne Allison, Amanda Archambeau, Nicole Barnes, Nima Bassiri, Taylor Black, Jeremy Boomhower, Lou Brown, Tracie Canada, Christina Chia, Leo Ching, Rey Chow, Sam Daly, Prasenjit Duara, Sophia Enriquez, Shai Ginsburg, Erdag Göknar, JP Gritton, Amy Laura Hall, Michael Hardt, Iyun Harrison, Matthew Hayes, Guo-Juin Hong, Hy Huynh, Tsitsi Jaji, Douglas Jones, Shambhavi Kaul, Ranjana Khanna, Hae-Young Kim, Michael Klien, Maya Kronfeld, Sharon Kunde, Renate Kwon, Christina León, Justin Leroy, Courtney Lewis, Ralph Litzinger, Cecilia Marquez, Louise Meintjes, Eli Meyerhoff, Johann Montozzi-Wood, Alex Nickley, Jolie Olcott, Michael Pascual, Sarah Quesada, Heidi Rodeffer, Carlos Rojas, Pete Sigal, Harris Solomon, Maira Uzair, Priscilla Wald, Gennifer Weisenfeld, Robyn Wiegman, Joe Winters, and Julie Wynmor. I am especially grateful to comrades and coconspirators who organize with Duke Academics and Staff for Justice in Palestine.

Material support is vital and too few and far between. I do not take for granted the generous funding and resources that made this book possible, including a Career Enhancement Fellowship for Junior Faculty from the Institute for Citizens and Scholars, an Assistant Professorship Award from the Andrew W. Mellon Foundation, a Dissertation Completion Fellowship in Asian American Studies at Dartmouth College, and a McNair Graduate Fellowship and All-S.T.A.R. Fellowship at the University of Maryland. Many thanks to the Asian/Pacific Studies Institute at Duke for funding travel for research.

Contact and conversation are also vital. I am indebted to the many audiences who listened, read, and offered generative responses to this book project. Thanks to Thiên Nguyễn, Chris Suh, and the Asian Pacific Islander Desi American Activists at Emory University; to Paige Pendarvis and the Wolf Humanities Center at the University of Pennsylvania; to James McMaster, Dwayne Wright, and participants in the seminar on Intersectional Masculinities at George Washington University; to Rana Jaleel and the cultural studies graduate students at the University of California, Davis; to Paniz Musawi Natanzi and participants in the roundtable on Knowing War at Duke; to Joanna Yeh, Divya Aikat, and the students in Asian American Coming of Age at the University of North Carolina (UNC) at Chapel Hill; to Elizabeth Apple and the graduate students and faculty in the Duke/UNC Americanist Speaker Series; to Rachel Adams, Jennifer Ling Datchuk, Jared Packard, and attendees at the Bemis Center for Contemporary Arts Summer 2023 Lecture Series; to Axelle Miel, Elaijah Lapay, and Duke's Pamilya; to Linda Galvane and the speakers and attendees at the Human Bod(il)y Waste and Aesthetics Symposium at Duke; to Erica Kanesaka, the organizers of Color Crossings, and the Pembroke Center at Brown University; to Ranjana Khanna and Duke's Franklin Humanities Institute; to Andy Choi and the students in Asian American Psychology at the University of Massachusetts, Boston; to Eng-Beng Lim and the students in Gender and Sexuality in Asian American Literature at Dartmouth College; and to Terry Park and the students in Asian American Performance at the University of Maryland. These pages, and my scholarly life more broadly, benefited from time spent with scholars at a summer research program at the University of Michigan in 2013, a summer institute in performance studies at Northwestern University in 2018, as well as from the engagement of fellow panelists and audience members at meetings of the American Studies Association, Association for Asian American

Studies, Association for the Study of the Arts of the Present, Canadian Association of Cultural Studies, Capacious: Affect Inquiry/Making Space, Critical Mixed Race Studies Association, DC Queer Studies, and the National Women's Studies Association.

The seeds of this book were sowed when I was a graduate student at the University of Maryland, College Park. I still remember that afternoon in early 2014 when Michelle Rowley called me with the exciting news that I had been accepted into the PhD program in women's studies. During my time as a graduate student, I grew as a thinker and as a person thanks to the guidance of faculty and staff. I owe a great deal to Bobby Benedicto, Lynn Bolles, Melissa Blanco Borelli, Elsa Barkley Brown, Robert Burgard, Laurie Frederik, Brittany Fremaux, Perla Guerrero, Eva Hageman, Christina Hanhardt, LaMonda Horton-Stallings, Luke Jensen, Seung-Kyung Kim, Katie King, Esther Kim Lee, Marilee Lindemann, Alexis Lothian, Karla Mantilla, Kai Kai Mascareñas, Nancy Mirabal, Robin Muncy, Rhea Nedd, Jan Padios, Christopher Pérez, Cliffornia Pryor, Iván Ramos, Deborah Rosenfelt, Michelle Rowley, Shige Sakurai, JV Sapinoso, Catherine Schuler, Martha Nell Smith, Ashwini Tambe, Catalina Toala, Sika Wheeler, Betsy Yuen, and Ruth Zambrana. Thank you, Katie and Ashwini, for your formative and lasting insights on feminist pedagogy; Nancy Struna and Martha Nell, for showing me what life could be; and Luke, for your vision and leadership.

To my dissertation committee, Alexis, Iván, LaMonda, Melissa, and Bobby, I remain in awe at your collective brilliance, and my thinking has benefited immensely from the time I spent in your office hours. Alexis, more than anyone else, saw this project in its earliest stages. As my chair, she read every draft and offered sharp comments, guiding me through its various iterations, and the PhD program overall, in a way that never made me feel inadequate. Somehow, I always left our meetings feeling like I belonged in grad school, a testament to her advising. Just as impactful, Iván helped me reshape disparate ideas into a cohesive project, allowing me to see the book's big picture while preparing me for the job market. Incredibly generous with his time and knowledge, he made each chapter and each cover letter stronger. I cannot overstate how special it was to have two advisers (both junior faculty, both Virgos!) be so incisive yet so kind. Thank you, Alexis and Iván, for setting the bar high.

As I was finishing my dissertation, I was fortunate to land a predoctoral to postdoctoral fellowship in Asian American studies at Dartmouth College. Gifted precious time and resources to focus on writing, I also met so many good people. Here's to existing on the same timeline in the Dartmouth diaspora: Charlotte Bacon, Shamell Bell, Alex Blue V., Kimberly Juanita Brown, Michelle Brown, Hazel Carby, Christine Castro, Alexander Chee, Carolyn Choi, Kelly Chung, Jorge Cuéllar, Misty De Berry, Marcela Di Blasi, Yui Hashimoto, Mingwei Huang, Sunmin Kim, Summer Kim Lee, Eng-Beng Lim, Najwa Mayer, Preston McBride, Jorell Melendez-Bandillo, Tyler Monson, Bethany Moreton, Lakshmi Padmanabhan, Aparna Parikh, Linette Park, Mark Ocegueda, Emily Raymundo, Israel Reyes, Evelyn Soto, Howie Tam, Michelle Thompson, MT Vallarta, Emily Walton, and all the faculty and students affiliated with the Consortium of Studies in Race, Migration, and Sexuality.

A project on Asian/white life would not have felt possible without the work of Wei Ming Dariotis, Camilla Fojas, and Laura Kina, who worked together to establish the Critical Mixed Race Studies Association. I thank them for generously taking the time to help me understand the field's history to imagine its potential. This is a potential I have long seen as already underway, in the scholarship of people who convince me that a *critical* mixed race studies (CMRS) is possible. For their vision and for their friendship, thank you to Alejandro Acierto, Bianca Nozaki-Nasser, Miya Shaffer, Alma Villanueva, and Roberta Wolfson. This book is better because of conversations and collaborations with them, as well as with other folks in CMRS, including Amanda Lee Adams, Sarah Barzak, Nancy Carranza, Greg Carter, Corrine Collins, Chandra Crudup, Lawrence-Minh Bùi Davis, Kevin Escudero, Eleanor Glewwe, Rudy Guevarra, Kelly Jackson, Naliyah Kaya, Nicole Leopardo, Lakia Lightner, Tisa Loewen, Thomas Lopez, Minelle Mahtani, Christopher Malafronti, Jasmine Mitchell, Andrea Kim Neighbors, LeiLani Nishime, Brittany Prince, Clare Ramsaran, Steven Riley, Casey Lu Simon-Plumb, Curtiss Takada Rooks, Ken Tanabe, Myra Washington, and A. B. Wilkinson.

In a similar vein, I could not imagine writing this book without the revitalizing work of Jennifer Ling Datchuk, Chanel Matsunami Govreau, Vanilla Honey, Maya Mackrandilal, Chanel Miller, Isamu Noguchi, Naomi Shihab Nye, Paisley Rekdal, Emma Sulkowicz, and Ocean Vuong. While it is their work that appears in these pages, my gratitude extends much wider to the many artists, writers, and activists who transform the way I see the world.

Scholarly life rarely feels easy to navigate, but when it does, it is because of people like Karen Tongson, a mentor to me and my PhD advisers. I affectionately call Karen (also a Virgo!) my academic *lola*. So much gratitude is owed to her helpful guidance and encouragement. For providing direction and reassurance at critical times, my thanks to Leslie Bow, Iyko Day, David Eng, and Julietta Singh. As I reflect on the decade-long process of writing this book, it feels special to have spent time in so many spaces, and I do not underestimate the impact of the people I spent that time with. In addition to those mentioned above, I want to acknowledge an intellectual community forged while breaking bread, sharing ideas, and commiserating on walks and over drinks: Aimee Bahng, Christine Bacareza Balance, DB Bauer, Rachelle Berry, Sony Coráñez Bolton, Sandibel Borges, Keva Bui, Long Bui, Silas Moon Cassinelli, V Varun Chaudhry, Andy Choi, Sylvia Chong, Athia Choudhury, Emmanuel David, Pawan Dhingra, Josen Masangkay Diaz, Patrice Douglass, Chris Eng, Ethan Fukuto, Linda Galvane, Irving Goh, Siri Gurudev, Jack Halberstam, Karen Buenavista Hanna, Huan He, Jennifer Ho, Rebecca Hogue, Grace Kyungwon Hong, Heidi Hong, Michelle Huang, Vivian Huang, James Huỳnh, Douglas Ishii, Rana Jaleel, Boram Jeong, Linshan Jiang, Aura Sofía Jirau, Moon-Ho Jung, Erica Kanesaka, Laura Kang, Simi Kang, Ronak Kapadia, Sarah Kessler, Kareem Khubchandani, Heidi Kim, Kevin Kim, Rachel Kuo, SunAh Laybourn, Wendy Lee, Mellissa Linton-Villafranco, Jonathan Magat, Martin Manalansan, Anita Mannur, Hana Maruyama, Daryl Maude, James McMaster, Victor Román Mendoza, Durba Mitra, Christine Mok, Amber Musser, Lisa Nakamura, Cheryl Naruse, Paniz Musawi Natanzi, Ly Thuy Nguyen, Patricia Nguyen, Trung Nguyen, erin Khuê Ninh, Mark Padoongpatt, Whit Pow, Nat Raha, Tania Rispoli, Takeo Rivera, Ramon Rivera-Servera, Cole Rizki, Laura Rodríguez, Elizabeth Hanna Rubio, Sasha Sabherwal, Nitasha Sharma, Mejdulene Shomali, Chad Shomura, Cara Snyder, Meshell Sturgis, Chris Suh, Kim Tran, Gina Velasco, Setsuko Yokoyama, and Sunhay You. I am grateful to so many others, especially folks at the Violence Prevention and Women's Resource Center, the Queer People of Color Collective, the LGBT Equity Center, the Speakers Bureau, and the people I grew with in classrooms in Pomona and College Park, on the dance floor, at the potluck, and at the dive bar. For this incomplete list, please blame the fault of my mind, the times, and not my heart.

Writing about the intimacy of violence has been taxing. Over the past decade or so, I have moved through old traumas and chronic pain, and certainly that will not subside just because a book is published. If it were not for care workers, healers, and doctors, I would be emerging from this work in a much more compromised position. I am forever grateful to Melissa, Ashley, Alexa, and Emma for listening and offering help and kindness. Time spent with Melissa, especially, has been transformative and grounding. I feel like I won the therapist lottery. She has helped me see and hold close the lessons I have learned over time, lessons about instinct, ritual, and endurance. Because of her, I hold even closer the people who have taught me these lessons and whose impact has gone the distance. To me, the hardest part is acknowledging what is no longer. We build intimacy with others, and sometimes that closeness meets its limit. Ties are severed. Companions become strangers or worse. How am I to acknowledge torn bonds? I could leave vacant the following lines, holding space for the unnamed for whom our paths do not cross in the way they once did. I could dare to spell out those names, bringing light to faded pain. I could even eschew the past altogether, acting as though bitterness has run its course, acting as though time heals all wounds.

Scars form. I remember.

So, what I will do instead is say *ingat*, take care, and mean it.

Now to the best part, acknowledging the people who bring me joy, calm me down, and lift me up. For your lasting friendship and so much more, thank you, Jaime. For making me feel at home no matter where I find myself, thank you, Amaya, Ana, Athia, Bianca, Cara, Chris, Cynthia, DB, Eric, Frances, Jess, Justice, Kate, Kathy, Kenny, Kevin, Khanh, Kim, Liv, Minnie, and Rachelle.

I dedicate this book to my family. I am enormously lucky to have been raised by a village and to have had elders like my *lolo*, Jesus M. Moncada, whose guiding light emblazons each page, and my *lola*, Aurea Jante, a matriarch who continues to nurture all of us with her warmth, stories, and love. I owe an immeasurable amount of gratitude to my *nanay*. Mom, thank you for your grit and generosity, for doing the hard work, and for teaching me what strength looks like. Dad, your endless support moves my goals within reach. Thank you for the time spent outdoors and for always making me laugh. Michael, you are my favorite guy. I'm so proud of who you are and will always admire how you bring our family together. One thing I treasure most about this life is being your big sister. To Mama and Papa, Tita Pachie, Tita Ana, Tito John, Tita Alma, Angela Joy, Matthew, Renuka, Tashi, Ajith, Maya, Nathan, Shane, Micaela, Phuong, Tito Alex, Tita Thais, Debbie, Tita Rose, Tita Bubut, Aunty Lydia, Uncle Mark, Jack, Daniel, and the many others whose love extends across a great distance and a long time, thank you. *Mahal ko kayo*. Speaking of love, no one more than mine deserves all the praises and pleasures of this world. Sasanka, your love is a kind that reassures, frees, and anchors, a kept promise I never thought was possible. Thank you for reading each page, easing my worries, and keeping me afloat. With Sesame, our home is a cocoon, your love a haven so nourishing I can breathe deep, come undone, and reemerge feeling better than before.

INTRODUCTION
Torn, Together

Strange how one can see the self as a collection of pieces. Strange, too, how disparate pieces, like the fragments of a life, can form into something neither broken nor fixed but whole. In *Half,* contemporary ceramist Jennifer Ling Datchuk builds a literal and figurative container for grappling with such thoughts. Part of the permanent collection in Houston's Museum of Fine Arts, *Half* is a pair of porcelain powder puffs with porcelain-molded chicken feet as their handles. On the left, a puff made of purchased black human hair stands on a blue-and-white Jingdezhen pattern, a style synonymous with Chinese porcelain. On the right, an unmarked white puff with hair from her father's blond toupee. The puffs, used to conceal faults on the skin, deliver a flawless rendition of the artist's race. Like me, Datchuk is of both Asian and white ancestry. Two halves make a whole. Joined together but in clear distinction, the puffs also invite speculation on the history of Asian exclusion and the present-day ruse of diversity, equity, and inclusion. Observe the blue-and-white patterned puff. Pay attention to its position, its edges. It is firm, resolute, and alongside the white edifice. There is touch. There may even be a bond, but there is no subsuming into the other. The line where

FIGURE I.1. Jennifer Ling Datchuk, *Half*, 2014.

color meets white is a border marking a rupture, an ending, a tear. I catch sight of a refusal to unify or belong. Despite what structurally appears as one cohesive piece, there is a split. Although the two puffs in *Half* meet to form one, the demarcation of difference remains stark.[1]

Coveted by the West for its pure-white color, porcelain originated in China around the tenth century and played an integral role in imperial trade when it was introduced into Europe through Asian imports in the fourteenth century. Renowned as white gold, porcelain's ascension into a global luxury item galvanized Europeans to discover the secrets mastered by the Chinese for working with porcelain in spite of its seemingly impossible properties, both strong and delicate, impenetrable yet receptive to color. That the chicken feet, a delicacy in many Asian cuisines, stand tall as handles on these objects of domesticity and beautification gestures to something explicit. Asianness remains even as it changes. With the middle finger pronounced, there seems to be an underlying gesture of defiance in this rendition of ornamental femininity.[2] Rather than force fusion, which here might mean condensing two halves into one lone puff, Datchuk interprets mixture as a process of becoming twice as much. In doing so, the artist tends to the irreparable—that which has reached its limit—not to surrender to negativity or cynicism but to insist on self-determination. On her terms, Datchuk fashions Asian/

white racialization as a synthesis between difference, touch, and the imperial conditions that brought Asianness and whiteness together. Strange, indeed, how one can see the self as a collection of pieces: torn, together.

To speak of being *torn, together* is predictably to speak of violence and to speak of intimacy. But suppose we take this analysis further to consider it a sign of the *intimacy of violence*. A deceptively simple combination of words, the intimacy of violence theorizes the pervasiveness of violence through the language and practice of intimacy. Whereas intimacy conveys closeness, sexuality, and a method of connection, violence subsists through a more excruciating variety—it can be described as colonial, imperial, state sanctioned, epistemic, racist, sexual, gendered, to name just a few—making it profoundly challenging to fully escape and account for. Resisting any easy definition, intimacy and violence both name amorphous relations. Brought together, the *intimacy of violence* extends an invitation to study violence through the ways it courses through patterns of intimacy, including romantic love, sexual desire, domestic living, national belonging, and other relations of closeness. As the theoretical framework for this study, the intimacy of violence reveals the more subtle and obscured harms of the imperial past. More pointedly, I propose it as a conceptual site to interrogate how and why US empire endures as a quotidian and durational feature of social life.

Reading for the intimacy of violence prompts attention onto how the harms of the US imperial past and present refuse neat conclusion, living on as a set of afflictions within the very bodies of empire's historical subjects, broadly construed. Attending to the long-standing effects of US imperialism, this book assembles an archive of empire, a record of objects and subjects—torn, together—that I have come to know quite intimately as a scholar who has devoted over a decade to searching through its files and, first and foremost, as a member of the archival record myself. The intimacy of violence names an inventory of embodied, psychic, and affective impressions caused by imperialism, be it war, militarism, forced migration, displacement, or a nation's exclusionary laws. I piece together this living archive to make the following argument: US imperial expansion transpires not solely on the shores, land, and sea of America's territories or colonies but through the everyday lives of the US citizenry and, more strikingly, within the psychic lives of its subjects.

That empire shapes the lives of its subjects is not an original position. There is a rich tradition of scholarship that accounts for the ways minoritarian life has been subjected, negated, and targeted by imperialism, and how minoritarian subjects have managed to outlive such forces.[3] What I seek to add to this is twofold. On the one hand, I focus on how imperialism cycles through the ordinary. This is not to ignore the role of imperialism in seismically shifting the earth's climate, refugee crises, and rise in fascism but to elevate mixed race embodiment as a key site for understanding the magnitude of US empire and its role in such catastrophe. On the other hand, in calling attention to the more obscure remnants of the imperial past such as the internalized contradiction conveyed in Datchuk's *Half*, I do so with an interest not in recovering, reclaiming, or recuperating that past but in tracing how one might otherwise attempt to contend with what often feels irreparable or incessant. I take as my point of departure the notion that racial mixture is an enduring social friction despite growing acceptance and demographics of racially mixed people and families. From this starting point, I make a claim for the importance of understanding the tensions and lingering effects of imperial violence particularly as they manifest in subtle, seemingly ordinary enactments of mixed race life.

Given that my project concerns racial mixture, readers may think of it in connection to the interdisciplinary field of critical mixed race studies (CMRS). Formed in 2010, through the intellectual and administrative labor of queer women of color based in the arts and humanities—Wei Ming Dariotis, Camilla Fojas, and Laura Kina—CMRS is marked by a biennial conference where scholars, artists, organizers, and practitioners contend with the flexibility of racial categories, account for the relative marginalization of the mixed race perspective, and reflect on the impact our racial world has on mixed race people, transracial adoptees, and members of interracial families. In its growth, the field has ostensibly developed a social scientific bend. Much of its research conforms to a positivist tradition where qualitative and quantitative studies on mixed race identity drastically outnumber those offering insight into mixed racial subjection. I see problems with this imbalance. Not only does a focus on identity, be it ruminating on the growing multiracial demographic or exploring an understudied group, align with the feigned anti-racism of liberalism as well as the more conservative racism of color blindness, but it also fails to meet the critical undertaking of the field. In my view, the *critical* in critical mixed race studies ought not to stand for an elaboration of identitarian difference but a pursuit of why that difference exists and how that difference becomes incorporated into structures of colonialism, racial capitalism, and heteropatriarchy.[4] Before all else, I am interested in empire's remnants, in their shape, guise, and contours, and in how one seeks to liberate oneself from their continuity. To arrive at this knowledge, I attend to the imperial forces that form contemporary Asian/white life, which is to say that I approach mixed-raceness as a means not to interpret mixed race living but to better comprehend the intimacy of violence. If, reader, you are to classify this project as a critical study of racial mixture, perhaps it will be because it has been my aim to deprioritize the mixed race *experience*, triggering an enactment of CMRS that has its eyes set on deciphering the inner workings of white supremacy, shared struggle, and the potential for solidarity beyond formal racial markings. Harkening back to the field's roots in humanistic inquiry, I examine Asian/white life as a means for tracing what I see are our world's *mass tensions*, the strains of subordination that are distinctly yet collectively felt across all forms of life.

Tension, therefore, is a key concept that arises throughout this study. At base, I strive to make clear how US imperialism simultaneously produces and subsists through bouts of tension—unmitigated yet nondescript moments of duress, strain, or inner striving—that shift how race, gender, and sexuality are inhabited by its survivors. Empire, to put it differently, has a material effect on subject formation. For my purposes, Asian/white racialization becomes the representative case study for such claims. Consider, then, as another example the following scene in Ocean Vuong's 2019 novel *On Earth We're Briefly Gorgeous*, a queer coming-of-age and refugee family history in the form of a son's letter to his mother, Rose, the daughter of a Vietnamese woman and a white American soldier. It is late in the day and Rose is settling in at home, lying face down on blankets spread on the floor as her mother is straddling her back, "kneading the knots and stiff cords" from her shoulders after a long day at work.[5] Rose's mother calls for her grandson to help her help his mother, and soon it is the two of them, one on each side of Rose, "rolling out the hardened cords" in her upper arms, wrists, fingers.[6] "You groaned with relief as we worked your muscles loose, unraveling you with nothing but our own weight."[7] This muscular tension certainly, most immediately, arises as a result of Rose's work at the nail salon, hunching over for hours on end, but "the knots and stiff cords" that her mother and son help to knead out result in a "relief" that is also, more pointedly, a sign of an intergenerational intimacy where the tension, while not permanently relieved, is transformed.[8] "For a moment almost too brief to matter," the son writes, "this made sense—that three people on the floor, connected to each other by touch, made something like the word *family*."[9]

The above scene illustrates the intimacy of violence as one of empire's quintessential attributes. Torn, a family is displaced from a homeland; together, they navigate a new country with one another. There is isolation and intimacy, tension and violence. How might one seek to contend with these afflictions? One mode is to give language to the pain. Trauma has become one concept used both in clinical and mainstream spheres to encapsulate an unending assortment of injury and suffering. A pervasive feature of social life, trauma is critical to the ways scholars have sought to understand the human condition. Where psychoanalysis claims there is no easy elimination of trauma, queer and feminist studies build on perspectives gleaned from holistic therapies, which provide tools to learn how to acknowledge, accept, and live with trauma, recognizing the impossibility of eliminating it altogether.[10] What I seek to account for, on the contrary, are the ways one might encounter trauma (and all it stands in for) beyond the acts of preventing, eliminating, or adapting to it. How, in other words, do diasporic subjects touched by empire otherwise contend with the intimacy—the closeness—of its violence? To answer this question, I engage tension as an epistemological measure and methodological anchor. My focus is on how one moves through tension, reconfiguring the shape of empire's residue. Think of the meditation on wholeness and animacy encrusted in Datchuk's porcelain powder puffs or the scene in Vuong's novel: "Three people on the floor, connected to each other by touch, made something like the word *family*." In the latter case, Rose's muscular pain becomes an occasion for familial intimacy where tension is neither destroyed nor disavowed but transformed, made into something that, as noted by the son, evokes family but also calls to mind what Datchuk summons in *Half*: an embodied state of having been touched and *torn* by imperial contact, and yet *together* as though to be torn is simply a sign of being part of something larger than oneself.

Torn: Asian/white Life and the Intimacy of Violence puts an ever-growing archive of Asian American aesthetic, literary, and cultural representations of racial mixture, such as Datchuk's porcelain sculpture and the character of Rose in Vuong's autobiographical novel, in conversation with feminist and queer critiques of US imperialism, violence, intimacy, and repair. My chief objective is to trace the ways Asian Americans knowingly or unknowingly contend with the divisive logics of US empire. More precisely, I set out to study the lingering effects of historical violence that translate into physical, psychic, and affective tensions in the bodies of empire's subjects. To do so, I follow a distinct racialized subject, the Asian American with white heritage. A figure with many names—war baby, love child, hapa, Eurasian, Amerasian, wasian—the Asian/white subject is not always born from militarized encounter or sexual violence but is nonetheless marked by a history of imperialism, which repeatedly places Asian and white bodies in close proximity, so close, in fact, that they touch, and through that touching they are thought to meld. Asian/white life is often measured against a common assumption:

that being of two or more distinct racial histories is to be rendered a body in tension, torn between two ancestral lineages. Rather than refute this stance, I propose a conceptual shift toward tracking racial mixture as an enduring social friction. In doing so, I observe the ways artists, cultural figures, and writers have either sought to or failed to contend with all that arises from living in the legacy of empire and, most specifically, America's unrelenting war machine.

Set predominantly in the years following the Vietnam War, this book argues that imperialism, like violence writ large, is ontological, giving form to racial and sexual tensions that signal the permanence of war. Given this permanence, I do not explore injury, trauma, or suffering as afflictions to be healed from or adapted to. Instead, I ask how subjects touched by imperialism employ an array of psychic and aesthetic strategies to piece together what empire has scattered. I narrow my focus onto Asian Americans with white heritage neither with the intention to dismiss the many other racialized experiences formed as a result of imperial encounter nor to suggest that members of this particular group somehow represent an ideal point of reckoning with empire's fragments. Rather, my preoccupation with the distinct subjectivity of being both Asian and of white ancestry is to create a lens with which to expose the fundamental logics of whiteness as an accumulating racial form, which is to say that white, as Haunani-Kay Trask has articulated, is "the color of violence."[11] In this sense, *Torn* shows how whiteness attempts to ideologically and fetishistically consume Asianness and how mixed race Asian Americans have either been willing or unwilling to accept that kind of capture. Chapter by chapter, I assemble a series of case studies revolving around subjects who can trace, in a matter of generations, some kind of connection to US imperialism, including America's colonization and imperial intervention in the Philippines, Vietnam, Korea, and across the Pacific, as well as its exclusionary laws, targeted incarceration, and allyship with other imperial powers. Documenting the leftovers of imperialism as they materialize in those belonging to diasporas across Southeast, South, West, and East Asia, I follow Asian/white life as an analytic with which to account for the obscure, unquestioned, or seemingly ordinary relations that have come to define twenty-first-century Western liberalism and the fallacies surrounding its compromising project of multiracialism. If the mixed race body is central to liberal claims boasting the benefits of an increasingly multiracial society, what I seek to make visible are the ways Asian/white racialization may challenge, even as it is thought to exemplify, the promise of US multiracialism. Throughout, I point to a number of cultural and political tensions, from accusations of appropriation and movements raising awareness on sexual violence to the rise of the far right, and I elucidate their connections to the permanence of imperial war. As host of these tensions, people of Asian and white ancestry become a timely and timeless point of reckoning.

Enduring Tension: Intimacy, Violence, and the Permanence of War

Let no one mistake us for the fruit of violence—but that violence, having passed through the fruit, failed to spoil it. —OCEAN VUONG, *On Earth We're Briefly Gorgeous*, 2019

Imperialism, which today is waging war against a genuine struggle for human liberation, sows seeds of decay here and there that must be mercilessly rooted out from our land and from our minds. —FRANTZ FANON, *The Wretched of the Earth*, 1961

An autobiographical novel, *On Earth We're Briefly Gorgeous* pieces together a series of letters written by a son, Little Dog, to Rose, his mother who was never taught to read. The letters, then, are never meant to be read, only to be written, provoking a confrontation with the rules of language and the desires it promises to satisfy. Folded into each page are fragmented recollections of refugee life in Hartford, Connecticut, woven together as an ode to Vietnamese life. Readers learn of a family who made a life in America following a war that lingered in memory and spirit. The matriarch of the family is the boy's grandmother, Lan, who worked as a sex worker for American GIs in Saigon. During those years, Lan became pregnant from a white American client and gave birth to Rose in 1968. Mixed, Rose stood out among her peers; "the children called her ghost-girl, called Lan a traitor and a whore for sleeping with the enemy."[12] These children would cut Rose's "auburn-tinted" hair and rub feces on her face and skin to make her "*brown again*, as if to be born lighter was a wrong that could be reversed."[13] At five years old, that same girl watches from afar as her schoolhouse collapses in a napalm raid. She never returns to school and thus never learns to read. By the time the family flees Vietnam for a refugee camp in the Philippines, it is 1990, and Rose is a wife with a baby boy, Little Dog. Once the family obtained asylum, they resettled in Connecticut. Not long after, the son's Vietnamese father is imprisoned for beating his mother. Rose and Lan both exhibit signs of post-traumatic stress. The first time Little Dog remembers being hit by his mother, he was four and he was teaching her how to read. In other beatings, Lan uses her body as a shield to protect her grandson from her daughter. "When does a war end?" the son writes.[14] This query summons Viet Thanh Nguyen's assertion,

"All wars are fought twice, the first time on the battlefield, the second time in memory."[15] For war's survivors, the intimacy of empire's violence persists even after asylum, which begs another question posed by Little Dog: "What do we mean when we say survivor?"

> I read that parents suffering from PTSD [post-traumatic stress disorder] are more likely to hit their children. Perhaps there is a monstrous origin to it, after all. Perhaps to lay hands on your child is to prepare him for war. To say possessing a heartbeat is never as simple as the heart's task of saying *yes yes yes* to the body.[16]

Here, the battles forged in the memory of war show that memory is not simply a faculty of the mind but an embodied affair where the aftermath of war produces bouts of tension ranging from sore muscles to domestic violence and laying a hand on a child. They also teach us something about survival—that it marks not only a beginning of a new life after war but a continuation of war's violence, causing one to question if there is in fact any afterward to violence.

Too often examined by its source, occurrence, and aftermath, the wars forged in imperial battlegrounds defy a linear narrative. Prone to reproduction, war and its violence are lodged within us, as survivors and as a culture. Here, the violence can fester even in spite of the passage of time or formal efforts to redress. War radically changes everyday life for Lan, Rose, and Little Dog, members of three different generations who witnessed and survived America's invasion of Vietnam. Imperial violence may subside on the battlefield, but it continues through PTSD and skewed life chances. For those of us indebted to and in pursuit of social transformation, there is much yet to learn about what imperial violence can look like and feel like, how it lingers, and how it may ripen into uncanny forms. To begin that work, one must first come to terms with a conceptual plight, which I stake as a central concern of this study: there is an intimacy to violence when surviving violence (as we all have to varying degrees) means not that the violence has come to an end but that it has begun a new trajectory where the living is left with the burden that is the fortune of living in spite of a violence that ceases to end. Survival, that is, names a condition of finding intimacy with violence's permanence.

As skilled as scholars, healers, artists, and organizers have become in differentiating between the many deployments of violence, noting the contradiction within their ties to narratives of liberty and freedom and building transformative movements to confront abuse at multiple levels, it remains undertheorized how one might confront what is arguably that most intimate form of violence: the one within.[17] While the mere mention of violence incites theoretical debate and conjures a familiar arrangement of injurious acts and harrowing affects, it not only names a threatening force or object of critique but a breeding entity that impacts our politics and our desires, even those we might be quick to deem nonviolent, anti-racist, queer, feminist, or otherwise liberatory. To suggest that there is violence inside each of us may seem pessimistic or obvious, and it may seem to evoke singular instances of psychic distress or mental unwellness, but it is rather to say that violence is an ontological experience, a relation of everyday life that elucidates just how *differently* at risk *we all are* under racial capitalism. In my conceptualization of the intimacy of violence, I attend to this difference through intellectual traditions like women of color feminism and queer of color critique, which assess race, gender, and sexuality in relation to indigeneity, migration, and diaspora. I am informed by conceptual vocabularies such as "the intimacies of four continents," "the affective consequence of colonialism," "the wake," and "remaindered life," because of their ability to frame the enduring effects of dehumanization as material and residual processes in need of address.[18] In seeking clarification of a culture's "residual" elements—that is, of how and why pieces of the past remain often hidden or undetectable in the present—I search for "strange affinities," discerning the nuances of "complex personhood" and "group-differentiated vulnerability to premature death."[19]

To help ground the stakes of the project at hand, I will now steer us toward an exercise in juxtaposition. I ask that you please review the two epigraphs that open this section. The first transports us to Vietnam and American invasion by way of Vuong's *On Earth*. "All this time I told myself we were born from war—but I was wrong, Ma. We were born from beauty. Let no one mistake us for the fruit of violence—but that violence, having passed through the fruit, failed to spoil it."[20] Here is a passage that points toward diasporic possibility, a rupture that releases the body and its bloodlines ever so slightly from the hold of violence, which in this case takes the shape of war, the United States, and whiteness, different names for the same thing. Little Dog confronts America's imperialist force with a sensorial recognition, pointing toward the body's ability to store past injury. Violence enters the fruit, but this arrival need not be a death sentence. While Vuong's words do not supply the details of violence's escape, they reassure the reader that it can in fact depart, leaving the body intact. It enters. It passes. Even as this rendition of poetic justice fails to apply to every refugee story, Vuong makes a world in which it is possible, overwhelming me with a series of questions: What must one do for the violence to pass through the fruit? If the fruit indeed is not spoiled, does it taste the same as it did before?[21] I wonder about the undeniable smell of rotten fruit and where the violence goes when it leaves. Does it vanish, fade, or dissolve? Like sweat, does it evaporate from the skin, becoming salt waiting to be rinsed off? Or does it scour to find another and go in for the kill, like salt to a wound? For Vuong, the intimacy of violence is that it punctures us, but it can leave us too. To scholars of queer and Asian diaspora, his words summon the unique injury ignited by the many arms of US militarism, articulating a grief with a potential neither to transform nor transport but rather to shift the gaze back toward us, an urgent lesson in survival and self-determination.

For Frantz Fanon, the mood is quite different. If Vuong's characters are simultaneously touched and untouched by violence, the subjects of Fanon's once-banned *The Wretched of the Earth* (1961) are instructed to be the sinner that sinks their teeth into violence, that forbidden fruit. Through a psychoanalytic inspection of colonialism, Fanon is famous for arguing that colonized populations—people who, in the colonizer's eyes and enforcement, exist outside the bounds of humanity and its moral codes—must resist colonization through the only language the colonizer understands: violence. Speaking specifically about the Algerian struggle against French colonial rule in the mid-twentieth century, Fanon defends the use of violence as the only true counter to a dominant military presence. Of crucial importance, however, is his resolution that using violence to facilitate decolonization will prove incomplete unless the residue of violence is removed from within: "Imperialism, which today is waging war against a genuine struggle for human liberation, sows seeds of decay here and there that must be mercilessly rooted out from our land and from our minds."[22] Imperialism leaves behind *seeds of decay*. That is to say, violence enters the fruit. In raw detail, Fanon records what happens when it festers within. Briefly gorgeous, the wretched of the earth are susceptible to "indelible wounds" that mar and threaten to spoil the fruit.[23] Like Vuong's *On Earth*, Fanon's *The Wretched* offers another lesson in life's prerequisites: Anticipating the power of nations that wield violence on a devastating scale means to become intimate with violence, learning its expanse and continuation so as to acknowledge how violence, like imperialism, leaves behind *seeds of decay* that one must *mercilessly* attend to, which as this book seeks to clarify, becomes a process of attending to the tensions that stem from the permanence of war.

Before I elaborate on how violence and intimacy coalesce as conceptual tools to track tension, let me first explain what I mean by the permanence of war. The phrasing is one I glean from feminist scholars of empire who conceptualize the ongoing effects of imperial war, globalization, and minoritarian resistance. Experts on the Philippines, in particular, have illustrated how incommensurable declarations of independence are with the continuous reverberations of US colonial and imperial rule.[24] Scholars of Asian diaspora more broadly have signaled the importance of thinking racial mixture as a central site for grappling with colonial and imperial haunting.[25] In addition to academic texts, memoir and life writing has seen a flourishing in work that seeks to explore the permanent effects of war as ghostly remnants or a life lived in fragments.[26] Whether through haunting or durability, imperial war refuses easy conclusion as evidenced by how its violence endures through affective, embodied, and psychic channels. The permanence of war, then, alludes to a set of interlocking global forces where subjectivity is made and unmade alongside the dynamics of nation, citizenship, and belonging that emerge after the official and supposed end of war or colonization. For my purposes, I track tension as the evidence of the ongoing-ness inherent to the permanence of war.

Understood as a state of stress, strain, and apprehension, tension brings one to consider the body and its ability to process, hold, and if one is so lucky, release whatever it is that causes one to tense up, be it a long day, a looming deadline, an eagerly anticipated date, or an unwanted touch. Just as one may seek relief from a tension headache, one may seek aid to help tightened muscles relax, which is to say that when one speaks of tension, one must also speak of release and relief. As embodied a phenomenon as tension is, however, it is also a social, cultural, and political relation. Racial tensions, for instance, reference a collective feeling felt by many, an awareness that things are off, on edge, or on the brink of disruption. That tension can sometimes be sensed by others may seem an obvious statement of fact, but it is precisely this sensing of tension that is central to the concerns of my study. Think here of the phrase *you can cut the tension with a knife*. This saying suggests an atmosphere is so tense that not only is the tension palatable but that there may soon be a break, snap, or sudden release, an eruption of stress rather than an easing or softening of the tension. Herein lies an important distinction: relief and release ≠ repair. If release connotes liberation or a freeing of pressure and if relief evokes comfort and the ephemeral, repair speaks toward remedy, redress, resolution. Release and relief, in contrast to repair, encapsulate brief, fading, and fugitive engagements, gesturing toward tension's opacity. What I'm after is precisely this sensing of tension.

For Rose, the tension that settles in after a long day of work calls to mind a claim raised by Laura Hyun Yi Kang in *Compositional Subjects*: "The bodies of Asian women . . . bear a promiscuous range of afflictions."[27] Here, Kang uplifts the Asian woman as a site to explore the epistemological and methodological directions of various disciplines, which then enable and constrain the composition of Asian and Asian American women as objects of study. In *Traffic in Asian Women*, she further takes on the figure of "Asian women" as a locus to tell a larger story about US empire in the twentieth century.[28] For many others, Asian women as a group differentiated by ethnic origin, class, and citizenship have been central to the formation of Asian American feminist critique.[29] The focus on Asian women, to be clear, is not sourced through an inquiry solely related to the experience of being racialized as Asian and gendered as woman.[30] Rather, the Asian woman is taken up as an analytic to observe and think through the ways gender and sexuality are factored into empire's racial calculus. By applying this logic to subjects of racial mixture, I propose that Asian/white racialization inheres as an imperial knowledge object, which helps to unravel how empire collapses into the lives of its subjects, manifesting as racial, sexual, and gendered tensions, not unlike how when a star collapses in on itself it creates a black hole.

My study is not the first to consider the ways history leaves its mark on its subjects. In my consideration of the multivalent meanings of tension as a physical, psychic, and sociocultural relation ripe for understanding the legacies of violence, I take a cue from Avery Gordon's elaboration of the cultural phenomenon of haunting, a sociopolitical-psychological state, "an animated state in which a repressed or unresolved social violence is making itself known, sometimes very directly, sometimes more obliquely."[31] In Gordon's account, haunting is seen to symbolize the complex legacies that find themselves existing, whether subtly or overtly, outside of their historical contexts. Gordon sets forth to understand how a legacy such as slavery has been inherited in the present moment, encouraging deep engagement with haunting's affective terrain as a starting point for critical inquiry. "To study social life one must confront the ghostly aspects of it."[32] What better way to begin than turning to Patricia Williams's *The Alchemy of Race*, as Gordon does, noting "the paradox of tracking through time and across all those forces that which makes its mark by being there and not there at the same time."[33] As I search for the intimacy of violence in muscle aches, conflict, controversy, political organizing, and self-doubt, I attempt to trace tension to its source much in the same way Williams does in the context of Blackness as she looks "for her shape and his hand," an endeavor to "track meticulously the dimension of meaning" of her great-great-grandmother and the white man who owned her and fathered her children.[34] To *track meticulously the dimension of meaning* is to confront the ghostly matters of social life with a precise attention to the ways colonialism, slavery, and war remain within the body. Insofar as I understand tension as unmitigated yet nondescript moments of duress, strain, or inner striving in which a person may soon give way to the pressure tension builds, I see tension as a state felt not only in the body but as a manifestation of imperial temporality. I view *moments* of duress, strain, or inner striving as epistemological openings for reconciling with historical violence and the ontological dimension of being torn, together. Throughout this study, I trace tensions through a mode of noticing akin to *conjuring*, what Gordon names a "particular form of calling up and calling out the forces that make things what they are in order to fix and transform a troubling situation."[35] Whereas Gordon has sought to link repair to transformation, I seek to sever these ties, employing *deidealization*, "a form of the reparative that acknowledges messiness and damage."[36] Moving away from the impulse to fix, I glean from engagements with Melanie Klein's theory of reparation, lingering with the irreparable qualities of tension that range from recurring aches and bad memories to the persistence of racism.[37] Sensing tension and efforts to ease or transform it rather than repair or redeem it therefore are my methodological imperatives for unveiling the intimacy of violence.

To this end, I theorize violence through the language of intimacy and thus I align my thinking with feminist and queer theorists who defamiliarize how we come to understand intimacy as an ideology mediated by national cultures and publics. When Lauren Berlant sought to make sense of intimacy in a 1998 special issue of *Critical Inquiry*, the underlying purpose was to reframe the ways intimacy had become an issue demarcating the public from the private, the personal from the collective.

> How can we think about the ways attachments make people public, producing transpersonal identities and subjectivities, when those attachments come from within spaces as varied as those of domestic intimacy, state policy, and mass-mediated experiences of intensely disruptive crises? And what have these formative encounters to do with the effects of other, less institutionalized events, which might take place on the street, on the phone, in fantasy, at work, but rarely register as anything but residue? Intimacy names the enigma of this range of attachments, and more; and it poses a question of scale that links the instability of individual lives to the trajectories of the collective.[38]

Berlant's sense that intimacy raises a "question of scale" similarly explicates what Lisa Lowe has shown when considering intimacy as a heuristic to discern the seemingly disparate processes of colonialism, slavery, war, and liberalism.[39] Shifting attention away from the *intimate* sphere of empire, which encompasses sexual, reproductive, and domestic relationalities, Lowe's use of intimacy offers a means to begin charting a *colonial division of intimacy* which unsettles the singularity of intimacy—which she traces to C. B. Macpherson's notion of the possessive individual—and thus makes space to examine the interrelated histories of colonialism that connect Africa, Asia, the Americas, and Europe. Contrary to intimacy's more colloquial understanding as a sense or feeling of closeness and a euphemism for sex and sexuality, for Lowe, intimacy endures as a political economy, a "constellation of asymmetrical and unevenly legible 'intimacies.'"[40] Likewise, Berlant proposes an engagement with intimacy's unevenness. By acknowledging the history of intimacy's public life, Berlant references Jürgen Habermas's formulation of the intimate spheres of domesticity, tracing the ways in which "liberal society was founded on the migration of intimacy expectations between the public and the domestic."[41] Intimacy, in other words, is a private affair living a public life.

Understanding intimacy as neither solely individualized nor private but collective and public is a prerequisite for discerning the intimacy of violence. Violence, by all means, is perpetrated by individuals as well as the state. While I discuss singular cases and acts of violence in the historical present, I do so with the larger aim to link those seemingly isolated instances to the structures that discipline subjects into committing violent acts. I treat violence as an accumulating process that not only inaugurates new and disproportionate effects against minoritarian subjects but also regulates the infrastructure of belonging that makes the US multiracial imaginary so distinctive in its ability to position its subjects, even and especially those deemed exceptional, outside the bounds of intimacy's promise.

Subjected by Empire: Asian/white Racialization in the American Century

At the turn of the millennium, *Time* magazine Asia made a bold claim. In their April 2001 issue, the faces of three entertainers—Tata Young, Maggie Q, and Asha Gill—grace a cover carrying the following caption: "All Mixed Up. Half Asian, Half Caucasian and 100% Cool. Why Eurasians Are the New Face of Asia." Uplifting Asian people with white heritage as a visual representation for a new, more cosmopolitan Asia, *Time* Asia takes notice of what seems to be a changing of the guard, a shift from monotony toward a *cooler*

FIGURE I.2. Eurasian Invasion, *Time* magazine Asia, 2001.

future.[42] In doing so, the periodical evokes a standard albeit eugenic interpretation of racial mixture: Asian/white life as an exemplar of hybrid vigor.[43]

In a striking parallel to *Time* Asia, the cover of *Time* USA's 1993 issue, "The New Face of America," features not three faces but one computer-generated figure known as Eve who personifies the issue's message: "How Immigrants Are Shaping the World's First Multicultural Society." Whereas *Time* calls Eve a woman, scholars have long shown how Eve functions more as an avatar representing a move away from the past peril of interraciality toward the contemporary moment's celebratory rise in multiracial citizens.[44] Indicative of how a "practical heterosexuality" is used to solve the latest crises of immigration, *Time*'s "New Face of America" cover dispels common readings of intimacy—like how we are often taught that intimacy is confined to the private realm of the bedroom or the domestic space of the home—to show instead how intimacy may function as a symbol of national identity.[45] Here, the product of interracial intimacy allows for the very interrogation of what it means for bodies to exist in relation not only to other bodies but also within

FIGURE I.3. A remarkable preview, *Time*, 1993.

or outside the larger body of the nation-state. The cover's direct attention to the mixed race body's role in shaping the future coincides with predictions seen in other publications, such as *National Geographic*, whose 2013 special issue on the "Changing Face of America" projected that by 2050, the average American will be mixed race.[46] Again and again, turn-of-the-twenty-first-century narratives of racial mixture veer away from anti-miscegenation discourse and embrace the seductive rewards of hybridity, which as I explain later in this section, reify and rely on utopian narratives of racial harmony rooted in eugenic interpretations of racial mixture. What remains significant about *Time* Asia is that it dives deeper into this fraught terrain, identifying the future of the Asian century with a Eurasian face.

Beyond one lone magazine cover, examples abound where Asian/white life epitomizes an ideal archetype marking the transition between the so-called *American* twentieth century and the *Asian* twenty-first century. Many of these narratives resort to techno-orientalist tropes as seen in Keanu Reeves's character Neo in *The Matrix* franchise or Sonoya Mizuno's character Kyoko in *Ex Machina*.[47] Others, like the popular photography books *The Eurasian Face* and *Part Asian, 100% Hapa*, join *Time* Asia in showing an appreciation of the mixed face, an aesthetic choice that works toward undoing harmful stereotypes associated with racial mixture only insofar as they incite a tendency for readers to view such figures as embodying the *best of both worlds*. This personification, the best of both worlds, emerges in subtle instances, like in *Time* Asia, and in more explicit ones, like in a phone call I held with Nancy Kwan in spring 2022. A self-proclaimed Eurasian and film star most known for her lead roles in *The World of Suzie Wong* (1960) and *Flower Drum Song* (1961), Kwan used this exact phrasing to articulate what she sees as "a benefit" of our shared racial identity.[48] Ann Curry, the American journalist, communicated the same sentiment in her foreword to *Blended Nation: Portraits and Interviews of Mixed-Race America* (2010): "For me it is impossible to say I am Asian or Caucasian, as choosing one would mean denying the other. No, the only way to honor the courage of my Japanese mother and white father to love in the face of adversity is to embrace both equally. As dad would say, 'You are the best of both worlds,' and so are the people you see on these pages, who cannot but strengthen America's dream, as they are living proof it comes true."[49] Being both white and Asian is seen to grant one the ability to understand two different ways of life, and herein lies a problem. To conflate Asian/white racialization into a net positive may refuse the older racism that criminalized interracial intimacy but at a cost. Not only is there an erasure of ethnicity's nuances, but there is a disavowal of the imperial history without which there would be no Asian/white subject as we have come to know it: the face of the future.

Broadly speaking, Asian/white intermixture can be traced to colonization, militarism, trade, global labor migration, sexual tourism, and international overseas study. In the twentieth century, the case of Asian/white racialization functions as a lens with which to understand the role race, gender, and sexuality play in America's empire building. One need only to recall the effects of the nation's landmark cases on immigration and interracial marriage. A dramatic shift from the nineteenth century, which saw the Page Act of 1875, the nation's first restrictive immigration law targeting Chinese women, twentieth-century laws such as the War Brides Act of 1945 allowed American servicemen to bring their spouses to the States following World War II. The War Brides Act helped to dismantle the era of Asian exclusion inaugurated by the 1882 Chinese Exclusion Act and reinforced by the Immigration Act of 1924, which limited the number of immigrants through a national quota system. In 1965, the United States abolished its quota system and opened its doors to those who President Lyndon B. Johnson deemed most able to contribute to America, "to its growth, to its strength, to its spirit."[50] Prioritizing family reunification, the 1965 Immigration and Nationality Act produced a wave of Asian migration to the States. By and large, people from Asian countries, particularly those most tightly held by the grip of American imperialism, began to immigrate into the country, a growth magnified after the Vietnam War and subsequent legislation like the Amerasian Homecoming Act, which facilitated the entry of applicants born in Vietnam and fathered by a US citizen. During these years, the Supreme Court overturned anti-miscegenation laws through the passage of *Loving v. Virginia* (1967). As interracial relationships and Southeast Asian immigration became more commonplace, the numbers of Asian children with white heritage began to rise.

Subjected by empire, people of Asian/white descent evoke the legacy of American intervention in Asia and the Pacific. A brief appraisal of the terminology associated with this figure makes this clear. Beyond the descriptors of biracial, multiracial, and mixed, Asian people with white heritage have been referred to by a variety of terms. *Eurasian* is most often used to denote mixed European and Asian ancestry. The term tends to be attributed to mixed race people born as a result of global labor migration and trade between China and the West in the mid-nineteenth century.[51] *Amerasian* emerged as a term in the twentieth century as a result of World War II, the Korean War, and the Vietnam War, each of which saw scores of children born to US servicemen and Asian women.[52] Amerasian has been used to describe children born as a result of America's military presence in countries like Japan, Korea, the Philippines, Vietnam, Thailand, and Cambodia. While Eurasian denotes part-white ancestry, Amerasian may describe an Asian American with either white or nonwhite ancestry, depending on the race of the American soldier. If Amerasian invokes a history of war and militarism, the terms "war baby," "GI baby," and "love child" take on a more derogatory connotation. On the flip side, the term "hapa" conjures an idealized version of racial and ethnic blending. An indigenous Hawaiian word that translates to "half," hapa has been used to reference those with mixed heritage in general with multiracial Asians taking a particular liking to the term, a history of appropriation I explore in chapter 1.[53] In the 2020s, Gen Z popularized the term "wasian"—that is, a "white Asian" typically of East Asian ancestry—with trends on TikTok such as "the wasian check" in which a child of a white and an Asian parent proves their racial identity by sharing family photos, removing sunglasses to expose Asian eyes, or revealing an assortment of Asian food in their home.[54]

Despite the variety of terminology, I opt for the descriptor "Asian/white." More than shorthand, my use of the solidus follows David Palumbo-Liu's move to recognize the constant and lasting rearrangements that have long designated the construction of *Asian/American*. Attentive to the porosity of multiracial whiteness, I utilize the solidus as a representation of the "*sliding over* between two seemingly separate terms."[55] That is to say, Asian/white racialization signifies multiple histories and embodiments of ethnicity where a person's phenotype is often understood as ambiguous. With *Asian* in the foreground, the slash invokes a possibility for ambiguity, while the secondary and lowercase *white* denotes a subsidiary position. Asian/white life, to be clear, is a form of Asian life no less Asian in spite of whiteness and its traces. To this end, Asian/white life constitutes both an identity and an analytic with which to examine the intimacy of empire's violence through the perspective of those partially responsible for shifting racial demographics.

The politics of multiracialism therefore name an important cultural and temporal backdrop to this project. Following the landmark cases discussed above, the racial makeup of America began to change. Growing numbers of interracial families resulted in the "biracial baby boom," which signaled a new division in American racial politics.[56] A largely ubiquitous interest in legally recognizing multiracial people and families created a divide between a conservative advocacy of color blindness and a liberal investment in establishing "multiracial" as a protected class.[57] Although the emergence of mixed race community organizations, university courses, family support groups, and artistic and academic writings—collectively regarded as the multiracial movement—stems from political activism during the civil rights era, the majority of the movement came into fruition during the Reagan years, coinciding with the rise of neoliberalism.[58] By the 1990s, these communities and organizations pushed for representation, and after years of deliberation, the US Census Bureau decided to offer a "check more than one box" option on the 2000 US Census. As expected, demographics culled since project a future nonwhite majority.[59] Obscuring the enduring legacies of colonialism, slavery, and empire, these statistics obfuscate how historical violence occasioned interracial encounter in the first place, helping to proliferate racial mixture. The pre-*Loving* peril and illegality of interracial heterosexual sex shifted into a celebratory rise in multiracial citizens, where Asian people with white heritage in particular were met with a peculiar enchantment. These racial subjects function as "servants of culture" or "children of the future" who usher the nation into "a new, more colorful sort of 'melting pot,' where racial groups do not separate and segregate, but marry and have babies."[60] As Kina and Dariotis argue, "the figure of the 'love child' has been transformed subversively into a positive (but still stereotypical) image of mixed race people as harbingers of racial harmony—even as 'racial saviors.'"[61] Asian/white life clarifies how race is not just a fixed subjectivity but rather a way of describing how certain bodies stick to certain spaces, inciting an account of racial mixture along the logic of interpellation, which yields the following interpretation: Asian/white life is simultaneously stuck *to* the future and hailed *as* the future.[62] Scholarship about multiracialism perpetuates this fixation on what lies ahead, specifically how the reproductive product of interracial sex is regarded as evidence of the "world's first multicultural society," a phenomenon variously identified as "national heterosexuality," the "general economy of racialization," the "hybrid future," "*la raza cósmica*," "the browning of America," and the "mulatto millennium."[63] The popularity of wasian celebrities may have prompted *Time* Asia to endow the Eurasian as the new face of Asia and, by association, the Asian century, but there is in fact a deeper set of circumstances at work.

On the one hand, the exceptionalism granted to the Asian/white subject evokes a privilege assigned to those with a proximity to whiteness.[64] Interracial encounters between the so-called East and West are seen to have changed the world for the better, producing a clear and uncompromising message: the twenty-first century is less white, more Asian.[65] For *Time*, this is cause for celebration but not without dangerous insinuations, ones rife with anti-Blackness, indigenous erasure, compulsory heterosexuality, and even anti-Asian racism. Where are Black, brown, and Indigenous people in the mixed future? Are Asian people more palatable or attractive if they're mixed with white? Colorism and white desirability inform such progress narratives with the assumption overwhelmingly being that the mixed child is born from a white man and a woman of color. What of the mixed race people neither mixed with white ancestry nor raised in a cishet nuclear family? Periodicals like *Time* and *Time* Asia may depict an important shift in a changing global citizenry, but they also illustrate a curious susceptibility surrounding specific embodiments of mixture. Vulnerable to whiteness by nature of a supposed proximity to it, Asian/white life sees that vulnerability evolve into a whitened Asian exceptionalism, an advantage granted to those who can conform to white standards of beauty through light skin and normative gender performance with just the added touch of difference, that allure of being half.

On the other hand, the racial and sexual logics at the center of Asian exceptionalism begin and end with whiteness, writ large. A construct of colonialism, whiteness is the standard and default for which other races are compared and measured up against. In the Americas, we can refer to the Spanish *casta* system, which delineated a racial hierarchy that named and ranked various forms of intermarriage against those with the "purest" Spanish blood. Even earlier, in the 1700s, the Swedish naturalist Carl Linnaeus developed a taxonomy of race, which classified humankind into four distinct races corresponding to the four continents known at the time: Europe, America, Asia, and Africa. Germinal work on racial formation has given us language to understand such modes of social stratification as a product of sociohistorical processes where racial categories are constructed, reconstructed, and dismantled.[66] Although whiteness is widely understood as a racial identity, it also functions as a basis for the right to property.[67] The rise of the far right as well as stringent work in critical race studies on such phenomena as "white rage," "white fragility," "white tears," and "white feelings" denotes whiteness as a porous omnipresence, encompassing a racial form, a nationalist agenda, and a structure of feeling.[68]

In the context of twentieth-century Asian America, whiteness functioned as the rubric for which Asianness was defined. From a legal standpoint, the Supreme Court cases of Takao Ozawa and Bhagat Singh Thind, as well as the California Supreme Court case of Salvador Roldan established legal parameters for determining Asianness in relation to whiteness. In a more everyday or *mundane* sense, the Asian American's unique ability to assimilate and be branded as a model minority allows access to a proximity to whiteness foreclosed to other racialized groups: "The paradox of Asian American racial formation," writes Ju Yon Kim, "is sustained through the mundane's ambiguous relationship to the body: it is enacted *by* the body, but may or may not be *of* the body."[69] Whiteness lingers within Asian America not simply as a rubric, a racial standard, or a residual marker of interracial intimacy. The whiteness inside Asian America functions as a lens with which to expose the fundamental illogics of white supremacy. Whiteness, without question, is a "bad habit" and a "truth game" that is "rigged insofar as it is meant to block access to freedom for those who cannot inhabit or at least mimic certain affective rhythms that have been preordained as acceptable."[70] It bears repeating that my preoccupation with the distinct subjectivity of being both Asian and of white ancestry is to explore how whiteness attempts to ideologically and fetishistically consume Asianness and how mixed race Asian Americans have either been *willing* or *unwilling* to accept that kind of capture.

Let me be very clear here. I turn to Asian/white racialization as a site to apprehend how racial difference becomes a nexus for laying bare the shifting terrains of white supremacy. Racial mixture, then, becomes the grounds for conceiving empire as a structure of racial subjection. What *Time* Asia and *Time* gloss over are the ways racial mixture continues to operate as a tool for maintaining the boundaries and falsifying hierarchies of race. Racist science has been paramount in this regard. Fabricating racial norms, racist science has sought to naturalize the construction of racial mixture as a means to uphold racial and colonial hierarchies.[71] Building on work demonstrating how such histories shape discursive understandings related to interracial heteronormative sex and the mixed race body, I side with criticism that suggests "we have yet to truly encounter the body, to learn precisely what it is or, rather, what it can do, to think creatively about its *becoming* rather than to pronounce upon its *being*."[72] Exercising an intention to observe more pointedly the effects of enduring a racially mixed life through processes of racialized sexuality and gender, I refuse and refute the preoccupation with mixed race representational narratives including demographical projections and statistics. Also, I operate from the premise that the psychic and embodied ways of analyzing race and genealogy deeply unsettle how we have come to understand racial formation as a sociohistorical phenomenon crudely assumed, by some, to be a biological fact. To this end, my study attempts to not merely delineate an alternative mode of understanding mixed-raceness but uses mixed-raceness to open up how we might come to understand race and racial form at large.

My stake in this work is to offer a critical examination into how the felt dimensions of Asian/white life unveil the structure of imperialism as an embodied palimpsest of past, present, and future. I glean from racially informed posthumanist thought, new materialism, and object-oriented ontology where the ontological conditions surrounding the organizing logics of race and racialization continue to redirect us to sites of matter, object life, and materiality.[73] In doing so, I address the flexible, perhaps unsettling ways in which racial mixture inheres within systems of oppression. It is not only that mixed-raceness emerges from the logics of whiteness but that the imprint of those logics converge and compound at the site of embodiment, objecthood, and traumatic feeling. From this angle, I attend to the subtleties of Asian/white life, eschewing the racial scientific study of racial mixture in order to trace how the violent history of imperialism emerges as an embodied remnant within the very body in which Asianness is thought to converge with whiteness, be it the literal body of the daughter of an

American soldier and a Vietnamese woman or the more obscure pair of porcelain powder puffs.

Epistemological Tensions: Race, Repair, Embodiment

There are three interrelated epistemological tensions that arise throughout this book. The first is one I have gestured to in previous pages and will now elaborate on at length, and that is the study of racial mixture and the emergence of CMRS. As a field of knowledge, CMRS takes the fluidity of race as its starting point, and as an association, it is most known for its biennial conferences and flagship journal, the *Journal of Critical Mixed Race Studies*.[74] Its mission statement foregrounds a commitment to critique "dominant conceptions of race" and "to undo local and global systemic injustice rooted in systems of racism and white supremacy through scholarship, teaching, advocacy, the arts, activism, and other forms of social justice work."[75] In its growth, CMRS has created as many members as skeptics, and in my view, the field has veered away from its queer origins given the trend to pronounce upon mixed race experience without seeking to problematize racial mixture as an object of analysis.[76]

A contested theoretical tension, racial mixture is both a fallacy and a lived experience. As a racial ideology, racial mixture has historically been operationalized as a scientific discourse developed through settler colonial processes of extinction and racial purity. Leftovers from racist science, both racial categorization and racial hybridity are grounded in the idea that race is biological, resulting in the fabrication of race into a eugenic knowledge object utilized to discourage heterosexual interracial sex for the purposes of preserving Eurocentric notions of white superiority. It was under such circumstances that racial mixture became inherent to the logics of genocidal conquest, racial slavery, and imperialist war. Racial mixture was not only the taboo consequence of the forbidden interracial relation, but it was also a strategy used to "whiten" nonwhite races through the reproductive labor of women of color who would birth children from white colonizers, settlers, or servicemen. The legacy of anti-miscegenation laws, the one-drop rule of hypodescent, mestizaje, and the documentation of indigeneity via blood quantum mark a path for interrogating the subject of racial mixture alongside the logics of whiteness, which view the "mixing of races" as both prohibited and imperative. That is to say, racial mixture not only became the central narrative in eugenic efforts to preserve the boundaries between races or even "whiten" nonwhite races, but it has also been used as evidence supporting the myth that the harm and peril that pervaded the anti-miscegenation past has been relieved through growing demographics of mixed people.

When faced with the biological, political, and cultural history of racial mixture, it is reasonable to note the propensity for whiteness to linger at the center as many in CMRS do. It is certainly the case that too often with discourse on racial mixture, there is a tendency to prioritize US-centric narratives of people mixed with white.[77] As a result, some in the field strive to "decenter" whiteness and uplift the voices of nonwhite multiply marginalized people of mixed race.[78] This endeavor to know more about the subjugated histories, imagined futures, and aesthetic alliances across nonwhite multiracial diasporas is necessary and pressing. As much as I align politically with the call to decenter whiteness, I likewise fear that decentering whiteness without also acknowledging its central role in the structural implications of racial mixture is to come short of a critical mixed race study. A disavowal of whiteness emerges in what is called a decentering. To fully understand the phenomenon of racialization, specifically multiracialism, we must come to terms with race's shifting forms and the role that whiteness plays in that reorganization of power. Whiteness, to put it simply, is the very sign of the intimacy of violence. Even though I am all for *decentering white people*, I remain more interested in a racial politics *in opposition to whiteness*, and thus I write toward a critique of whiteness in an attempt not to decenter it but to contend with its imperial life. To do so, I seek not to reinforce its hegemony but to tease out the methods in which whiteness deepens its hegemonic hold through narratives of racial mixture. Decentering whiteness in CMRS is not enough to eliminate or resist whiteness, which I would stake is a central aim in any field concerned with race and racism's death-dealing logics. Whiteness is the condition of possibility for the idea that races can mix. A critical study of racial mixture therefore must reckon with the conditions in which subjects become racialized as mixed. To that end, I treat multiraciality not as a white-free, white-marginal, or off-white beacon of liberal progress but as the colonial production of new race categories that utilize whiteness in the formation of racialized subjects who fail to fit neatly into already established racial categories.

My chief interest with CMRS is whether a field purporting to foster a critique of racial mixture in fact reinforces both the eugenic pronouncement of hybrid vigor and liberal progress narratives that suggest the ends of racism manifest through heterosexual reproductive futurity. Like multiculturalism, some interpretations of CMRS reify biological determinism, allowing white supremacy to go unchecked. Fixated on experience or identity, CMRS can precipitate an inability to acknowledge mixed race subjection as an embodied phenomenon that results when multiple racial histories converge in one body. Rather than cede an engagement with CMRS, I shift attention away from the boundedness of both the field and the mixed body to pursue an interdisciplinary critique of racial mixture. As with any identitarian field, CMRS will have growing pains.[79] It will fail, reinvent itself, and come up short again, as identity knowledges do. Insurgent modes of inquiry in CMRS are possible—they must be—insofar as its practitioners and theorists think more carefully about the habits of our thinking, which are, for better and for worse, intent on using scholarship to deliver us from an unjust world. For there to be a *critical* mixed race studies, that field must thoroughly reckon with the ways in which whiteness propels our treatment of racial categories as discrete entities. Deprioritizing mixed race *identity*, I propose turning to the "critical" in mixed race studies as a means of tracing shared struggle across and beyond formal racial markings. Doing so tends to the interiority of racially mixed life without prescribing it as inherently reparative or injurious.

This brings me to the second epistemological tension: the genealogy of repair and reparation. The reparative turn has shaped feminist and queer studies since the 1990s when theorists began shifting toward a reparative mode of criticism as opposed to a paranoid reading practice, a dichotomy laid out by Eve Kosofsky Sedgwick in her influential essay "Paranoid Reading and Reparative Reading, or, You're So Paranoid, You Probably Think This Essay Is About You." While some feminist and queer theorists have taken up the call for reparative reading, others conceptualize the limit of healing or "the ruse of repair," as Patricia Stuelke puts it.[80] Paranoid critique and reparative criticism are often understood as contradictory stances, and it is this assumed binary that my book seeks to unravel.

Like many Asian Americanists, I am drawn to the ways Asian Americans are negatively impacted by American imperial intervention, Asian exclusion, and racial fetishism, but I seek to examine such harms beyond the dichotomy of paranoid and reparative reading. Rather than search for the ways Asian Americans seek to recover from feeling torn (reparative reading) or insist on Asian Americans' internalized complicity (paranoid reading), I spotlight the unsettling affinities that emerge from empire's afflictions. How do some Asian Americans manage to sympathize with US imperial endeavors, the same ones that produced such devastating acts of violence against their own lineages? Why do political polls show that Asian Americans are growing increasingly more conservative? What fuels the desire for assimilation and national belonging? Whereas some may deem these questions the epitome of paranoid reading, I understand them as attempts to locate the paranoia festering within normative approaches to repair. I examine sympathy, belonging, and assimilation as dangerous reverberations of the reparative turn. The reparative, therefore, emerges in my study not only through critical inquiry and genuine efforts to heal but through what I see are its dangers: acts of disavowal or spiritual bypassing that in turn have the potential to convince us that repair is underway even if the harms have not let up. Ultimately, my attention on mixed race Asian America and the array of its unsettling affinities with whiteness, the nation-state, and neoliberalism—as I explore in chapters on serial rapist Daniel Holtzclaw, spree killer and incel Elliot Rodger, and the popular interior designer Joanna Gaines—argues for the importance of contending with the irreparable. Doing so, I insist, is not a paranoid stance but a prerequisite for ever reaching all that is promised within the broad rubric of repair, from joy and catharsis to the potential for justice and liberation.

What conjoins multiracialism and the reparative turn as epistemological tensions, it seems to me, is a mutual interest in moving past violence. That is, both multiracialism and the reparative turn, albeit differently, shape notions of historical harm and social change. On the one hand, multiracialism structures the central telos of racial progress, but as an ideological site, it can also lay bare the shifting terrains of white supremacy. In my study, I give language to the ways Asian Americans either challenge or internalize the logics of racial progress that have long fueled US empire. I ask how Asian/white life is folded into systems of domination. I ask how artists, writers, and cultural figures refuse, rework, or reify stereotypes of assimilation and complicity. In doing so, I regard the mixed body not as evidence of progress but as a recurrent site and source of tension. Multiracial literature, visual culture, performance, and installation art become critical indexes to detect the formal strategies and failures of attempting to ease tensions that stem from white supremacy and the permanence of war. On the other hand, the reparative turn has been instrumental in efforts to reconceptualize the meanings and enactments of survival. As students and teachers seeking to survive a violent world, we have only to remember Sedgwick's call to turn away from paranoid critique and toward reparative reading while—and this is vital—heeding Stuelke's repositioning of the reparative turn alongside US neoliberal empire. Doing so unearths how deeply implicated political, cultural, and theoretical investments in repair have been in colonial and imperial histories as well as emergent activism. Taking seriously the limits of reparative criticism, both in and out of the academy, as a response to state violence, I have found that tension reverts the focus away from healing, repair, and punishment in favor of a politics of relief summed up evocatively by Alexis Pauline Gumbs in the foreword to *Beyond Survival: Strategies and Stories from the Transformative Justice Movement* (2020): "You have survived. Numerous disastrous harms that could have destroyed you did not quite destroy you. You live. Beyond that, you must also acknowledge that the relationships, organizations, and spaces you have moved through have survived *you*, a person like other people, shaped by systems of harm."[81] Within these words lie what I see as a refusal to resolve, which in turn creates a potential to alleviate the pressures that burden multiracialism and reparative reading. If violence is pervasive, the human condition names a relation of enduring the unbearable. I am interested in how subjects have sought to make life beyond the category of repair. How, in other words, might a refusal to resolve animate the most promising enactments of tension relief?

The challenge in forwarding any theory on violence is to allow it the affordance to perceive the theorist's complicities. Another challenge is more methodological, which is to elucidate violence without replicating it. I seek to meet these challenges. That is to say, *Torn* is driven by the ontological implications of empire's pervasive nature, and although I will confess my own desires to reach the other side of violence—freedom, safety, forgiveness, return—I am more interested in formulating a conceptual framework for venturing through violence's expanse, slowing down the process Vuong describes as "the violence passing through the fruit." This endeavor not only necessitates a writerly comportment of pace and patience, moving deliberately to notice the violence as it evolves into bouts of tension, but—and this is of utmost importance—it means that any critic of violence, myself included, must acknowledge the ways that violence impedes all aspects of life, intimacy and knowledge production notwithstanding. To be clear, I am not making an argument about eliminating violence, what Fanon describes as *mercilessly* rooting it out. That, quite frankly, is outside the scope of any one book project. I also do not give attention to the revolutionary modes of resistance that keep so many of us alive in spite of it all. There is a long and growing list of queer, feminist, decolonial, and trans of color work on such life-sustaining and life-giving practices.[82] Instead, I underscore just how pervasive, normalized, and ordinary violence has become even in light of powerful healing-centered work.

I say this to explain my reservations surrounding a growing interpretation of healing, which has been encapsulated by some as "wellness capitalism" or "deadly biocultures."[83] Healing, in this sense, has become a cultural paradigm that informs the care economy and holistic health alike, impacting movements of restorative and racial justice. These paradigms of healing under capitalism elide and even replicate violence. Our present is saturated with positive psychology and desires for mindfulness, wellness, and willpower, forms of productive denial that take precedence over a critical heuristic for understanding how ordinary violence and harm have become. I have suspicions about the ways healing functions as a neoliberal distraction, deflecting attention away from the body, the worker, and the human where there is much to *nourish* and less to mend. In healing, the onus is on the human. My interest lies more in attending to that which extracts from the human, producing the very imposition to heal.

To that end, embodiment is the third epistemological tension that arises in this book. In critical theory, the body functions as a theoretical lacuna, a "blind spot" in spite of the abundance of scholarship surrounding it as a figure.[84] Feminist and queer scholars have long argued that the body is a socially constructed entity too often rendered male, cisgender, and heterosexual and, moreover, that there remains a tendency to regard the body, in all of its corporeal materiality, in discursive terms. Theories on affect have sought to bridge this gap.[85] Interchangeable with emotion and feeling, affects are sticky and visceral, and they are as attached to individuals as they are to the social and political world. The affective turn denotes a call to historicize subjectivity, accounting for differences like race and gender or class and ability along the lines of emotion and sensation. What this means for studies on embodiment is that the body functions not only as a critical epistemological tool but as a matter of methodology. Rather than focus solely on what the body can do, affect theory proposes an interrogation of what bodies are "made to do."[86] It is this query into bodily "doing" that I seek to explore.

To carry out this venture, I join theorists whose vibrant documentation of the historical present epitomizes the move to consolidate the study of race, diaspora, and colonialism.[87] I use intellectual tools—namely, queer of color critique, aesthetic inquiry, and critical promiscuity—to track the material effects of imperial violence by situating queer theories of temporality and feminist perspectives on positionality in relation to Asian Americanist investments in empire, performance, and memory.[88] Drawing on and departing from critical theorizations of the body, I approach Asian/white racialization through a queer reading practice concerned with bodily doing, where bodies are understood not simply as sites that store present and past pain but as entities capable of being folded into national discourse and nationalist agendas ranging from far right conservatism to neoliberal multiculturalism.[89] Challenging the traditions of critical theory, queer scholarship invested in race and diaspora wields a perspective primed to grapple with historically subjugated knowledge and marginalized subjectivities.[90] Here, the body represents a cultural form, historical site, and a mechanism for political expression where terrains of race, gender, and sexuality are seen as constitutive of imperialism, racialization, nationalism, and the impossibility of assimilation. With embodiment as a focal point, I utilize methods of literary analysis, movement analysis, visual cultural analysis, artist interviews, and historical contextualization to compile an archive of empire that functions as an instructive site to consider the political and ethical ramifications of multiracialism. By delving into this archive, I reveal moments in art, record, and practice in which the body—its literal surface, its embodied histories, and the ways writers and conceptual artists have creatively traversed and stretched beyond its borders—becomes the very site in which relief may become possible. To this end, I am especially drawn to scholars of minoritarian performance who follow in the Muñozian tradition of searching for the *hermeneutics of residue*.[91] Thinking of the wake of performance, José Esteban Muñoz asks, "What is left? What remains?" and offers the possibility that "ephemera remain. They are absent and they are present, disrupting a predictable metaphysics of presence."[92] I consider ordinary enactments of everyday life an especially ripe arena to track such affective correspondences.

By means of an example, I return once more to Vuong's *On Earth*. Part 2 of the novel opens with words once spoken by Rose: *Memory is a choice.* Little Dog wonders if it really is.

> There are times, late at night, when your son would wake believing a bullet is lodged inside him. He'd feel it floating on the right side of his chest, just between his ribs. *The bullet was always here,* the boy thinks, older even than himself—and his bones, tendons, and veins had merely wrapped around the metal shard, sealing it inside him. *It wasn't me,* the boy thinks, *who was inside my mother's womb, but this bullet, this seed I bloomed around.* Even now, as the cold creeps in around him, he feels it poking out from his chest, slightly tenting his sweater. He feels for the protrusion but, as usual, finds nothing. *It's receded,* he thinks. *It wants to stay inside me. It is nothing without me.* Because a bullet without a body is a song without ears.[93]

Is the bullet, this phantom figment of an unlived past, merely the violence passing through the fruit? Recall that statement. "Let no one mistake us for the fruit of violence—but that violence, having passed through the fruit, failed to spoil it." Somehow, we are told, violence passed through the fruit, sparing it from destruction, but perhaps it is rather that a choice was made, and it was this choice that, in a son's eyes, helped to facilitate the violence outward. Having passed through the body, the violence remains, though smaller and less harsh, like a memory. To survive is to live on with violence after the fact, easing tension time and time again.

> Yes, there was a war. Yes, we came from its epicenter. In that war, a woman gifted herself a new name—Lan—in that naming claimed herself beautiful, then made that beauty into something worth keeping. From that, a daughter was born, and from that daughter, a son.
>
> All this time I told myself we were born from war—but I was wrong, Ma. We were born from beauty.[94]

In Lan's renaming, beauty took the place of violence. For violence, then, to have passed through the fruit means not simply that an act of naming, an act of defiance or self-love eliminated the violence, but rather that a conscious choice, a steady attention to the violence was held by its person who then introduced something else—beauty—into the equation. Now recall the scene when Lan and Little Dog massage Rose. Tension relief is more often than not a collective affair, like intimacy and violence. If the bullet in the son's chest is older than himself, banishing it necessitates a return to its source, his mother, for it is her body that this particular violence entered. What he feels is not his but hers. Theirs.

Soon after the son's dream, he is asked by his mother again to tend to her back and he obliges, "releasing the bad winds" from her body.

> Through this careful bruising, you heal.
>
> I think of Barthes again. A writer is someone who plays with the body of his mother, he says after the death of his mother, in order to glorify it, to embellish it.
>
> How I want this to be true.
>
> And yet, even here, writing you, the physical fact of your body resists my moving it. Even in these sentences, I place my hands on your back and see how dark they are as they lie against the unchangeable white backdrop of your skin. Even now, I see the folds of your waist and hips as I knead out the tensions.[95]

Roland Barthes's *Mourning Diary* functions as a touchstone throughout Little Dog's letter, and it is worth reflecting on Barthes here. His notes on grief written in the two years following his mother's death illustrate a mode of reading intimately and against Western epistemology. For Little Dog and for Barthes, the mother's body should not be abandoned in life or in death but recognized and addressed for all its markings. In writing their works—for Little Dog, the letter, and for Barthes, the diary—they refuse the very methodological sign of Western epistemology as knowledge becoming Knowledge insofar as it is consumed. Their mothers will never read these works, but that is not the point. The point of reckoning is the body and its remembrance. Again, it is Rose's body that hosts the violence, and even though a family kneading out the tensions does not eliminate past injury, it does serve as a form of recognition, a kind of rehearsal or inauguration of continued living. Tension is a sign, which is to say it can be engaged as an invitation. You can say yes, no, maybe, or ignore it altogether. Tension may also break, a possibility that can produce feelings of anxiety or relief. Just as a mother's tension provokes a family to aid in bodily relief, my endeavor with this book is to notice tensions as they are and to follow how people have sought relief, not to claim that tension relief is ever enough to undo the harms of empire but rather that this is the place we must start in order to get to the place we want to be.

Attentive to Asian/white life, I cull from an archive less attuned to an official or legitimate collection of a people or a place but to what Julietta Singh has termed the *body archive*. In *No Archive Will Restore You*, Singh offers a sustained reflection on the urgency of assembling an archive of the body, "a way of thinking-feeling the body's unbounded relation to other bodies."[96] Part memoir, part theoretical prose, Singh's journey into the body's historical crevices begins with a summoning by the Italian intellectual Antonio Gramsci: "The starting point of critical elaboration is the consciousness of what one really is, and is 'knowing thyself' as a product of the historical processes to date, which has deposited in you an infinity of traces, without leaving an inventory. . . . Therefore it is imperative at the outset to compile such an inventory."[97] Gramsci's call to compile an "inventory" with "an infinity of traces" precipitated Singh's reckoning with Asian/white life, pain, and pleasure outside the strict limits of The Archive. The body archive attends to what our bodies have been trained to disavow like the bullet in Little Dog's dreams. Through a sensorial relation to oneself as a "messy, embodied, illegitimate archive," Singh dislocates the archive from the past, illuminating how archival labor necessitates an engagement with our own pain, sound, waste, and pleasure.[98] That such a feat is "imperative at the outset" matters for a political project inspired by Gramsci's revolutionary thought and requires one's curation to be neither complete nor selective but attuned to the body as an open and malleable archive containing traces of history. If, as I argue throughout this study, Asian/white life is imbued by multiple racial histories, then assembling a body archive attuned to mixed-raceness must acknowledge the body's capacity to cross borders delineating race, nation, and language. That Asian/white life blurs the lines of difference in this way gestures to something peculiar, perhaps even spectacular, about how mixed people may come to understand their unbounded connection to others, including those that came before them.

In the pages that follow, these three epistemological tensions collapse and break against one another. My focus on Asian/white life denounces postracial rhetoric claiming that mixed race citizens will repair racist histories as it also remains critical of the residual and oft-forgotten effects of imperialism that manifest in embodied living. Each chapter, overviewed in the next section, inspects an ordinary afterlife of violence, drawing attention to the varied dimensions of all that lives on in the wake of harm: nonbelonging, disavowal, complicity, mass violence, intergenerational trauma, femme uprising, and an urge to think, feel, and remember otherwise. What arises is twofold: an archive of tension and a cautionary tale warning of what may ensue depending on the methods in which one seeks to relieve tensions both singular and shared.

Tensions Unfolding

In *Half*, Datchuk fires clay into porcelain, reconfiguring one material into another. Her piece is a meditation on racial mixture and its peculiar relation to malleability. The aesthetic motives embedded within *Half* represent one of many strategic, instinctive, or unintentional modes of artistic and bodily expression enacted in an attempt to alleviate tensions that can be sourced back to imperial expansion and intervention. Throughout this book, I illuminate such processes of malleability—from Datchuk's ability to form clay into durable powder puffs to Vuong's scene of intergenerational tension relief. In doing so, I account for the ways one may confront the range and reach of traumatic feeling produced by empire. In each chapter, I focus on cases that exemplify the shortcomings of repair, and in turn, I think through the promise of orienting toward tension through a deliberate or latent attempt to alter the very form of American empire's strange afflictions.

Chapter 1 considers the affliction of not feeling whole in one's identity and explores the lengths one goes to manufacture a sense of wholeness. Through a critique of ethnographic photography, I recount how wholeness is pursued through the visual image, focusing on Kip Fulbeck's *Part Asian, 100% Hapa* (2006), Paisley Rekdal's *Intimate: An American Family Photo Album* (2011), and the Federal Bureau of Investigation's nationwide manhunt for Andrew Cunanan, the spree killer who murdered Gianni Versace and four others in 1997. A reckoning with the fragmented racial position and the ways racial mixture is folded into the infrastructure of settler colonialism, this chapter inquires into a seemingly banal act of cultural appropriation—biracial Asians and their identification with the term "hapa." I interrogate the complicitous tensions of this discursive co-optation as they arise in Fulbeck's work in particular. Turning to Rekdal, I highlight how one may pursue a decolonial recognition of settler complicity and familial legacy.

Chapter 2 studies the affliction of feeling out of place, traversing questions of national belonging, domesticity, and the reverberations of American empire present in home decor. I open the chapter with a vignette on Isamu Noguchi, the world-renowned sculpture artist, before I focus attention on the curious yet undeniable rise to fame of Joanna Gaines, a Texas-based TV personality most known for her role in HGTV's *Fixer Upper*, a home renovation show. Teased for being half-Asian, both Gaines and Noguchi struggled with feelings of shame throughout their childhoods. As adults, they turned toward art and design to cope and escape, enacting what I call *racial renovation*, an act of repurposing the racialized pain of past societal rejection, exclusion, or ostracism for the benefit of others' potential comfort and belonging. Reparative at times, racial renovation can also be suspect and, as seen with Gaines, deeply implicated with whiteness and the Christian right.

A brief interlude appears to mark a shift in the body chapters. Chapters 1 and 2 study Asian/white life through the arguably casual, more tolerable repercussions of empire, from cultural appropriation to racial renovation. The next two chapters turn toward overt but made-ordinary violences: Asian emasculation, sexual predation, misogyny, and racial fetishization. My hope is to guide readers in adjusting their analytical lenses to account for what lies beyond the most provocative and explicit details of a case, which tend to dominate our attention. Moving forward, sex is only part of the story.

Chapter 3 attends to the affliction of unjust treatment and the feeling of grievance in instances of sexual assault and misogyny. Specifically, I unpack the logics of heteropatriarchy that reside at the heart of the Hapacalypse theory, a joining of the words "apocalypse" and "hapa." The portmanteau speculates that Asian/white people in the twenty-first century will commit or be subjected to abhorrent acts of violence. The Hapacalypse theory originated on the subreddit r/hapa as a result of a series of cases in the mid-2010s—namely, that of Daniel Holtzclaw, a former Oklahoma City police officer convicted for his serial sexual violence against Black women, and Elliot Rodger, whose 2014 killings in Isla Vista, California, made incel (involuntary celibate) a household term. Attending to the details of each case, I juxtapose Holtzclaw and Rodger alongside the literary and performance work of feminist artists Chanel Miller, the author of the award-winning memoir *Know My Name* based on the aftermath of her assault by Brock Turner on Stanford's campus in 2015, and Emma Sulkowicz, the artist who carried the mattress they were raped on across the Columbia campus in 2014 through the durational performance *Mattress Performance (Carry That Weight)*. Through discussions of consent and accountability in the years preceding #MeToo and #TimesUp, I frame the Hapacalypse around a larger historical context of white supremacy, its investment in obscuring legacies of violence, and feminist opposition.

Chapter 4 addresses the affliction of being an object of racial fetish. Thinking racialized sexuality alongside anti-imperialist critique, I identify orientalist desire as a remainder of empire, focusing on the work of contemporary performance artists Chanel Matsunami Govreau and Maya Mackrandilal. By staging an encounter between white masculinity and Asian femininity, the two artists mobilize performance alter egos and queer aesthetics to rehearse the limits of bodily autonomy in the context of sexual fantasy. I argue that insofar as Asian femininity forms the object of imperial desires, it can also function as the basis for feminist revenge and resistance. This chapter locates Asian/white sexuality beyond the romance narrative, showing how it may labor toward minoritarian retribution for imperial harm. In doing so, I apprehend the ways neoliberal multiculturalism has further embedded itself within the infrastructure of everyday encounters, and I show how Asian/white life confronts the intimacy of that violence.

To close, the coda comments on shared struggle and the collective forms of relief present in the mass mobilization for a free Palestine. Israel's decades-long genocide of the Palestinian people cannot possibly be relieved. However, what I argue for is a consideration of relief as a relation of anti-imperial solidarity. I piece together protest slogans alongside Palestinian poet Naomi Shihab Nye's poems to decipher how the fleeting yet impactful moments of joy that arise in pro-Palestine demonstrations may signal a different interpretation of *torn together*, one not split by the punctuation mark of a comma, and thus not disjoined through pause, separation, or distinction, but rather one indicative of what it means to exist alongside or next to. Set apart only by a single space, *torn together* extends a culminating gesture to the book. Without the comma, the phrase offers a meditation on the ways genocide and ethnic cleansing—crimes against humanity too often minimized as global tensions in the Middle East—are resisted and challenged. Through mass mobilization and community organizing, these tensions are met with a momentary relief that may not undo excruciating levels of death and destruction but tend to the necessary conditions for shared struggle, keeping alive the enduring promises of multiracial solidarity and the antiwar movement.

1

SEDUCED WHOLE
Fragmentation, Asian Settler Complicity, and the Cultures of Appropriation

A whole cake, all for me —MITSKI, "I Don't Like My Mind," *The Land Is Inhospitable and So Are We*, 2023

We begin
whole. We corrode. —TAMIKO BEYER, "Dear Disappearing," *We Come Elemental*, 2013

In his Pulitzer Prize–winning novel *The Sympathizer* (2015), Viet Thanh Nguyen introduces readers to an unnamed half-Vietnamese, half-French undercover Communist agent who serves as the narrator of a story about duality and contradiction. Having survived the rise and fall of Saigon, relocation in Los Angeles, and torture and imprisonment back in Vietnam, the narrator adopts a skill in sympathizing with both sides of an argument. This ability, readers are led to presume, stems from the narrator's experience living a life of cultural hybridity.[1] The son of a Vietnamese woman and French Catholic priest, he is born in Vietnam and educated in America. For those on the outside looking in, these biographical facts become points of contention as detailed in one scene where the department chair of an American university shares his thoughts on the narrator's identity: "Ah, the Amerasian, forever caught between worlds and never knowing where he belongs! Imagine if you did not suffer from the confusion you must constantly experience, feeling the constant tug-of-war inside you and over you, between Orient and Occident."[2] In tension, East and West are thought to pull and tug at each other when they converge within the mixed body, *inside you. Over you,* the tensions between Asianness and whiteness call to mind an orientalist presumption that places white masculinity as the ideal counterpart to Asian femininity.[3] Regarded as "half" Asian, Asian people with white ancestry, like many people of biracial descent, field accusations of racial incompletion. Fragmented, Asian/white life is a life lived in two unequal but corresponding parts. Asian/white life, then, is susceptible to the seduction of wholeness, that elusive state so often denied to people of multiracial descent.

In the cultural milieu of mixed race art and aesthetics, examples abound where the pretense of halfness is interrogated, contextualized, and outright rejected. From the late 1980s to the present, American letters became an integral site to identify and reframe multiracial experience outside the bounds of dichotomy. Women of color feminists like Gloria Anzaldúa, Lisa Kahaleole Chang Hall, Cherríe Moraga, and the authors featured in Adebe De Rango-Adem's *Other Tongues: Mixed Race Women Speak Out* (2010) took to the written word to imagine a radical potential of hybridity, one that has proven to be as foundational to queer feminist consciousness raising as it has sometimes been complicit in the recuperation of coloniality and, in particular, mestizaje.[4] Quite different, texts such as Stephen Murphy-Shigematsu's *When Half Is Whole: Multiethnic Asian American Identities* (2012), Claudine C. O'Hearn's *Half and Half: Writers on Growing Up Biracial and Bicultural* (1998), and Teresa Williams-Leon and Cynthia L. Nakashima's coedited collection *The Sum of Our Parts: Mixed-Heritage Asian Americans* (2001) are more demonstrative of filling in the gaps of literary representation. Relying on liberal narratives of race and belonging, these works resist the splitting of identity that occurs in claims of halfness by ascribing wholeness onto mixed people who are perpetually rendered *not* whole.[5] Then there are the more informal embraces of half-hood that take place through casual messaging, such as the Subtle Halfie Traits and Subtle Mixed Traits groups on Facebook, which are branches of the original Subtle Asian Traits, or the "One Chopstick" group chat that features mixed-Asian students at my institution.[6]

While the literary world has proven to be a key domain to interpretate mixed race life, pop cultural representations are another site where artists have sought to contend with the implications embedded within insinuations of racial halfness. It may be that the written word is as vulnerable to reifying racist narratives of hybridity and blood quantum; however, visuality more readily conjures the racist history of racial science and, in particular, of anthropology and its colonial and imperial exploitation of the photographic image as a site of scientific evidence. Think here of Saartjie Baartman, the Black woman whose body was exhibited across Europe and subject to racist and sexual caricature. Think also of Dean C. Worcester's so-called expertise on the Philippines given his over fifteen thousand photographs of the nation and its people, and the colonialist work of Claude Lévi-Strauss, including but not limited to *The Savage Mind* (1962), his vast archive of ethnographic photography, and his photographic memoir *Saudades do Brasil* (1996). In contrast to anthropology's more explicit racist history, recent creative works use the camera for what seem to be good intentions. Kip Fulbeck's *Part Asian, 100% Hapa* (2006) and *Mixed: Portraits of Multiracial Kids* (2010), Mike Tauber's *Blended Nation: Portraits and Interviews of Mixed Race Americans* (2009), and Kirsteen Zimmern's *The Eurasian Face* (2011) feature a collection of portraits and responses by mixed race people as testimony to their existence, their humanity, and in the case of Fulbeck's *100% Hapa*, their wholeness.[7] In these works, the photographic subject returns the gaze as their portrait is juxtaposed with their own words on multiracial life. There is a drive to celebrate and depict a "new" group. There is assumed consent between photographer and subject, and yet, there remains a cruel resemblance between history and the present when a photograph is captured to produce a racial precedent. Consider these introductory words in *The Eurasian Face*: "Much of the glory in being Eurasian lies in being different, exotic even. Revelling in our uniqueness, we are nevertheless struck with anxiety over our identity and the human need to belong to an identifiable group of people. It was partly this contradiction which compelled me to create this book. Through the photographs, I hope to show whilst each Eurasian is unique, we all share a 'look' that is distinctively Eurasian, a look that lends us an ethnic identity of our very own."[8] Using the visual image as evidence, twenty-first-century photographic collections of multiracial life and interracial families seek to add more layers to the ways we have come to demarcate race. In hindsight, it is incontestable that early anthropological photography was inherently racist particularly when used to support scientific claims of racial inferiority and superiority. In the present, however, a portrait of a face and an interview combine to reclaim the mixing of races, a phenomenon now rendered "fresh and original," "timely," or "funny, touching, and sexy!"[9]

The mixed race portrait may satisfy a desire to be represented, a reasonable desire for anyone who has not felt seen, but it also, I argue, becomes a prime site to explore the enduring effects of America's colonial mission and imperial expansion, which are never not present even and especially within cultural objects deemed worthy of praise, purchase, and consumption. This chapter addresses the sociopolitical weight tied to the photographic image as a means to study the seemingly innocent desire for wholeness that emerges across Asian/white life. If wholeness stands in for belonging, community, and recognition, it also names a myth forwarded by racial science: whole > half. Critics and cultural producers have long demanded a refusal of hierarchies based on blood quantum by insisting on the wholeness of racially mixed life. Seduced whole, which is to say, enthralled by the lure of representation, Asian/white life can fall victim to logics of progress and disavowal, which linger in the frame of a photograph, reproducing the very dynamics that brought one to find solace in the visual image. In reaching toward wholeness, what exactly fills the gap? What is foreclosed? What remains in pieces? There is an unsettling fragmentation, in other words, to Asian/white life. This chapter traces the desires that unfold from the fragmented position, exposing the specter of imperial expansion that takes root and materializes in the spaces left unfilled by the affliction of *not* feeling whole.

At Face Value: Andrew Cunanan "Pushed to the Limit"

The largest failed manhunt in American history startled the nation with its share of sex and violence as it also marked the rise of twenty-first-century multiracialism and the cultural compulsion for seeking proof and validation in the photographic image.[10] It all came to a head in 1997. Just four years after *Time*'s "The New Face of America" issue hit the newsstands, the most wanted man in America was Andrew Phillip Cunanan, a twenty-seven-year-old gay Filipino and Italian American whose killing spree captured the attention of so many that summer of '97. From April to July, Cunanan had killed five men across such varied terrains as Minneapolis, rural Minnesota, Chicago, southwest New Jersey, and Miami's South Beach. One was brutally bludgeoned with a hammer, one was bound and stabbed multiple times with a screwdriver before his throat was slit with a garden saw, and three were shot. Each of his victims were white men; all but one inhabited same-sex desire. On July 23, the death toll rose to six when the spree killer shot himself in a houseboat on South Beach. It was only then when the police found him. Throughout those four months, Cunanan had avoided capture even after he became a fugitive on the Federal Bureau of Investigation's (FBI's) Most Wanted list in early May. Hiding away in Miami for the final two months of his life, he broke into the FBI's Ten Most Wanted list a month later, on June 12, a rather ironic christening on the anniversary of the historic court decision for interracial marriage, a day known as Loving Day.[11] Wanted and wanting, Cunanan lurked unseen as images of his face were broadcast across American TV screens. On the Most Wanted posters, his photos were joined with descriptions of his "white" race and a warning of his "ties to the gay community."[12] A grisly departure from the more melancholic or endearing stories of mixed race life we have come to expect since the turn of the century, Cunanan's case raises questions on the visibility and recognition of mixed race subjectivity that fall out of the heteronormative frame. A failed manhunt, yes, Cunanan's case also functions as a baseline in this chapter's attempt to make known the enduring though less explicit fragmentations brought on by American empire.

By the time Cunanan's story reached headlines, those who consumed popular print and television media within the premillennial cultural moment were growing more and more accustomed to news of racialized, sexualized, and sensationalized violence. His killings emerged three years after O. J. Simpson's heavily publicized murder trial, five years after the LA riots, and at the peak of HIV transmission. Commentary on Cunanan, however, repeatedly disavowed his race, even as it highlighted the killer's unique flexibility. The *Los Angeles Times* called Cunanan a "chameleon," and other news sources zeroed in on his ability to shapeshift.[13] We know now that Cunanan was not white in the way people thought he was, but this was clearly not a fact evidenced by pictures of his face, at least not to the masses. Circulating across TV and print media, Cunanan's face became the deracinated face of infamy where whiteness was wrongly taken at face value. Tales of his escorting, preference for BDSM, and gay-targeted murders were more newsworthy than his Asianness. Perhaps this is a justified attention toward scandal. Or perhaps the public needed more racial guidance. While *Time*'s 1993 cover provided a blueprint for tracking racial ambiguity, Cunanan's deviancy could never fit that reproductive mold. Pushed to the wayside, his racialization surfaced only by means of its operative function—an ability to roam under the guise of many names, marked by a lethal ability to adapt.

Without a race worth commenting on, Cunanan offers a stark contradiction to another integral though less rousing event of multiraciality that occurred in the same calendar year: the rise of Tiger Woods. At twenty-one years old and less than one year after turning pro, Woods became an international sensation when he won the Master's Tournament on April 13, 1997, making him the youngest and first person of color to win a major golf championship. Off the golf course, Woods was heralded as "America's son."[14] Born to a Black, Chinese, and Indigenous father and a Thai, Chinese, and Dutch mother, Tiger Woods was, for a time, the poster child for multiracial America.[15] His Nike sponsorship resulted in multiple advertisements geared toward issues of race and belonging. One ad titled "I Am Tiger Woods" features a number of children of all races taking a pause from playing golf to stare into the camera and declare "I am Tiger Woods." Tiger, with ancestry shared by so many, is mixedness personified. America's most wanted. His face is the reflection the future generation sees in the mirror. It is as though the children's declaration is paired with a rhetorical question: Aren't we all mixed, anyway? Another Nike advertisement narrates a number of his accomplishments alongside the fact that, at the time, he was not allowed to play on several courses because of his Black ancestry. Tiger was not only a rising champion but a glorified icon of the nation's more inclusive future. His professional success and growing fame landed him a seat as a guest on the *Oprah Winfrey Show* on April 24, 1997—three days before Cunanan's first murder—where Tiger famously identified himself as "Cablinasian," a meshing together of Caucasian, Black, Indian, and Asian.

Woods's Blackness did not afford him the ability to shape-shift, pass, or hide in ways Cunanan could, a privilege assigned to those with whitened phenotypes. Unlike the case of Asian/white life, ambiguous forms of Black life incite their own set of questions including ones that destabilize what we think we know about race, colonialism, and racial fluidity.[16] Whereas it would be more than a decade until the public would grapple with Woods's own sexual scandals, Cunanan's notoriety has waned as the years go on. In 1997, his motives were a hotly debated topic with some blaming his sadomasochism while others falsely speculating his drive to kill resulted from his being HIV positive. Autopsy reports evidenced that the murderer was in fact HIV negative, but those close to him confirm that the "gay gigolo" practiced S&M.[17] In the decades since his murder spree, facts and uncertainties continue to collide, but his story only rarely creeps into the present. One exception is FX's *American Crime Story: The Assassination of Gianni Versace*, a single-season special on Cunanan's case, which aired in early 2018. Indeed, Cunanan's last victim, Italian fashion designer Gianni Versace, is likely the man most remembered and most mourned in the spree killings, but it is Cunanan who continues to provide great clarity onto the transitional moment that saw the wake of the AIDS crisis and the rise of multiracial nationalism.

For these reasons and more, Cunanan has long been a figure of scholarly fascination. Queer and critical race scholars have shown how the man's notoriety incites a larger discussion on the colonial fantasies unique to Filipino America.[18] At the time of his killing spree, mainstream US media outlets were apt to discuss the most intimate details about the man's sexual life, but what evaded the American media frenzy was a thorough engagement with the killer's mixed Filipino and Italian heritage. Filipino American news outlets, however, did the opposite, focusing heavily on his Filipinoness never minding his homosexuality. Eerily voted by his high school classmates "Most Likely to Be Remembered," Cunanan was a clever, preppy, and precocious boy with an IQ of 147.[19] He relished being the center of attention, known to tell extravagant and irrational stories of his familial life that fed his reputation as a prolific liar. Could his lust for luxury and aspirational elitism be what made him so unforgettable? Or might it be that his status as worth remembering is contingent on what was withheld from those around him, on what escaped our collective memory of him? For all his boasting about his lavish personal life, Cunanan rarely invited friends into his home, shielding them from the humble life he wished was not his. By not disclosing his Filipino heritage to those nearest to him, Cunanan navigated his youth mostly unracialized, living on as the white-passing, vaguely brown, mixed race subject unaware of how his embodied imperial history haunted the colonial present. That Cunanan's multiracial ancestry so often went mishandled and unremembered—by US media unsurprisingly, by himself more significantly—provokes an exploration into the ways racial deception functions as a backdrop to the disavowed, the denied, and the oft-forgotten elements embedded within the cultural politics of American multiracialism at the turn of the century. His story, to be sure, demonstrates the intimate connection between US imperialism, transnational migration, and sexual politics, but it also proves instructive in examining what festers in one's pursuit of racial wholeness.

Born in 1969 to Modesto "Pete" Cunanan, a Philippine-born US Navy hospital corpsman, and MaryAnn Schillaci, an Italian American, Andrew Cunanan spent his formative years in San Diego, a racially diverse coastal city known both as a US borderland and a home for military families. As a child whose ancestry crosses the Pacific and extends across multiple generations of US immigration, Cunanan is more than a representative of American empire. The son of a Filipino father and Italian Catholic mother, Cunanan certainly carries the legacy of interracial desire, but with his labor in sexual economies, his is a legacy rooted in the "sexual fields of empire" as Emmanuel David puts it.[20] Seduced by fame and fortune, Cunanan was a seducer himself. Suffice it to say, he was attractive and men wanted him. Cunanan knew this and capitalized on it, working as an escort and traveling the world with his wealthy and much older white clients. According to Allan Punzalan Isaac, it was Cunanan's association with the "gay demimonde" that aided in his "glaring, if not blinding, whiteness."[21] Enraptured by stories of his illicit sex as both a gay man and sex worker, the American public could not place Cunanan as the Filipino he was, disallowing a thorough investigation into the imperial roots that were in fact the condition of possibility for his multiraciality, let alone his violent rampage. In *American Tropics,* Isaac begins with Cunanan as a means to reference the "unrecognizability" of the Filipino American.[22] Analyzing the enduring imperialism at the core of US fantasies about its former colony, Isaac reveals how a "U.S. American imperial grammar" produces, surveils, and patrols racialized and colonized subjects.[23] He writes, "One of the many trajectories of the Asian American body, Andrew's refuses closure and raises questions about the stability of 'ethnic' categories in light of an American colonial legacy and the movement and enfolding of fantasies and borders."[24] Cunanan's case does not only shatter the American public's mishandled conception of Filipino America, but it speaks to the nation's more comprehensive issues with race, sexuality, and colonialism's unending presence.

To consider Cunanan's story not only one of violent masculinity, therefore, not just of murder and US imperialism but of racial seduction and disavowal, is to understand that empire and sex go hand in hand. Eng-Beng Lim sums it up in his theorizing on the colonial dyad, a historically charged coupling between the white man and the native boy. The white man is a colonial subject "imbued with gravitas and mobility" while the native boy subsists as object, "infantile, tricky, and bound by tradition."[25] Like Isaac, Lim acknowledges Cunanan as a native boy indexed between unrecognizability and America's cultural amnesia, "a terrifying racial allegory" of queer Asian/white life where one may debate whether Cunanan stands as a successful or failed case of assimilation.[26] Like Lim, I suggest we not use Cunanan to make normal the narrative of the pathological native boy but to explore the seductive potentials of such "queer f(r)ictions," precisely the ones that animate and intervene into the tensions of the colonial dyad between brown people and the white subject.[27] How, for example, might we consider Cunanan as a convergence of the colonial dyad in one body? To pursue such a question, Lim's notion of the *tropic spell* is necessary grounding. Where Isaac utilizes tropic as a geopolitical term marking the terrain of the Philippines, Lim's notion of the tropic spell remains in constant negotiation between objectification and agency, seduction and failed cross-cultural understanding. The tropic spell is "a condition within which the queer coupling found a seductive scenario to play."[28] The spell, in constant negotiation, must then be traced with a queer reading practice tailored to the dyadic and thus not spellbound by the singular. Both sides of the equation matter here. To analyze Cunanan not just as a native boy but as a subject who hosts a colonial dyad—thus, as both white subject and an objectified brown body—is to begin to see how his living of an Asian/white life casts the tropic spell in more than one direction, onto the colonizer and the colonized, as well as toward the past, present, and future.

Be it a seductive scenario with Cunanan as the rigger and his white client as the rope bunny, or one more like the scene depicted in the FX series, Cunanan in control and straddling his client as he wraps the white face with duct tape, his tropic spell is an imperial residue not without a possibility for revolutionary sensation.[29] For all its potential to heal, sensation, as shown by Amber Musser, can be the material formation that sustains the queer brown subject as they are embedded in the relentless cycle of systemic domination.[30] Having only killed white men, Cunanan's murder spree could situate him alongside the likes of Tura Satana, the cult icon, busty badass, and exotic dancer trained in aikido and karate. Remembered most for her starring role in Russ Myer's 1965 exploitation film *Faster, Pussycat! Kill! Kill!*, Satana is revered for beating up men on screen, which is not unlike her own life where she exacted revenge on the five men who escaped prosecution after gang raping her as a child. Born in Japan, Tura Luna Pascual Yamaguchi moved to California at the peak of World War II and was interned at Manzanar with her father who was a Japanese citizen of Filipino descent. Afterward, the family reunited in Chicago with Satana's mother whose Indigenous (Cheyenne) and Scottish Irish heritage made assimilation during those postwar years all but possible. From here on, the plotlines thin. There was the gang rape at nine, an arranged marriage at thirteen, then a divorce and relocation to Los Angeles at fifteen. As a minor, she uses a fake ID to perform at clubs like the Trocadero, capturing the attention of silent-screen comedian and photographer Harold Lloyd whose nude images of Satana greenlit her short career in show business. When she is talked about at all, Satana is typecast as a racially ambiguous sex symbol with an attitude. Not often considered a pioneering Asian American actress, Satana's residence in cultural memory maps onto a similar kind of inscrutability that also describes the canonical writer of Asian/white life Sui Sin Far, the pen name for Edith Maude Eaton. Theirs is an *oriental inscrutability*, what Xine Yao describes as a "quintessential nonreactive Asiatic quality" that "threatens the good white American family and its health, its labor, and the foundation of its way of life."[31]

There is no record, none that I have found, that details what exactly Satana did to those men. Lost to the chaos of exclusion and the obstacles of youth, we have only fragments of her bad behavior to rely on in an effort to piece together empire's more scandalous intimacies.[32] The whiteness inside Asian America stands out in the same way that camouflage does and does not; be it mimicry or disguise, there is a potential for collusion when we choose another and are faced with the decision to either fuck, marry, or kill. Like Satana, one may question whether Cunanan's spree killings functioned as a sensational performance of retribution, an intentional and intergenerational undoing of the white men who occupied the positions of privilege, possibility, and safety denied to his queer brown diasporic body. Ruined, however, by a collective disavowal, Cunanan's unsettling three-month murder spree was too obscured by his glaring whiteness, a fraudulent wholeness, or what is more accurately described by Christine Bacareza Balance as "the distinctly Filipino capacity for adaptability" to be anything like a transformative act of racially informed sexual role-play.[33] Unlike Satana, his sporadic attacks are less obviously about retribution for sexual violence and thus more than a kinky fantasy gone wrong but a contemporary rendition of a fantasy "under the surveillance of the metroimperial gaze."[34]

Here, I invoke the work of Victor Román Mendoza whose understanding of fantasy is rooted in psychoanalytic thought where fantasy functions as a form of protection and as an ability to pinpoint the source of desire. Mendoza explains, "Fantasy protects one from the traumatizing truth of the impossibility of totalizing knowledge, of completely satisfying one's desire, by constructing and reconstructing desire with different configurations of historical knowledge and, once in a while, with new knowledge altogether."[35] Fantasy thus not only "shields" and "conceals" as it fills the gap made by the possibility of traumatic negation with something positive, but fantasy, as a scene, produces and "stages one's desire."[36] Cunanan, with his ancestral histories of US state governance and imperial violence, was in a way destined to engage in "the most improper intimacies."[37] It is as though his intimate life was fated to be a metroimperial one, geared to both follow through *and* resist the colonial regulation of Filipino bodies and desires. The act of inquiring "who is primed to become intimate with whom and why" drives the force of Mendoza's piercing study on the far-reaching nature of US empire.[38] Understanding intimacy as a zone of contact where forces of the metroimperial gaze and colonial state rule converge, Mendoza explores the US state's long-standing investment in constructing the Filipino subject as sexualized other and thus as sexually available. Cunanan encounters this legacy twofold, as product and successor: his mixed race facilitating its residual effects and his Filipino subjectivity always already suspended in the "historical undeniability of the U.S. white supremacist state's militarized detonation of Filipino life."[39] His glaring whiteness is never not devoid of this history, but due to multiracial politics and the "optics of globalization" present in those years surrounding the turn of the twenty-first century, the larger public could never see Cunanan for what he was—torn.[40] Whether he set out to kill or if he was overcome with his being "geared to calamity,"[41] Cunanan remains a Filipino subject, gay and diasporic, existing always in close proximity to America's colonial frontier and its imminent mixed race future. Keeping Cunanan's case in the back of our minds, I now turn to consider the spaces in which his face would never be found, on the pages in which mixed race Asian America's preoccupation with wholeness is at its most celebrated and controversial.

"The New Face of the Millennium": Mixed Race Futurity and The Hapa Project

Kip Fulbeck's *Part Asian, 100% Hapa* is arguably the most celebrated cultural artifact in mixed race Asian America. Published in 2006, the collection stems from The Hapa Project, Fulbeck's larger photography project, which includes a range of mediums—traveling portrait exhibitions, a published book, and a web-based archive. An artist and professor of art at the University of California, Santa Barbara, Fulbeck has been instrumental in capturing the growing population of multiracial Asian people, which he describes as hapas, an indigenous Hawaiian word used to denote mixed ancestry. Unlike other terms used to describe mixed Asian life—war baby, love child, mutt—hapa is not pejorative. With roots in occupied Hawai'i, the term, for some, connotes an idealized illusion of racial and ethnic blending. Here, colonial amnesia produces feelings of pride and a sense of community. It is precisely this interpretation of hapa that caused Fulbeck to create The Hapa Project. Conflating multiracial Asians with native Hawaiians, Fulbeck's borrowing of the word could be said to result from good intentions: to foster a sense of belonging for hapas, broadly construed, and to problematize the stereotype that mixed race Asian and Pacific Islanders are children of war. I should be clear at the outset that despite his role in popularizing the term "hapa," Fulbeck is not the first to use it. In Hawai'i, the term is often used to describe mixedness in general, a side effect of how normalized colonization can become. In the early 1990s, student groups on the mainland United States used hapa as a term to organize multiracial communities. In 1992, the Hapa Issues Forum (HIF), a student activist group, was established at the University of California, Berkeley to create a space for multiracial Japanese Americans. A year later, HIF became a nonprofit, and by 1994, it expanded to include all mixed Asian Americans.[42] In addition to student groups, the term entered into cultural media with the publication of *Hyphen Magazine*'s 2008 issue on hybrid identity and the Mixed Race Asian Media collective (previously named Hapa Mag). There is, however, no measuring up to the fame of The Hapa Project, which debuted a new exhibition documenting fifteen years of the project in 2018 at the Japanese American National Museum in Los Angeles, just two weeks following the finale of FX's *The Assassination of Gianni Versace.*

Without question, the term "hapa" has been received with open arms by many mixed race Asians who have long desired a label to group together the varied experiences of being part Asian. I myself recall the positive feelings of racial association when I first came across *Part Asian, 100% Hapa* in 2006. I was in high school, and for the first time I felt as though there was a word that captured all of me. Back then, I never questioned the term's etymology. It was not until college, when I first read Wei Ming Dariotis's essay "Hapa: The Word of Power" that I learned how the appropriation of the indigenous Hawaiian term by non-native Hawaiians exists within a colonial legacy where Europeans and Americans stole native land.[43] The term's appropriation has been met with unwavering disapproval from native Hawaiian scholars and mixed Asian allies who profess the damages that arise from using a term outside of its origination in a history of colonization.[44] Mixed Asians who continue to use the term assert that no one culture can claim ownership when it comes to language. If some Asian Americans understand hapa as a malleable identity, flexible enough to include nonindigenous Hawaiians, how can we understand multiracial Asian American community formation as compatible with colonial disavowal? What forms of settler colonial complicity traffic in the Asian American appropriation of hapa if indeed the Asian American use of hapa is an appropriation?

The Hapa Project, a traveling exhibition that has appeared in museums across the nation, debuted publicly in 2006 at the Japanese American National Museum in Los Angeles.[45] In the same year, the project's book form was published as a companion to the exhibit. *Part Asian, 100% Hapa* gathers approximately 10 percent of the project's participants and includes a foreword by Sean Lennon, the son of Yoko Ono and John Lennon. Unlike other photographic collections of multiraciality, Fulbeck's most resembles photography's tendency for turning race into a spectacularized piece of evidence. The signature look of the project strives for a minimalist aesthetic but evokes the anthropological colonial gaze. Fulbeck photographed each volunteer head-on, naked from the shoulders up, minimal if any makeup, and without any notable facial expression, jewelry, or glasses. The majority of the volunteers were photographed in California and Hawai'i, while others were photographed in New York, Illinois, and Wisconsin. The portraits feature mixed Asian and Pacific Islanders young and old and of multifarious mixes. Although those photographed were not all mixed with white, a majority were. There was also an overwhelming presence of women participants and those with Japanese heritage. Each portrait is joined with the model's handwritten response to the question "What are you?" The participants' responses to the question are unsurprisingly mixed. Some list their ethnicities, others narrate a life, write poetically, or attempt to draw a family tree, a few choose to express their answers in artistic sketch. The man on the cover writes, "I am exactly the same as every other person in 2500."[46] Another participant mixed with Chinese, English, Scottish, and German responds, "My last boyfriend told me he liked me because of my race. So I dumped him."[47]

If "the new face of the millennium is part Asian/Pacific Islander," as claimed by Fulbeck in the introduction to the book of portraits, how does Andrew Cunanan factor into that model?[48] Does Cunanan emerge as the heralder of Fulbeck's claims, or is he the exception or of a different breed altogether? Fulbeck's sample size includes celebrities like Keanu Reeves who exist in clear distinction from Cunanan whose queerness, criminalized labor, and bloody trail dirty his racial mixture's potential for progress. Neglecting the more controversial and complicated figures, Fulbeck's claims breathe life into a neoliberal agenda: that there is no more formulaic figure to define such a transitional moment, a shift from the American century to the Asian century, than the part-Asian, part-American subject, the *100 percent* hapa.

By pairing portrait with handwritten account, Fulbeck aimed to cultivate a space of agency for a growing population, inviting mixed people to be agents of their own identity, something that is denied to many including Cunanan. Take note of his representations on the FBI poster. Racialized as white, Cunanan is branded as an amorphous figure. Along with an added alias and a note that he has been known to fluctuate in weight and hairstyle, the three

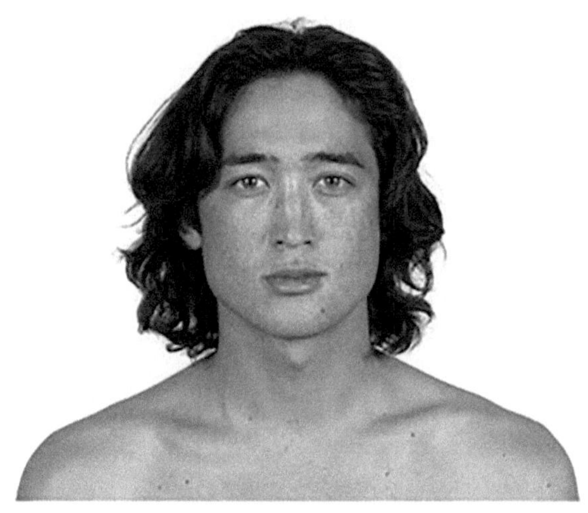

FIGURE 1.1. A glimpse into the future, *Part Asian, 100% Hapa*, 2006.

images display his range of appearances. There is a number for the Triangle Foundation, a Detroit-based gay and lesbian advocacy organization. Although it is right to doubt the FBI's racial comprehension in the 1990s and always, it is not as though the public did not eventually learn Cunanan's race. Asian Americans in the know certainly came to acknowledge his Filipinoness. Like Keanu and Tiger, Cunanan's was a famous face, a mixed Asian face.

As Cunanan's case falls deeper into cultural memory, Fulbeck's seemingly innocent move to define a movement by utilizing the anthropological gaze, one that also distinguishes the FBI's photographic methods, raises cause for concern. In the introduction to *Part Asian, 100% Hapa*, Fulbeck links an increase in representation to an ownership of time:

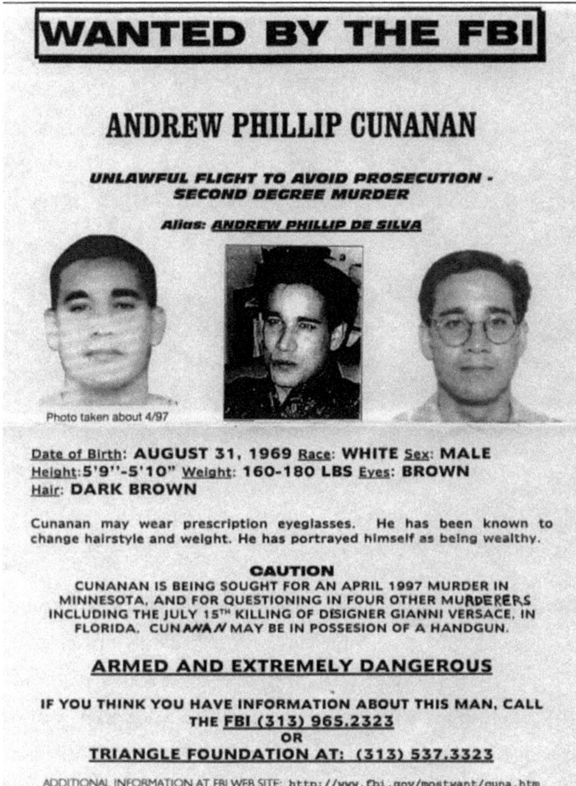

FIGURE 1.2. Wanted, FBI, 1997.

> We recognize a phenomenon around us, but until now it has been nameless. The new face of the millennium is part Asian/Pacific Islander. Modeling agencies clamor to sign the next Devon Aoki or Tyson Beckford. We watch Keanu Reeves, listen to Norah Jones, cheer Tiger Woods, read Aimee Liu, and get our news from Ann Curry. *Time Magazine Asia* goes so far to call Hapas "the poster children for 21st-century globalization." That's a lot of expectation placed upon a group that's been ignored for centuries. And now it's our time because we're in vogue? The way I look at it, it's always been our time.[49]

Is "the new face of the millennium" contingent on the "now"? Or is it a sign of a racial-temporal shift, that from now on it is the hapa's time? The supposed ownership of time is the first of two dangerous problems with The Hapa Project. To suggest that "it's always been our time" means either that historical and future time is for hapas *only*, or that "our" means everyone, suggesting that hapas are somehow representative of humanity.

The Hapa Project may push back on the misconception that racial mixture is a phenomenon unique to the present but only as it holds the racially mixed subject as a prototype for the future. Such claims of universal mixture participate in settler colonial and anti-Black projects of erasure insofar as the embrace of multiraciality targets the singularity of Blackness, indigeneity, and Asianness in the present. In the conclusion to the book, historian Paul Spickard reiterates this sentiment:

> "It's always been our time." Those are the last words of the introduction to this book. And they are true. Hapas, racially mixed people, have always been around. We are *all* mixed. Every so-called racial group—no matter how "pure" it thinks it is—has multiple ancestries. Go check your family tree. You will find ancestors you did not know were there. That we are all mixed has always been true. What is new these days is that people are owning up to being mixed. . . . There is something freeing in that, something celebrating.[50]

Writing "We are *all* mixed," Spickard proposes that Fulbeck's wording of "our time" lends a more thorough understanding of the human condition, but without mentioning the fundamental conditions that allow for racial mixture—settler colonialism, slavery, war—declaring that the hapa is paradigmatic of all people translates into a rationalization of systemic violence obscured into a mixed race future to celebrate. Doubling down, Spickard concludes the book with a definitive statement: "Now is the Hapa time."[51] Since the advent of Fulbeck's project, multiracial identity has indeed been on the rise. Such demographic shifts have often correlated with welcomed signs of diversity, even myths of post-racism. Nonetheless, to profess "Hapa time" is to misunderstand hybridity as a détente for racism's past rather than its condition of possibility. In spite of these faux pas, there has been an overwhelmingly positive reception to the project.

We are in fact not all mixed, which is to say *mixed* fails to gather an all-encompassing category of the human.[52] By suggesting that time, either as historical or cultural moment, is possessed by one specific group does less to offer refuge for all racialized bodies but more so bounds and confines the future terrain from those without access to the potential of phenotypical lightening via racial mixture. Traversing multiple racial borders is an act of racial crossing that renders invalid the statement "We are *all* mixed." An individual's ancestral variety is not indicative of what is a biracial or multiracial experience. Thus, to insinuate that historical time is possessed by anyone other than white is to fundamentally not know the severity of how white supremacy and coloniality continues to penetrate our times and bodies. As Sandra Ruiz so persuasively argues, "this is the affective consequence of colonialism—an active state in the here and now, looping forward and back into itself as if time never started or stopped ticking."[53] Indeed, the colonial clock neither stops ticking nor provides mercy by existing in linearity. Colonial time is never ending. And so when Spickard goes on to dispel two potential "misinterpretations" readers might have—one, that the book's images employ scientific racism's tactics of condensing race to visual markers, and two, that the book's use of "hapa" is cultural appropriation—the endurance of colonialism's reach is woefully neglected.

CMRS scholar Minelle Mahtani argues that for the proliferation of mixed race citizens to be seen as a sign of progress, a process of cultural amnesia must occur. Naming this form of cultural amnesia "strategic forgetting," Mahtani seeks to register the damaging effects that arise when mixed people forget their mixed histories.[54] When Fulbeck insists that the project's underlying theme is not race but identity, direction can be found through David Eng, who posits that "a constitutive violence of forgetting" occurs as racialized subjects are folded into a discourse of color blindness, one centered on a "persistent disavowal of race."[55] The romanticized view governing popular and personal narratives of Asian multiraciality contributes to the assumption that the growing number of mixed race people indicates a turn toward post-racism, indeed a moving toward a better future. The hapa's supposed ownership of the future only substantiates this point.

The kind of empty celebration present within such Asian settler claims occurs through colonial disavowal, specifically of Hawaiian history. In spite of its well-received contribution to Asian American cultural production, which includes complicating the misconception that all mixed people are tragic subjects bred from war, my scrutiny of The Hapa Project sets out to grasp how an exploration into mixed race subjectivity falls short when it does not comprehend the gravity of colonialism's grip on racialized otherness. Any attempt to portray racially mixed life must grapple with the embodied and inherited effects/affects that result when multiple racial histories converge in one body. Failure to do so renders complicity with "the foundational dialectic" of our times, "a disavowal of the ways in which the political protection of life is always predicated on the dispersal of death."[56] Multiracialism is not immune to the neoliberal incorporation of difference. What better way in fact to describe the celebration of multiracial kids born from heterosexual interracial couples than an invitation extended and accepted to join reproductive respectability? Contrary to discourse suggesting the imminent mixed race future will be a less divisive one, it is the painful and forgotten memories of colonialism, militarism, and exclusion that emerge as defining features in the making of racially mixed life.

Colonial Deception: Racial Liberalism and the Appropriative Grammar of Authenticity

The contemporary appeal fastened onto the mixed Asian subject is not a novel one. Historian Emma Jinhua Teng has shown how nineteenth-century Chinese utopian visions of racial harmony regard the Eurasian as the answer for racial conflict. In her study *Eurasian: Mixed Identities in the United States, China, and Hong Kong, 1842–1943*, Teng documents a range of Chinese literature published in the second half of the nineteenth century, arguing that Eurasians were not universally marginalized but that they in fact experienced varied levels of inclusion and exclusion.[57] In a striking correlation with the present, Teng analyzes *One World Treatise*, a utopian tract published in 1902 by Kang Youwei, a man known as late–Imperial China's preeminent Confucian philosopher. Written over the course of several decades, *One World Treatise* took its inspiration from growing levels of Western expansion. Concerned with China's ability to coexist with American imperialism, Youwei advocated the amalgamation of yellow and white races. For Youwei, Eurasians represented the perfect super-race of the future, strengthening the weaker Chinese race with an infusion of the vigor of European blood. In Youwei's One World utopia, Black and brown people would eventually become yellow through intermarriage with yellow and white people. In a resulting world of only Asian/white people, amalgamation between the two groups would produce the Eurasian of the future, a complementary pairing of European physical qualities and aggressive military and economic command and Asian intellectualism and moral sensibility.[58] As a staunch supporter of yellow-white hybrid vigor, Youwei was part of a growing Chinese reform movement that celebrated Chinese men and women for marrying Western spouses at the same time as they discouraged Chinese women from "lowering themselves" by marrying "men of darker races."[59] As Teng makes clear, Youwei's manifesto for hybridization was nothing other than "a mechanism for eugenic improvement and revitalization."[60] Unlike the West's fixation on hybrid degeneracy, Youwei believed fervently that hybridity was less a threat to racial purity but a mode of enhancing inferior nonwhite races, forming a Eurasian world of equality and racial sameness.

Representative more so of the *model majority* than the model minority, such depictions of Asian/white life crystallize the colonial logics of racial purity, gendered nationalism, and sexual violence that underline contemporary discourse on multiraciality.[61] Whether one retains, extends, or contests those colonial legacies depends not on correcting narratives of the past or in filling in historical gaps. Instead, it is whether one acknowledges that *the past does things*. Here, I repeat the words of José Esteban Muñoz who uses Ernst Bloch's model of studying the past through the Marxist tradition invested in historicizing, suggesting that "it is important to call on the past, to animate it, understanding that the past has a performative nature."[62] Muñoz's insistence is a powerful proposal for queer futurity, extending a critical engagement with utopian hermeneutics, which takes seriously how minoritarian life is "intensely relational with the past."[63] Evoking this Blochian practice, drawn out by Muñoz, let us put "the past into play with the present, calling into view the tautological nature of the present."[64]

To begin, I raise the case of the winter 2007 cover of *Hyphen* magazine. On the cover stands Kip Fulbeck as a centaur, upright and peering into the distance. Fulbeck, as creator of The Hapa Project and with his Cantonese, English, Irish, and Welsh heritage, is celebrated as "the face of hapa."[65] The provocative and contentious cover was no stranger to commentary. Some felt the cover portrayed an insensitive depiction of the mixed body as monstrous, an uncouth rendition of a racialized past that deemed people of mixed race as illegitimate hybrids of a nonhuman species. Indeed, as the cover image of *Hyphen*'s "Hybrid Issue," the centaur made mythical the representation of mixedness for a readership of Asian America. For all its display of muscular Asian masculinity, the image likens the sentiment of *Time* magazine Asia's "All Mixed Up" tagline: "Half Asian, Half Caucasian and 100% Cool." We need only apply half-man, half-animal to this equation for the manimal to apply.

Fulbeck is likely just one inadvertent successor of Youwei's Eurasian future, but his chimeric and legendary demeanor staged on the *Hyphen* cover certainly packs a punch. Armed with a spear in his right hand and a clenched left fist, Fulbeck is primed for battle. Surrounded by hummingbirds, messengers of love and healing, Fulbeck is perhaps on the brink of destiny, geared to give rise to a more racially harmonious world. The question remains: Is the centaur, with his eyes locked upward, peering toward the future or backward to the past? His head positioned away from his body's stance may suggest that the centaur is looking back to the past, but his watch remains forward and set. There is no head turned backward, only slightly tilted toward what

FIGURE 1.3. The Hybrid Issue, *Hyphen*, 2007.

lies ahead. Following Muñoz, I read the *Hyphen* cover as a glimmer of the future's archival form, which traces back to "flickering illuminations from other times and places."[66] The future, as they say, is mixed.

An orientation toward the future embodied by the centaur as an idealized reference to a mythical past offers a telling contradiction. Beyond the lines delineating past from future, a process of racial abjection lingers within the contours of mixed race Asian America. Julia Kristeva has most famously described abjection as a process of separation and rejection whereby the subject, in noting its corporeality, rejects horrific or grotesque parts of itself (the abject) into a liminal space between subject and object.[67] Cast out, the abject "is something rejected from which one does not part."[68] Thus, for Kristeva, "abjection is above all ambiguity."[69] Torn and fragmented, one may discard parts of the self, but one will always fail to abandon them completely. Racial abjection in mixed race Asian America, then, might be described as an ejection of that which makes one other, only for it to recoil back. Fulbeck's existence within a cultural moment that celebrates Eurasians is never detached from racist history's insistence that mixed bodies are of a monstrous breed. Some skin can never be shed.

I draw on the notion of abjection to follow the likes of Karen Shimakawa, whose engagement with abjection seeks to understand and describe the aesthetic, legal, and psychoanalytic modes that impact and chart Asian Americans' performance of national identity. Arguing that "Asian Americanness functions as *abject* in relation to Americanness," Shimakawa follows Kristeva to define the process of abjection as "an attempt to circumscribe and radically differentiate something that, although deemed repulsively *other* is, paradoxically, at some fundamental level, an undifferentiable part of the whole."[70] For Shimakawa, the abject embodies a "contradictory nature."[71] She explains, "Read as abject, Asian Americanness thus occupies a role both necessary to and mutually constitutive of national subject formation—*but it does not result in the formation of an Asian American subject or even an Asian American object*."[72] Instead, the Asian American subsists as national abject, made to be both present in multiculturalist discourse and excluded from an encompassing realm of protection.

For Shimakawa, contradictory stereotypes demarcate Asian Americans as either "foreigners/outsiders/deviants/criminals" or "domesticated/invisible/exemplary/honorary whites."[73] Asian/white life encounters such contradiction twofold, wavering not only within the range of Asian American stereotype but between the colonial discourse that positions the mixed body as a model of either hybrid degeneracy or hybrid vigor. Such colonial discourse, according to Homi Bhabha, is hinged on the concept of "fixity," which Shimakawa adds to, noting that "colonial discourse functions, through the racial stereotype, to establish a self in opposition to an other by making that other abnormal, monstrous, and thereby fixed and *characterizable*."[74] Colonial discourse creates a divergent pathway for the Asian American, mixed or not, each track paved by the derivative nature of race itself. Fulbeck—as centaur, as face of hapa, and as Eurasian—is not immune from such colonial discourse. The contradictory nature of Asian/white racial abjection is one that simultaneously makes hidden and glorifies the very colonial desire, which is the model majority's condition of possibility.

Compromised by its settler complicity, The Hapa Project disavows coloniality through the specific posture of appropriation. Again, Indigenous and allied critics have been forthright about the cultural appropriation present in the contemporary moment's use of hapa, explaining that the current deployment of the word disregards its colonial roots. Spickard responds to these concerns: "I sympathize with resentments some Hawaiians may have at their word being appropriated by Asian Americans. But that is the nature of language. It morphs and moves. It is not anyone's property. Continental Americans might just as well complain about Hawaiians using 'TV' and 'cell phone.'"[75] It is a loud and indecent comparison to liken colonial conquest with material object. For all its traction in twenty-first-century debates on cultural appropriation, the use of hapa resides within the conventional denial of the term's origins in colonial violence, indeed in colonial desire. Fulbeck insists the project is not about race but is one that uses race to discuss the book's overarching theme of identity. The Hapa Project adds a celebratory tone of inclusion, belonging, and progress, each a keystone of multicultural American discourse. In other words, the overlooking of complex diasporic histories is part and parcel of the colonial and imperial logics governing much of the discourse on racial mixing.

That these discourses converge in The Hapa Project at the site of photography is not surprising.[76] Scholars like Kimberly Juanita Brown and Tina Campt have shown how the practice of photography is inextricably linked to systems of colonialism, empire, and white supremacy, which rely on tactics of objectification and surveillance to justify state-sanctioned violence.[77] Beyond these explicit influences, the photographic image produces an effect in the viewer, as Roland Barthes has shown with the concept of the punctum and as Susan Sontag describes as chronic voyeurism.[78] Anne McClintock avers: "With photography, Western knowledge and Western authority become synonymous with the real."[79] If photography names an artistic, archival, and colonial practice of capturing and reproducing an image for use, is The Hapa Project's use of racial portrait inherently appropriative?

Given Fulbeck's photographic reworking of hapa, one could classify his adaptation of the indigenous Hawaiian term along the lines of what Paisley Rekdal has described as "marketplace colonialism," a standard if not underquestioned dynamic where the publishing industry supports an appropriative act at the expense of the community whose identity is appropriated.[80] Too often misread as an issue solely of cultural enfranchisement, cultural appropriation is, as argued by Rekdal, also a problem of remuneration. Profiting off The Hapa Project, in a monetary and reputational sense, Fulbeck not only benefits but has produced a template for narratives of hapa authenticity. The public's embrace of The Hapa Project only exacerbates this condition. As a result, the colonial and capitalistic backbones of appropriation fall even deeper under the radar.

A business, the world of publishing is not immune to "the pervasive and often invisible history of colonialism."[81] In *Appropriate: A Provocation*, Rekdal, an American poet and creative writing professor, discusses the controversial practice of cultural appropriation in contemporary American literature. Through a series of letters addressed to a white student, Rekdal traverses the fraught terrain of literary appropriation—from writing in the voice of another to fabricating identity on the page—in order to offer a more expansive framework for approaching appropriation, one less structured on the rights and wrongs of the action and more interested in the potential benefits of employing appropriation as a literary device. For Rekdal, appropriation may indeed function as a continuing practice of colonialism, but wielded as a technique, writers may use appropriation to abandon the grip of authenticity and thus kindle relationality. As an experiment, it can get us to think differently about how humans relate to one another, helping to kickstart new ways of resisting fetishization and preserving cultural practices. It matters, of course, what drives the impetus to approximate and identify differently than a writer's own, and to this, Rekdal offers a list of practical and challenging questions for writers in a postscript, which proves invaluable considering the long history and recent uptick of works concerning appropriation in Asian American art and culture.[82]

Cultural appropriation is, it goes without saying, a loaded and contentious topic, and Rekdal devotes an entire letter, "Letter Two: Setting the Terms," to explain its history. She cites literary criticism on the aesthetic practice of adaptation and pools together the arguments forwarded by scholars and critics who have published on appropriation, a breadth of work including that of America's most influential authors like James Baldwin, Toni Morrison, and Claudia Rankine, literary scholars Pascal Nicklas and Julie Sanders, philosopher James O. Young, legal scholar Susan Scafidi, and postcolonial theorist Edward Said. By the end of the text, Rekdal leaves the reader without positivist answers, only contextualized reflections and guidance, an example of pedagogical care: "If you approach appropriation with any ethical seriousness," she writes, "you will have to think deeply about aesthetics, history, and difference; you will reevaluate the literary and humanistic values you claim to hold, on the page and in the publishing industry, and you will have to consider the role that money and commercialism play in art."[83]

Rekdal herself is Chinese and white American. Throughout the text, she ruminates on how her identity as a biracial woman informs the way she both teaches and considers implementing literary appropriation in her work. Conscientious, she wonders how her race may inform her ability to sympathize with certain characters, surveying the risk inherent in pursuing a story based solely on the limits of identification:

> As a writer and a teacher, and most especially as a mixed-race woman, I don't believe that writing outside one's subject position is always and only a culturally appropriative act. Because to insist that a writer must be from the same group identity as the voice of the author has a dangerous flip side to it: while it warns off writers from blithely taking on subject matters outside their own experience, it also implicitly warns writers within the same group identity that an authentic experience of that identity *does* exist—to the group at least—and can and may be policed from within.[84]

If authenticity implies representation or embodiment of the real, genuine, or true, then how might feelings of inauthenticity—"I am not truly Asian," "I am not Asian enough," or "I am only half-Asian"—lead mixed Asians to identify as hapa? How do visual representations of hapa embodiment discursively construct hapa identity as exemplar of heteronormativity? Finally, if there is a potential utility of literary appropriation, does that same utility take place in acts of visual or identitarian appropriation?

The critique of the implied dichotomy between the authentic and the inauthentic, the real and the unreal, is not confined to contemporary literature. The empirical implications of authenticity—fact and truth—have long been questioned in postmodernist and poststructural thought, which understand reason itself as a historical formation. Postcolonial theory and queer theory, perhaps two of the most significant fields within poststructuralist thought, embrace postmodern notions focused on decentering essence as well as prioritizing meaning over origin. A brief survey of these two fields will further elucidate the depths of colonial complicity enacted in The Hapa Project's racial liberalism.

To begin, queer theory opts to deconstruct what is considered natural, original, or essential as well as rethink categories associated with oppressively normalizing societal conventions. With its investment in challenging essentialist thought, queer theory argues that what we often perceive as real or authentic ways of living in and studying society are in fact artificial and unstable. Queer theory approaches notions of authenticity by employing a counterhegemonic logic committed to a constant questioning and decentering of norms.[85] It also differentiates "the real" from a concept known as realness, which stems from trans and queer of color critique. Jack Halberstam states, "Realness—the appropriation of the attributes of the real, one could say—is precisely the transsexual condition. The real, on the other hand, is that which always exists elsewhere, and as a fantasy of belonging and being."[86] By arguing that the real is both standardized and expected, Halberstam dispels the seemingly authentic nature of gender and, through a focus on transgender bodies, conveys the inherent precariousness of the hegemonic gender binary. In a similar vein, Marlon Bailey examines ballroom culture, a queer of color subculture where queer Black and Latino/a members perform drag, arguing that ballroom's reappropriation of "realness" serves as a basis for successful performance criteria as well as a productive site to challenge normative kinship formation: "Realness requires adherence to certain performances, self-presentations, and embodiments that are believed to capture the authenticity of particular gender and sexual identities. These criteria are established and function within a schema of race, class, gender, and sexuality. Racialized, classed, gendered and sexualized performances, self-presentations, and embodiments, to a large extent, give realness its discursive power in both the ballroom scene as well as in society at large."[87] Bailey sheds light on the queered concept of realness to demonstrate how ballroom performances provide a space to craft nonnormative kinship structures that challenge hegemonic and heteronormative notions of identity, family, and community. In parallel, Halberstam contends, "queer genders profoundly disturb the order of relations between the authentic and the inauthentic, the original and the mimic, the real and the constructed," as Bailey asserts that the presence of "realness" disrupts the authority of the real.[88]

To be clear, authenticity is less a symptom of appropriation than an insinuation. Insofar as The Hapa Project appropriates an indigenous Hawaiian word, it creates a distinct look and spirit to mixed Asian life, blending assimilation with racial progress. Queer theory's critique of gender and sexual authenticity presents a productive mode of reference for The Hapa Project, a collection of portraits that is as much about race and ethnicity as it is about interracial desire. Coded in various forms, sexuality is always in excess on the pages of *Part Asian, 100% Hapa*. More than mentions of attraction and dating, like in the example discussed earlier in this chapter, or in the allure invited by the model's bare chest and "exotic" features, sexuality is mobilized by the very idea of mixed life. This sexuality is as for the taking as it is heteronormative, reproductive, and interracial. The assumption embedded in each portrait—a cishet man and woman of different races defied the odds, choosing love—lends toward a defaulted narrative: if mixed-raceness is a sign of progress, we have heteronormative, reproductive, and interracial sexuality to thank. There are deep affinities, complicities, and compatibilities between multiracialism and sexual politics. As evidenced by Siobhan B. Somerville, the intimacy between race and homosexuality in particular necessitates an acknowledgment of the late nineteenth century and the Black/white color line.[89] Race has historically been central to the invention of homosexuality. To this end, let us not forget that the Supreme Court case that ended the illegality of interracial marriage, *Loving v. Virginia* (1967), was, among other cases, used as precedent for the legalization of same-sex marriage in *Obergefell v. Hodges* (2015).

Moreover, postcolonial theory draws from schools of postmodern thought that both complicate the politics of knowing and analyze the structural intersections of social and political power that maintain colonialism in the present moment. In its approach to authenticity, postcolonial studies challenge the assumed dominance and perceived authenticity of Eurocentric discourse, exploring the fiction of an "authentic" postcolonial voice. As an example, Ella Shohat and Robert Stam examine Eurocentric discourse and multiculturalism in popular culture, particularly the role third world filmmakers play in constructing representations of postcolonial authenticity. Considering the moving image as a national project, the authors specify the concept of "relative powerlessness," an articulation of postcoloniality where each generation desires an "elusive 'authenticity'" in order to claim an authentic postcolonial condition.[90] They argue, "to abandon the language of 'authenticity' with its implicit standard of appeal to verisimilitude as a kind of 'gold standard,' in favor of a language of 'discourses.' . . . Reformulating the question as one of 'voices' and 'discourses' disputes the hegemony of the visual."[91] Opting to forgo a focus on authenticity, Shohat and Sham suggest that a focus on the multiplicity of postcolonial voices offers a potent critique of Eurocentric hegemony.

Whereas Shohat and Sham promote an analysis of voice, some practitioners of postcolonial studies contend that conversations about the authentic postcolonial voice demonstrate the alleged advantages of claiming postcolonial subjectivity. Much of this literature revolves around a desire to define and claim an authentic postcolonial condition.[92] Authenticity, then, is not simply employed as a theoretical caveat but functions as an appropriation of indigeneity itself. To this point, Alicia Arrizón explores authenticity in relationship to the native or indigenous body, focusing on the ideology of mestizaje, a concept that "epitomizes the in-betweenness of identities produced by the impact of colonial/cultural encounters and their intimate relation to social processes."[93] What is particularly pertinent about examining "authentic" native bodies through the ideology of mestizaje is how the analytic of queerness factors in the process. In *Queering Mestizaje,* Arrizón not only deems mestizaje as a condition of postcoloniality but establishes a queer critique of mestizaje, revealing the hegemony of Western epistemologies of race, ethnicity, and culture as well as the subsequent resistance of these dominant and normalizing ways of knowing. Arrizón states, "Knowledge of the 'native' body returns to its genealogy, cultural identity, and historical origination, resisting the type of authenticity that *performs* universal standardization, and thus creating a productive way to eradicate and silence racial oppression."[94] The very desire to categorize the native body shows the inherent instability of authentic categories. Arrizón's work on mestizaje exemplifies what I find to be a productive merging of queer theory and postcolonial studies; this amalgamation offers a key critique to essentialist discourses that arise within postcolonial studies' investment in "the postcolonial voice" and queer theory's critique on the presumed authenticity of gender and sexual binaries.

Epistemological undertakings on authenticity emerge within queer theory's critique of normativity and postcolonial studies' incisive arguments against Eurocentrism. Despite their alternative approaches, both fields insist that authenticity, with its maintenance of an authentic-inauthentic binary, limits the capacity to produce nuanced ways of knowing that are neither complicit with Eurocentric nor essentialist discourses. Queer theory and postcolonial studies serve as productive companions in critiquing authenticity because both fields constantly trouble binary categories and question the hegemony of Eurocentric discourse. Such theoretical principles work to challenge visual representations of multiracial identity as well as Eurocentric notions of authenticity.

The vast literature on authenticity gathers together a variety of perspectives and conclusions on appropriation that are often in conflict. More often than not, however, there is one understanding of appropriation that remains constant. While appropriation may offer aesthetic and relational advantages when employed as a literary device, for an author, artist, or scholar to venture further, taking on the identity of another completely, we are faced with an entirely different problem. Many have chosen to cross this line. White women from Rachel Dolezal to Jessica Krug and Andrea Smith have been found to fake racial identities as Black, brown, and Indigenous women. More than resorting to racial masquerade, some find themselves racialized by affinity or association. Think of singer-songwriter Gwen Stefani, a white woman who understands herself as "a little bit of an Orange County girl, a little bit of a Japanese girl, a little bit of an English girl."[95] Here, a power dynamic emerges between appreciation and appropriation, celebration and commodification.

If literary appropriation offers a potential to experiment with form and relation, what about photography? How does The Hapa Project, with its distortion of *hapa*'s literal translation and with its anthropological colonial gaze, measure up to what Rekdal has described as the potential of literary appropriation? What about Cunanan and his ability to pass and hide as white, utilizing ambiguity to evade capture? Simply put, there are stark differences between an author developing a character different than their own, Asian migrant settlers co-opting an indigenous term, and fabricating one's identity entirely. To judge appropriation as an act of colonial violence means considering both the intention behind the appropriative act as well as its impact. With Fulbeck, we see not a white person appropriating a community of color but a more intricate seemingly redeemable case, a mixed race Asian whose aim is to form community, positioning similarity over difference. Here, neither his intention nor description of the project include appropriation, and yet, neither good intentions nor an incomprehension of the subject can outweigh the fact of racial inequality, a fact that emerges clearly and without question in the colonial histories that distinguish mixed Asians from the indigenous people of the Hawaiian islands. Rekdal says it well: "Compassionate approximations, if they want to avoid becoming cultural appropriations, cannot first be sentimental projects."[96] In the marketplace of colonialism, which includes the publishing industry, hapa narratives are largely derived from The Hapa Project, where it is mixed Asian voices, not hapa voices, that are in the majority. What does accountability look like here? There seems to be two main routes: *apology* and a commitment to disengage with otherness, finding (or assuming) comfort with one's own, or *denial*, advocating for sameness and human universality and thereby disavowing the real differences between us. Hindered, for good reason, by conventions of authenticity and ethical imperative, appropriation perhaps is not the best word to articulate what is happening here. Racial deception, cultural embezzlement, and colonial delusion seem more apt to describe *the thing* that drives the seduction of wholeness.

"The thing that can be seen, but will not be spoken out loud."

I conclude this chapter with a provocation on how one may confront the legacies of Western colonial and imperial expansion—legacies, to be very clear, that are embedded in every American story—in the narrative of one's own life. If The Hapa Project is too beholden to the allure of wholeness, foreclosing any real potential to undo the harms of racial hierarchy, how might one approach Asian/white life otherwise? A distraction, wholeness is, we convince ourselves, a legitimate desire for minoritized lives who must work against overlapping legacies of dehumanization to demand full and legal personhood. Gleaned through collections like *Part Asian, 100% Hapa*, the pursuit of wholeness marks an appeal for personhood, a liberal temptation born of America's imperial and colonial past and its intimate connections with racial science. It is therefore a tainted desire too compromised to recuperate. Reading for the intimacy of such violence, I now turn to Rekdal's *Intimate: An American Family Photo Album* (2011) to offer a view into the ways Asian/white life may contend both with the unique feelings of racial incompletion experienced by those of racially mixed ancestry and with the colonial violence that courses through patterns of interracial familial intimacy. Writing against colonial disavowal, Rekdal produces a mode of life writing that situates her Asian/white life alongside the depths of American colonization. The seductive qualities of wholeness that seem to dominate mixed race cultural production are set to the margins of Rekdal's *Intimate*. Present but not at the center, wholeness takes a back seat to all that constitutes life in the American west from the entangled dilemmas of indigeneity, whiteness, land, and labor to assimilation and the photographic method.

Published in the Lineage Series from Tupelo Press, *Intimate* is part-memoir, part-photo album, weaving together the author's personal vignettes of her parents' interracial marriage with the work of American photographer and ethnologist Edward S. Curtis and his Apsaroke guide, Alexander Upshaw. Curtis (1868–1952), a white man born in Wisconsin, is known for his work taking and manipulating images of Native Americans in an attempt to depict precolonial life. Staging scenes, simulating ceremony, and paying Indigenous people to dress in garments, Curtis is celebrated and criticized for his work, which is regarded as a precursor to visual anthropology.[97] Upshaw (1874–1909) was a member of the Crow Nation and worked for Curtis as a translator and Native informant. As a child, Upshaw attended the notorious Carlisle Indian Industrial School, a boarding school with a mission to "kill the Indian and save the man." Through personal essay, poetry, photography, and historical writing, Rekdal streams together the stories of Curtis, Upshaw, and her family, evoking a "stranger intimacy."[98] To do so, she uses three different fonts: pages on Rekdal, her family, and her analyses appear in a serif font, pages on Curtis appear in sans serif, and pages on Upshaw are sans serif with bolded typeface. Rekdal works across form and voice, revealing the fraught limits of genre, life narrative, and settler complicity. A panoramic tapestry of America and family, race and ancestry, *Intimate* begins with Rekdal's voice:

> The photos are by the bed. Edward Curtis's first volume of *The North American Indian*: My father had laid the book on his night table beside a box of pills, an extra pair of glasses, and the novel by Conrad I'd bought for his birthday. I am at my parents' house alone, while my father is at the hospital with my mother, who is being prepped for an operation for her cancer. The fact that my mother has gone to the hospital at all and discovered this cancer is surprising: She has avoided doctors since my father's operation years ago on a tumor in his neck. She still talks about the smells there, the awfulness of his room, the way his attending nurse scrutinized her Chinese face when they first met, then looked over at my white father and at me, their child, and asked me, *Are you the translator?*[99]

Intimate features over two dozen photographs of Indigenous people and Native land captured by Curtis and included in his *The North American Indian*. The photographs are used as musings and insights into the self, the nation, and the cultural perceptions of American history. "Do we stare harder, trying to penetrate beneath the surface to what must be the realer face, lurking?"[100] Memoir, in the case of *Intimate*, means searching for one's life story through the very lens of colonization. It is not simply that Rekdal avoids neglecting the colonial past but that she demonstrates the impossibility of approaching any American family history without seeing it as one entangled with Indigenous dispossession.

Bearing in mind this chapter's focus, I want to underscore that *Intimate* includes passages of the author discussing photographs of herself. "I cannot see myself without seeing first my audience, those who are seeing me."[101] When asked by the University of Wyoming, her previous employer, to be photographed, she shares how the image is manipulated to make her appear, in her father's words, "*like a Hawaiian Air stewardess*."[102] When reviewing a series of book-jacket photos, she and her friends comment that when she faces to the right, she looks more Chinese.[103] Throughout, the author shares what others have said in regard to her racial appearance, one ambiguous enough to warrant attention. "Whenever I talk about the Edward Curtis photos, people ask if I'm Native American."[104] Ambiguity can be misleading.

> At my first job, the manager asks for my racial information to fill out the forms. He looks at me. Checks the little box marked "Other."
>
> The thing that can be seen, but will not be spoken out loud.
>
> You know, my father tells me, in some lights you could pass for Indian.[105]

Does ambiguity elevate racial passing into the realm of Indigenous relationality? Or is it simply "the thing" that need not be explored, "the thing" that is articulated just barely, through the look and recognition of a slight deviation from the norm?

> If I do not meet the requirements of Chinese authenticity, neither do I always meet the requirements of mixed-race authenticity, if appearance is that identity's defining factor. Strange facts, which other mixed-race people may have noticed as well: the face changes shape, the hair changes color. Some start looking more dark, whereas I've become more white.[106]

When she asks her mother if she is in fact Chinese, her mother responds, "*A part of you.*" Rekdal pursues further, "*What part?* She doesn't answer."[107] The author follows this passage with a story in bold sans serif, in the perspective of Upshaw, who is asked by Curtis if the photographer can join in on a snake dance, a ceremony in Hopi culture. For Curtis, photographs are everything. They are also not enough. More than document, he wants to experience: "Not to be merely an observer. Not to be on the outside of their beauty, but a part of their beauty. To be their preserver."[108] The following pages in *Intimate* move from Upshaw to Curtis and back to Rekdal, who analyzes her white father's "meritocratic idealism" as the grounds for which she came to remain silent about her mixed race: "In the end, my reticence's only achievement was to make myself more of a mirror."[109] What do we make of this mirror? I want to suggest that the mirror reflects, as mirrors do, a clear image of what is in front of it. Staying silent—that is, letting the visual markings of race say it all—Rekdal is made into a reflective surface: something others look into, something that reproduces the world as it is.

Writing can operate as a material and corporal practice. As modeled through forms of *necrowriting* and *disappropriation*, which offer a political disposition to the written word, some manners of writing invite an ethos attuned to paying toward the indebtedness writers have to others.[110] In a poem titled "Intimacy," Rekdal alludes to this tradition:

> If we can't know the boundaries between ourselves
> in life, what will they be in death,[111]

A question phrased as a pronouncement that can be read as despair or hopefulness, this stanza uncovers the ways in which relationality almost always involves reckoning with the boundaries that demarcate one from another.

If we are to answer this question and begin to speak of intimacy as a matter of knowing ourselves in relation to each other in both life and in death, then perhaps we are confronted again with the limitations and shortcomings of wholeness. More than reaching toward an individual sense of wholeness, what forms of relation take root in centering those who do not immediately seem to be included as our own? Kinship is a troubling concept when it assumes commonality and community simply based on specific points of connection. What I am suggesting is not to abandon the pursuit of wholeness and replace that desire with a vision that sees humanity as one race. Rather, I am slowly becoming more convinced by the promise of an aesthetics that provides a portal—a way in and a way out—of the intimacy of violence. In terms of the photographic method, this would mean placing the harms of US colonial and imperial expansion at the center of any American photo album, even and especially ones that purport to document the changing racial landscape. Bringing Curtis and Upshaw into her family's story, Rekdal emits an acknowledgment of colonial intimacy and Asian settler complicity. One can analyze this choice as a posture of solidarity or proof of clarity. At the very least, Rekdal foregrounds Indigenous dispossession, erasure, and the whiteness at the helm. Do not reduce this to pessimism for that would risk succumbing to a neoliberal delusion, the idea that any story is not always already a story about settler colonialism.

While Rekdal labors in the realm of American literature, *Intimate* gestures toward what Susette Min argues as a possible alternative to contemporary Asian American art, which requires "recasting the categorical imperatives of Asian American art as more than a historical recovery and conversation project . . . considering it less in terms of its aspirations to be seen and more in terms of how it can forge conditions for a politics to come."[112] Unlike the neoliberal multiracialism (i.e., aspirations to be seen) that lingers in the portraits of The Hapa Project, *Intimate* demands an interrogation of the colonial past, forging a politics to come. As Fulbeck's use of hapa removes the term from its roots in the colonial occupation of Hawai'i, it also transforms Hawai'i into a deracinated multiracial paradise of the future. This is a desire that has contributed to the displacement of Kanaka Maoli while billionaires like Mark Zuckerberg purchase Hawaiian land to build a 1,400-acre compound and 5,000-square-foot underground bunker.[113] Perhaps Zuckerberg, his Asian wife, and their Asian/white children are simply following the script laid out for them, planning to survive the postapocalyptic future in their rightful hapa homeland. Sarcasm aside, while some scholars like Nitasha

Sharma have shown the ways Hawai'i's identity as a paradise opens up conversations about anti-Blackness, The Hapa Project simply does not measure up to the kind of cultural production needed to combat racial exclusion.[114] Some forms of interracial intimacy can be liberating, but it matters what defines the bounds of that liberation. Unwavering in its political impulse, intimacy, as shown in *Intimate*, is not only a relation of intergenerational closeness unbound by blood or race but an instruction to interrogate how and why the colonial past refuses to stay there.

2

RACIAL RENOVATIONS

Isolation, Asian/white Domesticity, and America's Lifestyle Brand

I fold countries around myself, false familiarity, some serene carapace. —KIMBERLY QUIOGUE ANDREWS, "*n*: Shield, or Shell Covering," *A Brief History of Fruit*, 2020

I wanted to be like you
I wanted everything —MICHELLE BRANCH, "All You Wanted," *The Spirit Room*, 2001

At times, a metaphor can become a rubric. An example: being a bridge between East and West. A figure of speech long used to convey border crossing as a characteristic of the "third-culture kid," the bridge metaphor reifies the overly neat distinction between the Orient and the Occident while acknowledging hybridity's unique affordances.[1] However antiquated and overly simplistic, the metaphor persists, capturing what it means to live a life of dichotomy: both/and, neither/nor. To be a bridge is to embody an inherent skill set in translation. It also delineates the premises underlying a widely accepted belief: Asian Americans are prone to the feeling of *not* belonging. Like the bridge, Asian American life is rendered foreign and domestic all at once. For Asian/white life, this tension contains multiple registers. Too white to be Asian, too Asian to be white, the Asian American with white heritage comes across as both an outsider and an insider, belonging everywhere and nowhere, a form of isolation. Sometimes one passes as white. Other times the foreignness is apparent. These charades tend to be settled on visual terrains. Like other forms of mixed-raceness where racial difference converges at the site of embodiment, Asian/white life personifies the faults and limitations of standardized racial categorization. Malleable, race and racial identity are both chosen and conferred. Tasked to lessen the divide between how we see ourselves and how others see us, Asian/white life makes a bid for grappling with what it means to belong neither here nor there but to exist as a bridge, a middle ground, a threshold. Allow me to be clear. Belonging, like the concept of elsewhere, is merely a description of desire. It conjures the promise of space, like a home, and perhaps more significantly, the anxiety of absence, loss, and outsiderhood. *Where am I? Do I fit in? Will I be accepted*? Even as these questions center the self, they force confrontation with the nature of sociality and intimacy: belonging—be it through citizenship, community, or inclusion—is out of one's control. There will be uncertainty. How have Asian Americans with white heritage reworked, refused, or outlasted such moments of confusion?

As a preliminary case study, let us think back on the life of Isamu Noguchi, the world-renowned twentieth-century Japanese American artist and landscape architect. For Noguchi, the arts became the space to channel lifelong feelings of grief and exclusion. Sculpture, in particular, was Noguchi's claim to fame. Most known for his public works, which appear across the world in museums, parks, and gardens, Noguchi is just as celebrated for his influence on modern design. In 1947, he began a collaboration with Herman Miller, which resulted in the creation of his iconic Noguchi table, a glass top with a curved wooden base found in many American living rooms. In addition to furniture, he worked in lighting, designing the famous Akari lamps, paper lanterns that became a staple of modernist style. He also constructed stage sets for many Martha Graham productions and pushed the bounds of how the human form is captured in time, helping "to redirect attention to the potentialities of sculpture as a medium for portraiture."[2] Just as his artistic practice involved various forms and extended across disciplinary borders—from stone and wood to interior design and landscape architecture—his life overall proved to be a transnational one, a bridge between East and West.

Born in 1904 in Los Angeles, Noguchi is the son of Japanese poet Yone Noguchi and Léonie Gilmour, a white American editor. In *Queer Compul-*

sions, historian Amy Sueyoshi uncovers the racial and sexual frictions that governed the life of Isamu's father, an Asian man who managed to navigate the world of American art and literature through unexpected intimacies, from interracial sex to same-sex desire. Living in California at the turn of the twentieth century, Yone "proactively sought out romantic if not sexual fulfillment in unconventional ways," sustaining a passionate friendship with writer Charles Warren Stoddard, proposing marriage to journalist Ethel Armes, and impregnating Gilmour, his editor.[3] Months before Isamu's birth, Yone returned to Japan. Following the Russo-Japanese War and the resulting anti-Japanese racism in the United States, Léonie moved to Japan with their son, but by the time mother and son arrived, Yone had married a Japanese woman. As a child, Noguchi lived with his white mother, and the two moved several times throughout Japan. Yone was mostly absent from their lives. In reflecting on his childhood, Noguchi has described his upbringing in Japan as one that made him feel like a "waif," a "loner," and a "stranger."[4] In *Noguchi: East and West*, art historian Dore Ashton explains how Noguchi felt shadowed "by the duality of his origins."[5] Japanese with white American heritage, Noguchi always acknowledged this duality, paying homage to his mother's Irish ancestry and to his father's Japanese background, a racial inheritance more visually apparent. After the attack on Pearl Harbor, Noguchi formed Nisei Writers and Artists for Democracy. A year later, when Noguchi was in his late thirties, Executive Order 9066 forced over 110,000 Japanese Americans in California into internment camps. Aware of the threat of incarceration, Noguchi immediately fled to Washington where he met John Collier, the commissioner for the Bureau of Indian Affairs during the Roosevelt administration, who helped convince Noguchi to travel to an internment camp in Poston, Arizona to promote the arts. There, Noguchi voluntarily interned himself with the goal to build recreational areas for his fellow Japanese internees. While the world was at war, he wanted to make spaces for joy, play, and mourning. Participating fully in interned life, he drew up plans for baseball fields, swimming pools, and a cemetery but decided to leave six months later upon realizing that the War Relocation Authority had no intention of implementing his plans. While his exit from the Poston camp was not seamless—he was questioned for his role in the nisei writers collective, accused of espionage by the Federal Bureau of Investigation, and received a deportation order—he managed to make his way back to New York where he resumed his artistic career.

From a young age, Noguchi expressed a penchant for the arts, a path his mother supported. In 1918, she sent Noguchi back to the United States, to Indiana, to continue his schooling. Over the following years, he held an apprenticeship with Gutzon Borglum, the creator of the Mount Rushmore National Memorial, enrolled as a premed student at Columbia University, and took evening sculpture classes at the Leonardo da Vinci Art School. He eventually dropped out of Columbia to pursue sculpture full time. In 1927, he was awarded the Guggenheim Fellowship, which brought him to Paris, helping him gain international acclaim at what was only the start of a six-decade-long career. In his application for the Guggenheim, Noguchi concludes, "My father, Yone Noguchi, is Japanese and has long been known as an interpreter of the East to the West, through poetry. I wish to fulfill my heritage."[6]

Beginning in 1985, Noguchi opened up his studio to the public, becoming the first living artist to curate a retrospective display of their art. Open year-round, the Noguchi Museum and Sculpture Garden is located in the Long Island City neighborhood of Queens, New York City.[7] In his words, the museum exists "to define my role as a crossing where inward and outward meet, East and West."[8] Like much of Noguchi's work, this impetus seems to revolve around temporality and spatiality.[9] Even in a promotional video, the previous director of the Noguchi Museum, Brett Littman, described the space as "an oasis in time and space," one that reflects "his [Noguchi's] vision for a different way of being in the world."[10] Noguchi elaborates, "Sometimes I think I'm part of this world today. Sometimes I feel that maybe I belong in history, or prehistory, or that there's no such thing as time. But if you're caught in time, the immediate present time, then your choice is very limited. . . . But if you want to escape from that time constraint, then the whole world, you see . . . is someplace you belong."[11] When I visited the museum in July 2022, its stillness became a source of refuge. Full of visitors, the grounds remained quiet, tranquil, and cool even at the peak of summer. To no surprise, there was an intention behind every detail of the space's design. Noguchi wanted people to gather and unwind, a sign not simply of a willing host but a sacrificial one that I argue is unique to an enactment of Asian/white domesticity.

If you have visited a space curated by Noguchi or adorned by one of his sculptures, this is the sentiment that comes across: someone who felt so incredibly out of place (in space and time) made it their life's mission to make others feel completely at ease. Noguchi, contending with what Hayden Herrera describes as "his feeling of placelessness," recycled the distress of isolation and not belonging—the feeling, that is, of being torn between East and West—and created spaces of comfort, peace, and rest for others.[12] An expert in the art of sculpturing space, Noguchi did not need to rely on stone or clay to succeed in making others feel good. Think of the butterflies, a gift he gave Frida Kahlo. In the mid-1930s, when Noguchi lived in Mexico City to work on his first public commission, a sculptural frieze, *History Mexico* (1936), at the Mercado Abelardo Rodríguez market, the two iconic artists met and became lovers. The affair ended, to the delight of Diego Rivera, but Frida and Isamu remained lifelong friends. In Casa Azul, Kahlo's house-turned-museum in Coyoacán, a framed collection of butterflies is mounted under the canopy of her bed, the same bed Kahlo was bound to so often due to chronic pain. The butterflies, symbols of transformation, are captured in time. A promise of beauty and a sight of freedom, the butterflies await the artist's gaze, providing comfort in the midst of suffering. Visitors may notice words by Frida that appear on the back wall: "Never in my life will I forget your presence. You found me torn apart and you took me back full and complete." When Patti Smith, the American singer and poet, visited Caza Azul in 2012, she was so taken by the butterflies that she penned a song, "Noguchi's Butterflies," which I cite here in full:

> I can not walk
> I can not see
> Further than what
> Is in front of me
> I lay on my back
> yet I do not cry
> Transported in space by the butterflies.
> Above my bed
> Another sky
> With the wings you sent
> Within my sight
> All pain dissolves
> In another light
> Transported thru
> Time
> By the butterfly
> This little song
> Came to me
> Like a little gift as I stood
> Beside the bed of Frida.
> I give it to you with much love,
> Patti Smith

FIGURE 2.1. You found me torn apart. Noguchi's Butterflies, Coyoacán, Mexico City, 2023. Photographed by the author.

Noguchi's desire to comfort manifests, by way of the butterflies, as a direct offering to Kahlo and an indirect one to Smith. In doing so, he exemplifies what I term *racial renovation*, an act of repurposing the racialized pain of past societal rejection, exclusion, or ostracism for the benefit of others' potential comfort and belonging. For Noguchi, racialized isolation resulted indeed in negative feelings of nonbelonging, but it also became the impulse for his life's work: making spaces more hospitable for others. A bridge, Noguchi may seem to connect the East and the West, but what I find more worthy of critical inspection are the ways his feelings of nonbelonging dovetail into a performance of Asian American domesticity. Not removed from his own feelings of racialized exclusion, Noguchi's ability to repurpose internalized pain could be understood as a form of "proactive grief."[13] If, as Ashton explains, "The history of Yone Noguchi was like an ember within, always ready to flare up," then, for Noguchi, any act of racial renovation could be said to stem from his father.[14] However, renovation is not the same as restoration, which is to say, and here I again quote Ashton, "He was asking for more than the restoration of a rejecting father."[15] What Noguchi makes possible through the practice of racial renovation is an invitation to expand what we mean when we say home. In other words, Noguchi encourages living life otherwise, beyond the rubrics that are always already outside our making. As described by Bruce Altshuler, another former director of the Noguchi Museum, "Moved as a child between cultures, always treated as a foreigner in both America and Japan, Noguchi said that he could feel at home anywhere because he was at home nowhere."[16]

This chapter explores racial renovation as a form of agency enacted through the domestic sphere and taken up by those living Asian/white lives, those, in other words, who are seen to embody the bridge between East and West. I view racial renovation as a lens with which to analyze Asian/white domesticity, and I opt for the term "domesticity" because it conjures the intimacy of violence as it manifests in the gendered and racial connotations of home, hospitality, and care work. In Noguchi's case, his racial renovations are more or less universally celebrated. What I seek to explore in the following pages is a more dubious pursuit of racial renovation, whereby the imperial affliction of feeling out of place manifests into a set of complicitous associations with US nationalism and the Christian right. To do so, I turn to Joanna Gaines, the Korean American and Waco, Texas–based TV personality most known for her role in HGTV's *Fixer Upper*, a home renovation television show she starred in alongside her white American husband, Chip Gaines. Teased for being half-Asian, Gaines, like Noguchi, struggled with feelings of racial shame throughout her childhood. Also like Noguchi, Gaines found a home in the marketplace of domesticity. Where his was an aesthetic of highbrow modernism, hers is of a more mass-market variety. Credited for popularizing the American trend of buying and flipping houses for a profit, Gaines not only seeks to create welcoming and inviting spaces for others, but similar to Noguchi, her work can be found in many American homes given her partnership with the American retail corporations Target and Home Depot, which sell home goods by her exclusive brands—Hearth & Hand and Magnolia Home—at family-friendly prices. Whereas the nonconformity that Noguchi exhibited throughout his life may align more neatly with the radical potential inherent to Iván Ramos's theorization of *unbelonging*—"the embrace of a shared sense of illegibility" specific to Mexican and Latinx aesthetics[17]—Gaines, with her conservativism and associations with Christian evangelicalism, proves to be a much more complicated figure. Hers is a story of assimilation only insofar as assimilation names a specific form of complicity: an intimacy with white supremacy. In what follows, I focus on this intimacy, showing how one opts to survive in a world saturated in whiteness. This kind of survival, given it being individualized and not collective, may invite scrutiny. I endeavor to direct that critique not toward the individual—that is, Gaines—but to the source, which in this case is the whiteness inside Asian America. If this book's argument thus far has sought to unveil how the intimacy of US empire is refracted through the prism of its violence, let us now venture into the home and the American heartland, with a specific eye toward Central Texas, to assess how the reverberations of American empire can be traced through twenty-first-century home decor and the larger industry of American home and lifestyle brands to which arguably no one has left a larger imprint than Joanna Gaines, the so-called queen of Waco, Texas.

The Rise of the Magnolia Empire

"Are you ready to see your fixer-upper?" so goes Chip and Joanna Gaines, the married lifestyle moguls whose hit show *Fixer Upper* (2013–18) remains one of the most popular and influential series on HGTV. Each episode features Chip and Joanna, the owners of the remodeling and design business Magnolia Homes, as they help clients select a house, usually one dilapidated, to purchase for a bargain and refurbish within the client's budget. Quirky, goofy, and extroverted Chip oversees the realty and construction side of the operation, while poised and practical Joanna is the lead designer. Always with their hands full, Chip and Joanna often call on the labor of Clint Harp, the couple's go-to carpenter, contractor Saul "Shorty" Sanchez, and other mostly Latine workers. Like other home renovation shows, *Fixer Upper* creates a sense of what could be. Viewers from urban centers bask at the relatively affordable prices of land and property available in Central Texas. Aspiring homeowners begin to see ownership as a possibility so long as they are willing to look beyond a structure's imperfections. In making the pursuit of a dream home an affordable and achievable one, the Gaineses brought DIY restoration into the mainstream, turning the house flip into a trend for middle-class Americans. After their show launched, flippers came out from the woodwork and specific loan programs to finance and rehab a fixer-upper home became more popular, influencing sales, lending, and the types of buyers and investors interested in renovation.[18] This not only benefited the real estate market, since ownership could now be expanded to the lower and middle class, but it also expanded what became possible for homeownership, encouraging Americans to take more risks in making home and turning a profit. Although flipping opened the market for investing to the lower strata, it also meant that those not equipped with the right budget or construction and design skills could fail to break even. Marketed as a trend for anyone and everyone, the house flip requires expertise and a willingness to take a chance. An exponential growth in flipping produced a rise not only in shoddy workmanship but also in fast furniture and the resulting environmental damages associated with increased landfill waste and shipping emissions.[19]

Nonetheless, *Fixer Upper* completely transformed the home-buying market, which in turn impacted the types of reality shows featured on HGTV. Before the Gaineses, the most popular show on the channel was *House Hunters* (1999–present), a series pairing prospective buyers with agents as they navigate the home-buying process. Home makeover and improvement shows had been a staple on HGTV since the early 2000s, but something changed once the Gaineses arrived on the scene.[20] Pairing DIY with scenes of a married couple's banter and their family life in Central Texas, *Fixer Upper* has since influenced the creation and popularity of shows featuring husband-and-wife teams including *Renovation Aloha, Home Town, 100 Day Dream Home, Married to Real Estate,* and *Fixer to Fabulous*. What distinguished *Fixer Upper,* to be clear, was its focus on the Gaines family. In each episode, viewers get a glimpse into Chip and Joanna's home life, including scenes of their own years-long process of building their farmhouse and raising their four young children. Representing a mostly white, heterosexual America, sparing the mostly Latine construction workers and the small number of clients of color, *Fixer Upper* emerged alongside a renewed cultural attachment to normalcy. From frequent mentions of "the new normal" in the 2010s to aesthetic trends of normcore and minimalism, *Fixer Upper*'s authenticity, mediocrity, and farmhouse simplicity produce a reality TV version of what Karen Tongson has described as "normporn."[21] A kind of sedative that soothes the queer viewer, normporn materializes through the veneer of normality, allowing for an ability to process how the hardships of everyday life are connected to the trials and tribulations of a nation or a historical moment, such as the financial recession. In what follows, I consider *Fixer Upper*—a television show revering the mundane—in the context of normporn. I depict the rise of the Gaines empire, with a particular focus on Joanna, in order to think about agency, complicity, and the Asian/white domesticity of America's Asian mother. If Joanna Gaines sits atop the American industry of lifestyle brands, shattering both the glass and bamboo ceiling, let us dwell on the years leading up to her summit.

Chip and Joanna met in Waco, Texas in 2001, the same year Joanna graduated from Baylor University and three years after Chip did. Two years later, they married and opened their flagship store, Magnolia Market. In the years that followed, the two renovated and flipped houses, sold home goods, and built an entire home community. Joanna's blogging about the couple's work caught the eyes of a producer in 2011, and in 2013, *Fixer Upper* debuted on HGTV. It did not take long for viewers to fall in love with the down-to-earth Texas couple and the interior design trend they popularized, a style known as farmhouse chic. A mix of antique, contemporary, and raw materials such as distressed wood, exposed wood beams, barn doors, and large pendant light fixtures, farmhouse chic grew in popularity largely because of *Fixer Upper*. After analyzing 1.9 million home sales between 2016 and 2017, Zillow reported that homes with farmhouse features like the ones promoted on *Fixer Upper*—exposed brick and beams, wainscoting, shiplap, farmhouse sinks, and clawfoot bathtubs—sold as much as 30 percent higher than the expected value.[22] Becoming a staple of twenty-first-century Americana, the Gaineses took advantage of the public's love affair with all things farmhouse and launched their own cable network in 2022. A hub of lifestyle media, the Magnolia Network carries programs centered on the home, from interior design and landscaping to renovation and construction. Fan favorite programs include *Fixer Upper: Welcome Home* (2021), a reprise of the original show's format, *Fixer Upper: The Castle* (2022), a one-season special where Chip and Joanna restore a late-nineteenth-century Waco castle, *Fixer Upper: The Hotel* (2023), another single season where they renovate a historical Waco building into a boutique hotel, and *Fixer Upper: The Lakehouse* (2024), a six-episode special marking ten years of the *Fixer Upper* franchise with the couple transforming a mid-century modern lake house near Lake Waco into the Spanish revival style. One notable addition to the lineup is the cooking show *Magnolia Table with Joanna Gaines*.

The same success that led Chip and Joanna to become owners of a cable network paved the way for them to expand their brick and mortar. When *Fixer Upper* was still airing, the couple purchased land spanning two downtown city blocks and highlighted by two abandoned 120-foot-high cotton silos previously owned by the Brazos Valley Cotton Oil Company. It was here where they uprooted Magnolia Market to a larger and more central location with the hopes of generating business. Opening in 2015, Magnolia Market reported just under two million visitors in its first full year of operation, drawing an estimated thirty thousand visitors per week.[23] In 2019, the Gainses oversaw a $10.4 million expansion. Newly renovated, their 4.9 acre grounds now feature something for everybody: a 12,000-square-foot retail store located in a historical barn, food trucks, picnic tables, a baseball field, garden store, bakery, lawn, church, and an assortment of boutique shops. Like a mall, it does not cost anything to visit except during special events. It does, however, cost money to take a tour of the Silos grounds, which I did in April 2023. I brought my mom, a huge Joanna fan, with me. We were the only people of color. The tour lasted an hour and was led by a white woman volunteer affiliated with the Gaineses' church. Striking up conversation with workers, I asked about Joanna (who had denied my invitation to interview her but was honored by the request, per an email exchange I had with Magnolia's director of public relations).[24] Everyone I spoke to, not including the police officers and security guards patrolling the grounds, reiterated how *unique* she is, how she and Chip are just what America needs. They certainly seem to love the couple; distinct personalities and relatable persona are proof that opposites attract and that any normal American can rise to such heteronormative bliss. To them, and to many, the Gaineses are an all-American family, Joanna an American sweetheart. To others, hers is a name that may spark familiarity but is otherwise forgettable, blended into the monotony of suburban-centric reality TV. Still, the sentiment rings clear: It is Joanna at the helm of the Magnolia empire.

Beyond her obvious likability, what explains the public's appeal toward Joanna Gaines? Could it be the allure of her whitened Asian femininity, both inviting and unthreatening? Or could it stem from her race itself, and the ruse of color-blind racism that pervades American liberalism and its side project, the fixer-upper more commonly known as multiracialism? To this, I ask another question: What might we make of Magnolia's choice to make her face *the* face of the brand? If one were to roam the grounds of the Silos, the Target aisles featuring her Hearth & Hand brand, or even the grocery checkout lane where it is always her on the cover of the quarterly *Magnolia* magazine, one is sure to be greeted by an image of Joanna's friendly face. Warm and inviting, Joanna's smile also appears on the cover of her 2022 memoir, *The Stories We Tell: Every Piece of Your Story Matters*. When I visited the Silos, a promotion banner of that memoir hung on a brick wall. A quote from the book—"Imagine if all the worn-out, untrue, painful chapters of our lives started to quiet, and the beautiful, unique pieces of who we are were to rise"—is set alongside images of the author, one of her as an adult and another as a child. While present-day Joanna may pass as racially ambiguous,

FIGURE 2.2. Torn in two. The Silos, Downtown Waco, Texas, 2023. Photographed by the author.

images of her younger self present a more obvious Asianness. What if we presume that it is for these reasons that Joanna selected the two portraits as dual covers for the book?

The first picture is the one on the paper jacket, a smiling Joanna at forty-four. When you remove the cover flap, you'll see a picture of her at six years old on the hardback. A sort of touchstone, this second image stands in as a reference point throughout the pages, a piece of evidence that Joanna is part Asian, 100 percent herself. To be clear, it was not until she published *The Stories We Tell* that Joanna Gaines began putting her background in the center. In the early part of her career, references to her Asian heritage were sprinkled across a few episodes of *Fixer Upper*—often with Chip making a slight comment about how taking one's shoes off is a Korean tradition, that Jo could karate chop him, or with Jo mentioning her mom's Korean cooking.[25] In the memoir, she is as open as she's ever been, sharing "the short version of a very complicated yet beautiful love story."[26] Her parents, Nan and Jerry, met at a party in Korea in 1971 after her dad had been drafted to serve in the Vietnam War and was stationed in Seoul. They fell in love, and when Jerry returned to the United States, the two wrote letters back and forth, using a translator to understand the other's written language. A year later, Jerry mailed Nan a plane ticket with a note asking if she'd marry him. He was in his early twenties. A few months later, at nineteen years old, Nan landed in San Francisco, married Jerry that same day, and followed her husband from the courthouse to Kansas where they started their life together and raised three daughters, Joanna the middle child.

As a young girl in Seoul, Nan adored American culture, and upon landing in Kansas, she took note of the beautiful white women with, in her words, big eyes and perfect noses. She cooked Korean food for her family but committed to "American ways of living" and raising her children.[27] This was, to no surprise, formative for Joanna, to be part of a mixed race family in a small town outside Wichita in the '70s. Throughout the memoir and in the book's supplemental podcast, Joanna recounts the pressures she felt to hide the Asian part of her identity. She was a perfectionist, wanting nothing but to blend into the surroundings. After she was teased for eating rice at school, she followed her mother's lead and decided to do what she could to fit in, and she found success. Voted prom queen in high school, Joanna went on to graduate from Baylor, complete a journalism internship in New York, move back home, meet Chip, get married, start a business, and start a family. But at forty-four years old, she began feeling like she was "full, but running on empty."[28] *The Stories We Tell* functions as a turning point; decades of shame have evolved into pride for all parts of herself. As the author seeks to undo years of racial denial, the memoir extends an invitation to the reader to "come as you are. To join me, with a vulnerable and open heart, as we connect the chapters of our life stories and figure out where we go next, learning to move forward from within. Guard down, light shining."[29]

Needless to say, what is marketed as a memoir is, one can argue, a moralizing if not sanctimonious attempt at the self-help genre. Like the Gaineses' Magnolia brand, the memoir traffics in the inspirational and spiritual dimension of a minimalist, modern sensibility. Hidden behind rustic white spaces and motivational positivity, like the word "décor" that appears on the walls of their fixer-uppers is the evangelical infrastructure of their rising empire in neofascist times.[30] Although I will unpack the Christian connection later on in this chapter, let me briefly appraise the ways in which faith functions as a major theme in the memoir.

Each chapter of *The Stories We Tell* walks the reader through an overarching lesson learned from life's obstacles be it Joanna's trait of perfectionism, her insecurities and tendency to evade vulnerability, or even her discomfort with fame. Interconnected, these hardships can be traced to a racial shame that Joanna first experienced in childhood when classmates joked about the slant in her eyes and her mother's Korean accent. Without providing any substantive details—like the names her peers called her or the kinds of insults others would direct toward her Korean heritage—Joanna does make it clear that she "grew up thinking [she] had two options: fit in or be called out."[31] Choosing the former, Joanna quieted her Asian side, a choice not always available to mixed race people. It was not until her internship in New York that she was able to see "the beauty of being different and the thrill of being unique."[32] Writing from this vantage point, an enlightened Joanna relies on a gospel-like writing style that gestures to the religious basis in which she's been able to embrace her Korean identity, escaping the darkness of isolation. Consider the following excerpts: "Let's choose the rhythms that move us forward, toward the flow of gratitude and hopeful expectation."[33] Or, "None of us has to go on fighting monsters in the dark by ourselves. We can show one another that it's safer to live open-hearted after all. Out of hiding. Willing to step forward courageously even when there's no guarantee—only a hope that the life we're worthy of abounds on the other side. Whether we leap forward or put one brave foot in front of the other. Fear breaks. We rise."[34] Sentences like these abound within the text. Indeed, most of the memoir consists of preachy filler that emphasizes the faith she has in God. As Gaines writes, "My journal is where I talk to myself and to God."[35] Gaines is not a formally trained writer, and thus, I am less interested in critiquing the quality of the journaling but in drawing connections between Gaines's dependence on morality and virtue signaling and the implications these tactics have for her supposed pursuit in telling her story.

For all her focus on story, that is, readers will find it odd that Gaines, in actuality, does not tell many stories. There are morals and lessons but no substantive details, no conflict, setting, or plot. If, as the author clarifies, "When I say *story*, I don't mean history," then we would do well to analyze the text along the lines of what Roland Barthes posits in *Mythologies*: "To see someone who does not see is the best way to be intensely aware of *what* he does not see."[36] Turning to publishing, the Gaineses have consolidated the Magnolia brand into the written form, opening up a new site to assess that which remains unaccounted for in their various ventures: the synergies between the Magnolia empire and the US evangelical empire. Faux–Brené Brown, Gaines's desire to inspire the reader to lean into intention, vulnerability, and purpose is expressed through vague and redundant commentary mimicking the vernacular employed by the Christian right in their efforts to push for the reemergence of evangelicalism, triggering a "return to America's

Christian heritage."[37] God, as Gaines writes, "is the deepest anchor in [her] life," and it is through an ability to empathize that Gaines has found her "path forward."[38] Resting on faith and unity, she "believe[s] that at our core, we are all more similar than we think."[39] Elsewhere, I have written about the feminist potential of deidealizing empathy as an embodied knowledge intrinsic to the racial hybrid.[40] The idealization of empathy, like one's commitment to togetherness and belonging, is not inherently dangerous unless one fails to heed Audre Lorde's dictum that it is not the "differences between us that are separating us" but "our refusal to recognize those differences."[41] To this point, in *The Stories We Tell*, Gaines offers cultural commentary on the 2020 moment and "the racial injustices that still plague our country."[42] In the following excerpt, pay attention both to how Gaines acknowledges racial tension and the solution she offers:

> For me, these past few years have felt a bit like a maze, trying to navigate my way through where I stand on important issues, how much I should advocate for my opinions, what I should say and shouldn't say, who and what I should support. Maybe you can relate. It's as though opinion is the new currency of our culture—and ideas about right and wrong are expected and asked for, only to be praised or torn apart. I see the value of the collected voice, but when I look around at all the pain and hurt, the bitterness and anger that's spreading through our communities, I can't say it's opinions that we lack. We don't need more microphones on the stage or more views or judgements that aren't necessarily based on fact or knowledge, because those aren't always grounded in truth. The best thing we can offer one another is a listening ear—a brave soul.[43]

Championing an ethics and appreciation of a multiculturalism specific to the Magnolia brand of racial renovation, Gaines performs perfectly the role of a good neighbor through her ability to acknowledge "important issues" without venturing into the murky waters of sociopolitical critique. She exhibits this same demeanor in an episode of "Uncomfortable Conversations with a Black Man," when the Gaines family sits down with host Emmanuel Acho, former professional football player and current sports analyst, to discuss the importance of "seeing color." As Joanna and Chip each ask Acho questions about whether to raise children to be color-blind and how to teach community members about racism, two of their children, Ella and Drake, ask questions of their own, one about whether the host is afraid of white people and another about whether the host has any hope for the future.

Acho responds to this final question in the affirmative, citing Chip and Joanna's parenting, their willingness to initiate conversations about race with their children, as the reason he has hope. As of writing, Acho is the inaugural host for *Second Chance Stage*, a live talent show that premiered on the Magnolia Network in fall 2024.

The narrative of blind optimism that pervades the Magnolia brand, and Gaines's memoir in particular, amends a feminist political grammar, affirming Clare Hemmings's argument in *Why Stories Matter*.[44] As Hemmings convincingly outlines the political and ethical risks of feminist narrations of progress, loss, and return, she warns against potential adaptation or co-optation. Staged and filmed, the Gaineses' participation in America's racial reckoning following the murder of George Floyd can be understood as a conservative mobilization of the progress narrative. Like most businesses, the Magnolia brand defaults to the neutral and apolitical position, a position that always will lean rightward. In moments of unrest and uprising, companies may shift their stance and announce commitments to diversity, equity, and inclusion without ever veering into liberatory territory. In 2020, that is, discussing racism and anti-racism was good for business. For many families like the Gaineses, the conversation centered on Blackness and whiteness, leaving one to wonder why when an increase in anti-Asian racism took place during those same years, there was no comparable public engagement by the family. As much as it is not Joanna's responsibility to speak on such issues given her identity as a Korean American, it is telling that an Asian mother of mixed race children chose not to make a similar statement about the rise in anti-Asian violence. Was Joanna simply being a good ally, keeping the attention on Blackness and the family's presumed whiteness? Was it, in other words, that Joanna did not view herself or her children as the kinds of Asian bodies under threat? Either way, this is a sign of Barthes's observation: "To see someone who does not see is the best way to be intensely aware of *what* he does not see."[45] So much for the potential of racial ambiguity to unmoor the fixity of race, which Jennifer Ho has shown is integral to understanding Asian American racialization.[46] While Gaines is aware that she is "good at being malleable," perhaps there is a side to that malleability that she is unaware of.[47] As writer and activist Cherríe Moraga has written, "There is an accountability to what we know. If being mixed blood impacts what you know, and what you don't know, you're accountable to both of those sides of you."[48]

Why is it, then, that Joanna's story seems to evade the white side of the equation? Although Chip is as front and center as she is, in her memoir and even in the book's supplementary podcast (which features four episodes of her interviewing her mother, sisters, and Chip about their respective stories), there is little mention of her father. This seems to be a sign of the times. The white father takes a back seat to the Korean mother in two other memoirs written by two of Gaines's contemporaries who also happen to be mixed race women born to Korean mothers and white fathers: Grace M. Cho's *Tastes like War* (2021) and Michelle Zauner's *Crying in H Mart* (2021). For each author, familial culinary traditions mark significant memories between daughter and mother, and for Gaines, these recollections appear scattered throughout the pages of her cookbooks, *Magnolia Table: A Collection of Recipes for Gathering*, inviting speculation into (1) the gender and racial configurations that bind Asian women to the scenes and practices of domesticity and (2) the almost disappeared specter of the white father.[49] This is not a critique but a curiosity. One can procure vast intel in silences. It could be that Joanna is intentionally decentering whiteness, a commendable but limited act. Although readers learn of the white father's settler roots, his aspirations, and his faults, he is present only through the margins.[50] Elsewhere, we do in fact learn that her father, Jerry, is of Lebanese and German heritage. In "A Family Tradition" (2021), the first episode of *Magnolia Table with Joanna Gaines*, Joanna cooks her paternal grandfather's fatayer, a classic Lebanese meat pie, with a side Lebanese salad, hummus, and baklava, and at the end of the episode, we get to meet Jerry when Joanna surprises him with leftovers. Joanna even dedicates the third volume of her cookbook to him.[51] Notwithstanding these facts, Jerry lingers on the margins. A critique not of the choice to decenter the father but of the ramifications of failing to contend with him as part of one's story, my concern, particularly in Joanna's case, is that to tell the full story, one must commit to surveying all sides of oneself.[52] This includes her, her mother, and her children's phenotypically different Asianness as mentioned in one of the book's podcast episodes in which Joanna laughs with pride when recounting a story about how her children express a wish that their eyes were more slanted and that they use makeup to look more Asian.[53] Here, the mixed Asian anxiety of not looking Asian enough produces a desire to be captured by what Asian American comedian Jes Tom calls "wadar," a witty play on gaydar that speaks on an intuitive ability to sense that someone is wasian.[54] Such attempts for authenticity or visibility like TikTok's Wasian check are as much a story about whiteness and its porosity as it is about being half. Joanna accentuates her Asianness, spotlighting her Korean mother while the white American father measures up to no more than a supporting cast member. One reading is that this is a feminist and racialized act of repair or overcompensation: filling in the gaps produced by white ancestry and a male-dominated world. As praiseworthy and justified as it may be to opt to decenter whiteness, it does not align with the book's subtitle, *Every Piece of Your Story Matters*, leaving much to be desired about the stories she does not offer about whiteness. Is it that whiteness bears no story to tell? Is it that the story has already been told?[55] Perhaps it is because whiteness is so normalized and naturalized that one may not even consider it as a story to tell. Or is it that whiteness is precisely where the story ends because it is where the narrator has come up against a wall? Rather than inquire into what Laura Kang explores as the Asian woman as method, Joanna dabbles instead in Leslie Bow's provocation of racist love, an anxiety that manifests into a kind of fetishistic attachment Asian American women may have for other Asian American women.[56] To tell the full story might require consenting to Julietta Singh's credo that *no archive will restore you*, even and especially an archive of the body that represents a bridge between the best of both worlds: the fortitude of the Occident and the hospitality of the Orient, if you will.

Alas, it is restoration that Joanna stumbles upon in the process of journaling: "I didn't think that writing down my story would heal me, but it did."[57] Given that the Magnolia brand made a name for itself with palatability, simplicity, and uplift, the preachiness of the memoir should be expected, to the disappointment of her fans, many of whom turned to Goodreads to critique the book's lack of sincerity, "stream of consciousness" writing style, and its "faith-based approach to Godly living." There is no denying that Jo, like Chip, is an entrepreneur. The tactic is business expansion, diversifying ones operations into new products and markets while remaining light, fresh, and family oriented. A *New York Times* best-selling author of an assortment of cookbooks, interior design books, children's books, and a cowritten book with Chip, Joanna has built an empire, one that transcends the grounds of the Magnolia Silos and enters the homes of all who either purchase an item of theirs from Target, remodel their home with an eye toward farmhouse chic, or even tune in to the Magnolia Network.

My aim here is to question the peculiar incarnations of America's love affair with restoration for which Joanna Gaines has played a major role in influencing. I do not mean to suggest that Joanna's aim is malicious—in fact, I argue quite the opposite, that her desire is to make others feel what she has only begun to feel: comfort, belonging, whole. One issue with this is that these feelings of homeliness are not made accessible to all. Another is that there are consequences to restoration, a risk in hiding or embellishing what has yet to have undergone a true reckoning. For a town like Waco to house Magnolia—a place, a lifestyle, a philosophy—we ought to worry about the impact of the urge to revamp, modernize, update, or freshen up. What gets swept away or covered up with a timeless look? If Joanna's claim to fame is her preference for all things classic, then in this nation, and in that city, that is a dangerous desire. Nothing is more classic, more typically American than genocide and racist violence, two staples in Waco's history. Her acts of racial renovation signal more than an aesthetic gesture or taste but a curious complicity with an old and explicit white supremacy. To put it simply, race is no fixer-upper.

The Big Reveal: Race and Revival in Waco, Texas

Nestled in the heart of Texas, the city of Waco is situated alongside the Brazos River, which marks the boundary between East and West Texas. A ninety-minute drive from both Austin to the south and Dallas to the north, Waco is home to Baylor University and the Dr. Pepper Museum. If you know of Waco, you know the city boasts a complicated history. In the 1700s, the land was home to the Waco, a band of the Wichita tribe who forged an agrarian style of life. In the nineteenth century, white settlers began occupying their land, and soon after, government treaties forced their displacement onto a reservation in Oklahoma. In the beginning of the twentieth century, racial segregation was common, so common that it was not until 2016 that Waco's Greenwood Cemetery put an end to segregated burials that divided Black graves from white ones. The year 2016 also marked a century since Jesse Washington, a seventeen-year-old Black farmhand, was tortured and lynched in front of Waco's city hall. His hours-long torture was treated as a celebratory spectacle to white Wacoans, while it was condemned by newspapers around the country. As of February 2023, a historical marker branded with the title "The Waco Horror" can be seen at the front of the city hall, a meager attempt to raise awareness of racist lynching in Central Texas. Toward the end of the twentieth century, Waco again captured the attention of Americans with the Waco siege: a fifty-one-day standoff between the US Bureau of Alcohol, Tobacco, and Firearms and the Branch Davidians, a paramilitary religious cult whose compound was set ablaze, killing seventy-four people, including controversial leader David Koresh.

Waco, Texas, a city whose history of the present boasts legacies of colonialism, spectacularized state violence, the evangelical right, and white supremacy, including a Ku Klux Klan chapter active since 1986, is a particularly ripe site to investigate what historian Kathleen Belew has shown is the white power movement's origin in the aftermath of the Vietnam War.[58] As Belew elaborates in *Bring the War Home*, disparate strands of American white supremacy were brought together in the wake of the Vietnam War due to a growing distrust of the federal government. Louis Beam, the Vietnam War veteran and neofascist author of *Essays of a Klansman* (1983), went so far as to urge white power activists to "bring it on home," referring to "a literal extension of military-style combat into civilian space."[59] With the rise of the Magnolia empire, Waco is undoubtably undergoing a renovation. Rebranded and refurbished into an unlikely but popular tourist destination, the city now carries a new reputation, the center of American domesticity, resulting in a rapidly gentrifying Waco, a town whose population has increased by 18 percent since 2010.[60] The Gaineses are rightfully credited for Waco's transformation, but like any space touched by American settler colonialism, the past finds a way into the present. To analyze the Magnolia empire alongside Waco's militant, racist, and nationalist history is to seek confrontation with what haunts the present-day vision of the American home.

Let us begin by reviewing the very name of the brand: Magnolia. The story behind the name is not especially meaningful, other than the fact that Chip and Jo had two magnolia trees outside their first home together and that Jo has always loved magnolia trees and their blooms. However, in *The Magnolia Story*, Chip and Jo's 2016 coauthored book, Joanna makes a startling comment, remarking on the way magnolias "just seemed so entirely Southern. They reminded me of drinking sweet tea on the big wraparound porch of a nineteenth-century plantation home or something. The name *Magnolia* just fit my business and the feeling I wanted to create."[61]

Magnolias are indeed a prominent and magnificent sight in the southern landscape, but to use Magnolia as the name and to associate that name with a feeling of plantation life begs a question asked by literary scholar Michael Chaney: "How is slavery remembered here?"[62] Chaney is referring to the tourism surrounding the Magnolia Plantation in Charleston, South Carolina, which has grown to become a staple of the area's booming economy. While, as Chaney writes, "many plantations are in fact places of history, marking sites where many Americans go to reflect on this country's vexed past," the Magnolia Silos seem privy to diverting attention away from a difficult past, focusing instead on the possibility of revival as performed by *America's first family of renovation* (as they are referred in the book's marketing) and as manifested through their sterile aesthetic of post-race all-white everything.[63] This is an affective curation, a disavowal turned timeless. In her memoir, Joanna tells the reader what any fan of hers already knows, that she has "an instinct for creating spaces that said something about the people who lived there."[64] Tense is important; she is concerned with rewriting the past in real time. If, as Joanna writes, "a house becomes a home when it tells your story," what stories get airtime and which ones turn ghostly when one brings home a piece of the Magnolia brand?[65] This is a question targeted less toward consumer complicity than the market and mass appeal, and although Joanna would be the first to say that not all stories are packaged up neatly and without controversy, she would also say that every piece of the story matters, and if there is one piece, a literal material object that defines the Magnolia brand, it is not the magnolia tree but the side paneling known as shiplap.

Shiplap is a type of lumber marked by a groove cut at the top and bottom of each board, which allows individual panels to overlap and form a tight seal. Originally used on ships given its ability to protect against water and wind, these slabs of wood can be reclaimed and used in interior design as side paneling on homes. Since the mid-2010s, shiplap became popularized by the house-flipping team. The material simultaneously disappears the past as it exposes a made-over present, contributing to a dangerous practice of renovation seen not only in the installation of one panel atop another but also in the repetition of recovery and restoration. Buying, flipping, and pushing color away, Joanna resists criticism that her style is one-dimensionally shiplap, noting in *The Stories We Tell* that she and her style are "always evolving."[66] Her renovations are revelations that everything can be made over, that nothing should be discarded.

In an evocative engagement with the Gaineses, race and media scholar Eva Hageman's documentary video essay titled *shiplap* begins with clips from *Fixer Upper* to analyze shiplap beyond its ornamentality. In just under seven minutes, the video essay uses the material as a way in to examine how race haunts the race-neutral portrayals in reality lifestyle television.[67] Reflecting on the popular home renovation material, the piece recenters the systemic racism that lingers on the fringes of American lifestyle television, and it is Hageman's voice-over that guides the viewer through this "American nightmare."[68] In the creator's statement, Hageman explains, "The piece highlights how the *Fixer Upper* narratives of transformation, hospitality, and normative family values are used to obscure stories of displacement and marginalization in the representation of Waco. In these affective visions of *Fixed Up* transformations, the histories and lives of Black and Brown people in the Waco area are pushed to the margins or swept out of the frame altogether."[69] Through use of critical and clear-eyed speculation, Hageman's *shiplap* reframes *Fixer Upper* in order to question how its focus on restoration disavows structural realities of American racism. "What histories are pushed out of the carefully constructed frames of lifestyle television? What are the stories behind the open concept walls of their fixed-up houses?"[70] To answer these questions, Hageman turns to the history of shipbuilding, regarding shiplap as a commodity never not disconnected from the Black Atlantic slave trade. Dwelling on the intertwined history of shiplap, maritime history, and racial capitalism, Hageman restores the racial pain superficially glossed over in seemingly apolitical narratives of home restoration. In a review of the video essay, Terri Francis decodes Hageman's piece as a reminder "that houses have histories and neighborhoods too have histories and, though hidden, the grief will eventually be heard."[71]

In any endeavor to repair, disavowed histories are necessary to not only reveal but to reckon with, and if, as Joanna writes, "it may be no surprise that I love a good reveal," then what Hageman offers is an assurance that the racialized grief once hidden can yet become uncovered.[72] Following Hageman's example, one may make room for reparative revelation in other corners of the Magnolia empire and surely in its most prominent towers, such as the case of *Fixer Upper: The Castle* (2022). The six-part miniseries documents Chip and Jo through the process of their most challenging venture to date, the restoration of a 6,700-square-foot, late-nineteenth-century castle. Located in the historical neighborhood of Castle Heights, the Cottonland Castle broke ground in 1890, a time when Waco's cotton-based economy flourished.[73] A local stone contractor, John Tennant, conceived of the build as a way to invest in local property. This lone castle represented a growing interest in residents to break from Waco's urban center, matching the national trend of suburban development in and around city centers.[74] Tennant sold the land to Ripley Hanrick, a cotton broker, in 1906, and then to Civil War veteran Alfred Abeel in 1908, who oversaw an architect's completion of the castle's tower, three stories, basement, and eight fireplaces.[75] In 2019, Chip convinced Joanna to purchase and renovate the castle always with the intention to sell it. The couple ultimately decided to keep the property and as of writing, they are still the owners.[76]

In a blog posted on the Magnolia website, Joanna recounts her first impression of the property, that it was haunted, but then goes on to reflect on what she's learned from following Chip: "If you look past the cracks in the masonry, past the rotted floorboards, past the wilderness taking over the backyard, there is a lot of beauty to be found in this old castle."[77] Beauty, as the saying goes, is in the eyes of the beholder. For the couple to own a castle erected at the apex of the US South's cotton industry and to see potential rather than outrage or shame is staggering but unsurprising given their approach to restoration: "We believe in home, that it should restore us from today and ready us for tomorrow. . . . We believe in unearthing beauty, however hidden or subtle it might be." These sentiments are expressed in the Magnolia Manifesto, a passage found at the end of each issue of the Magnolia quarterly magazine. Notice the strategic removal of the past in the manifesto's focus on today and tomorrow. Notice the preference to unearth the good, never minding the bad or the ugly. What if Joanna had refused the fairy-tale ending and instead held on to her first impression, letting the castle's ghosts guide her? This is no simple task. A white environment is extractive, isolating the person of color and pressuring them to second-guess, deny, or undermine racism. From a young age, Joanna navigated whiteness in its most extreme sites. When children called her names, she made the conscious decision not to share those experiences with her mother so as to shield Nan from the racism she too endured. It may be that Joanna sought to protect her family from racism as she herself sought protection from racist microaggressions by looking away, blending in, and honing a positive outlook, three arenas she could control. At home, there was no other example to follow. Conditioned to see racism as singular events of explicit and overt violence, white family members "cannot be a resource" for mixed race people as Samira K. Mehta sums it up in *The Racism of People Who Love You*, a collection of essays on mixed race belonging.[78]

There are, however, moments where one can sense Joanna pressing back against the whiteness of her environment, refusing its direction and force. There are her annoyed yet playful facial expressions, like the eye rolls she directs toward Chip when he airs a questionable comment. There are the anecdotes in *The Magnolia Story* about how Chip was never Joanna's type because she was always attracted to quiet guys with dark hair.[79] She even pushes back on whiteness as an aesthetic taste as seen in an episode in the first season of the original *Fixer Upper* where Joanna and Chip help their friend and woodworker Clint Harp and his wife find a house. We can read Gaines as torn between her instincts and the incredibly white-saturated setting she finds herself in when she says, "I mean, I love white, but I need a little bit of a break." Given her design style, white does seem to be her color of choice. Chip certainly thinks so. In the third episode of *Fixer Upper: The Castle*, he jokes, "Jo likes a lot of different colors. She likes white, and then she likes a version of white that you would have thought was white, but it was in fact some alternative to white. Then of course don't forget the gray white. She loves the gray white. (Jo: I'm into color, guys.) White. Beige, beige

FIGURE 2.3. "Family Craves Urban Feel," *Fixer Upper*, 2014.

white, woof that makes her go nuts."[80] A woman of color, Joanna navigates Waco through a racial and gendered lens, managing to make life in a space deeply entrenched in all things racist and sexist. In spite of her complicity and intimacy with whiteness, which I clearly have chosen to concentrate on in this chapter, she still offers us an example of how one can survive in a toxic environment, even if it fails to amount to a refusal strong enough to amend any real historical damage. Hers is a story of assimilation, success, and survival. Hers, though not a path I would brand as one to follow if one prioritizes collective over individual survival, remains important to review if only to assess the ways in which we too may find ourselves moved by whiteness and, on occasion, moved so far as to steer away from our own instincts. Rather than shame her, it is imperative to attack the source (i.e., whiteness) that informs her experience in the *interstitial*.[81] I move now toward opening up space to discern how disorienting it can be to live within what sociologist Elijah Anderson has termed "the white space."[82]

In a 2024 article in the *Journal of Interior Design*, design strategist and consultant Jacquelyn Ogorchukwu Iyamah forwards the concept of interior race theory, "the theory that we can stimulate *or* hinder racial liberation in our interior spaces through objects that we use in our daily lives such as homeware, furniture, and décor."[83] Reviewing work at the intersection of material culture and critical race theory from bell hooks's writing on how

Black people could heal from racial domination through the "task of making homeplace" to Bridget T. Heneghan's study on the American consumer's preference in the antebellum period for white-colored goods, Iyamah suggests that the interiors of our homes can function as sites to "restore, remember, and resist."[84] If home is, as Iyamah writes, "a set of practices," then what practices does the Gaineses' Magnolia brand exercise?[85]

Answers can be sourced in the owners' very words. On Oprah Winfrey's *Super Soul Sunday* podcast, Chip describes Joanna as guarded, someone who "doesn't love to be transparent and honest."[86] In *The Stories We Tell*, she gives context: "For a while, I was good at building fortresses, good at establishing one sturdy wall of self-protection after another. I knew how to retreat, and for most of my life, I considered it a safety measure."[87] Call it avoidance or self-preservation, Joanna's tendency to view the home as shelter, as a kind of shield, may suggest that hers is a life of fabrication or deception, one that prioritizes the image over the story. More likely, it could be understood as a form of refusal, a way for a public figure to cultivate privacy, a return to isolation where one keeps their most intimate memories at a distance. As a guest on Jeremiah Brent's *Ideas of Order* podcast, Joanna reflects on one of her dictums—that home is not a place but a feeling—before explaining how she creates tangible moments of connection in the home, like placing puzzle pieces on a green card cable in the middle of a room, a subtle invitation for her family to take a break from their screens, sit down with one another, and create moments of "togetherness."[88]

Beyond these practices of suburban domesticity, there are more incriminating ones where colonialism loiters in the decor.[89] Joanna, like most designers, has a penchant for accumulating vintage goods like old wooden doors and antique lamps to use in her fixers, but as any student of feminist materialism can tell you, there is a "vital materiality" that conjoins human and nonhuman things.[90] The materialist perspectives forged in Jane Bennett's *Vibrant Matter* (2010) and Mel Chen's *Animacies* (2012) and *Intoxicated* (2023) are, in their own right, case studies on the intimacy of violence, explorations of the ways in which nonhuman forces challenge what we think we know about the order of things. It may come as no surprise, then, that Joanna's guilty pleasure concerns material items.[91] As Bill Brown argues in *The Sense of Things*, things possess us much more than we possess them.[92] When it comes to household objects, Joanna has a wandering eye, amassing wooden boards, old buildings, and storage bins full of flea market finds that await their destiny in the Magnolia universe. To invoke Iyamah, how might the relatively innocent practice of accumulating things stimulate *or* hinder racial liberation?

To her husband, the hoarding is endearing, but say we were to employ Brown's "thing theory" onto Joanna's love of things.[93] Following Brown's direction that "we begin to confront the thingness of objects when they stop working for us," allow me to use as a case study the Old Church that stands on the grounds of the Magnolia Silos.[94] You might say that a church is not a thing but a place; however, the history of the church's relocation to the Silos would prove otherwise. Built in 1894 as the Second Presbyterian Church, the structure had been vacant since 1989 before Chip and Joanna decided to purchase it in 2017.[95] One of Waco's oldest buildings and a centerpiece in the Silos 2020 expansion project, the church had been designated as a historical landmark by the local historical commission, a designation that would drop following the relocation. Its rotting frame and structurally unsound foundation meant that in order to transport the structure approximately one mile from its original site (N. Thirteenth Street) to the Silos grounds (between S. Eighth and S. Sixth Street), the church would need to be moved piece by piece, which is what happened. The original bell tower and steeple were demolished, and Magnolia opted not to preserve the stained glass windows for budgetary reasons, but with restored pews and hardwood floors, the Old Church now stands on a new frame and foundation, both constructed at the Silos.[96] While Magnolia framed their plan as a "deconstruction" rather than a "demolition," the relocation process caused a minor uproar from the city's preservation board members including Kenneth Hafertepe, a professor of museum studies at Baylor University, who viewed the Gaineses' project as "the antithesis of historic restoration," branding the Old Church as "a completely new building with a few salvaged fragments."[97]

No longer with its historical marker, it is not as though the structure has lost its history, for "things may still lurk in the shadows," as Brown puts it.[98] When I sat in the new church, observing the wainscoting and exposed beams, a fellow guest expressed disappointment upon learning from our tour guide that the space was not available to rent for her wedding. Nevertheless, as we were reassured, its presence offers a space for all Silos visitors to take a "pause, reflect, and behold the beauty of a place with such a rich and meaningful history."[99] In taking that pause, what shadows come to light? Thinking with Saidiya Hartman's tool of critical fabulation, my effort to address the historical omissions made even more opaque through the church's relocation brings me to remember the murder of Jesse Washington, the Black farmhand brutally lynched outside Waco's city hall on May 15, 1916.[100] The next few lines include gruesome details of his lynching, details I have opted to include to illustrate how the violence with which he succumbed is a violence that restoration could never make over. After castrating, dismembering, burning, and killing him, white Wacoans chained what remained of Washington behind a horse. Cheering and celebrating the illegal lynching, fifteen thousand spectators gathered to watch as the corpse of a seventeen-year-old was dragged throughout the town. It was the lunch hour on a Monday, which meant that children could attend. I wonder if those same spectators went to church just the day before. What gospel was preached at the Second Presbyterian Church that Sunday? I wonder if any of the children who attended, the same ones who snapped Washington's teeth out of his jaw and sold them as souvenirs, were baptized in the church. From May 9, when Washington was escorted away to the neighboring county as to quell a rising vigilante action, to May 15, when the trial and lynching took place, who sought solace or divine intervention in that place of worship? Dragged behind horseback, did Washington's charred body pass by the white church that once stood on N. Thirteenth Street? What about places where Black people found worship? Toliver Chapel Baptist Church and New Hope Baptist Church, at the time one of the largest Black churches in the South, were both founded after emancipation and were places of refuge. Like Waco's segregated burial grounds, the Old Church was without a doubt a church that did not welcome Black people. It is in light of this history that the Old Church, now remade into a space where Silos visitors can find reprieve from the Texas heat, can never truly exist outside the shadows of American anti-Blackness. Here, racial renovation carries no moral justification. Erected in 1894, four years after Washington's birth, the church may look different now, but fresh paint and new windows could never bury the spirits that call us forth. There is, in other words, no redemptive renovation of the church on Thirteenth Street without a reckoning of the centuries-old practice of white supremacy that the people of Waco embodied in their dehumanization of Washington during an era when slavery, though abolished, endured in its afterlife. *We begin to confront the thingness of objects when they stop working for us.*

In May 1953, a series of at least thirty-three tornados tore through the heartland with the most deadly hitting Waco, Texas on May 11, killing 114 people. Some Black people in the area considered the event, which took place almost thirty-seven years to the day, an instance of divine retribution for Washington's lynching.[101] For people of color and white people alike, the presence and evocation of God is an undeniable staple in the Bible Belt. In that region and beyond, the church is associated with conservative family values, an umbrella term that allows homophobia and racism to fester. To end, I contemplate the ways Christianity functions as a site with which to further accentuate the connections behind the Gaineses, their Magnolia brand, and the nation's long-standing white supremacist traditions.

In the twenty-first century, Christianity has been at the center of America's divisive culture wars. Marie Mutsuki Mockett's *American Harvest: God, Country, and Farming in the Heartland* (2020) offers an elaborate portrayal of Christian theology in a post-2016 America, exploring the intersection of race and faith through the Asian/white perspective. On her father's side, Mockett comes from a line of farmers who have owned a seven-thousand-acre wheat farm in Nebraska since 1895, which the author has recently come to inherit. On her mother's side, Mockett is Japanese. Born and bred on the coasts and a self-identified "nonbeliever," Mockett was invited by Eric Wolgemuth, a devout evangelical farmer who long worked on her family's farm, to join a group of conservative white Christian wheat harvesters along their route across the heartland.[102] Wolgemuth's intention was to lessen the country's widening "divide": "Eric told me he wanted to share his America because he feared how little we have come to understand each other," and soon enough, Mockett accompanies farmers in wheat fields and in church, witnessing the divide not only between the Right and the Left, the religious and the secular, but between the city and the country as well as the historical tensions between whiteness and indigeneity.[103] A text that traces the overlapping history of genocide, displacement, farming, and Christianity in the American West, *American Harvest* shows the author struggle through difference while acknowledging her own embeddedness in the nation's colonial past and present. Moments of mixed race angst can be traced throughout the book. The only person of color on the route, Mockett traverses the familiar Asian/white terrain of passing, ambiguity, and a proximity to whiteness. Reflecting on her journey with the farmers, she asks herself, "Have I, in trying so hard to build a bridge, simply erased myself?"[104] The bridge metaphor appears again. When Mockett writes about Juston, Eric's son and an English major at Cairn University, a Christian university outside Philadelphia, she finds herself surprised at the similarities she sees between herself and Eric's son, a white man who "enjoys critical thinking and discussion around the things that make us all both different and similar."[105] Like her, Juston is "a bridge between worlds."[106]

No matter which dichotomy those worlds are thought to define, the bridge proves ubiquitous. When it comes to Christianity, one can argue that the bridge is based in the heartland, stretching from the West to the East.

There are levels to this metaphorical extension. On the surface, we can recall the origin of the term "heartland." Halford Mackinder, a British geographer, coined the term in his 1904 article "The Geographical Pivot of History."[107] Mackinder's theory was that whoever controlled the "heart" of the Eurasian land mass was then poised to wield geopolitical control over the rest of the world given that the heartland boasted the center of power, industry, and natural resources. It was not until the mid-twentieth century when the term began referring to the Midwestern American region.[108] Digging deeper, as Helen Jin Kim does in *Race for Revival* (2022), one may observe how the rise of both American modern evangelicalism and South Korean Christianity hinged on America's religious presence in Asia during the Cold War.[109] Bringing it back to Joanna Gaines, we can conceive of her faith and its presence in her lifestyle brand as operating within the framework of "reencounters," Crystal Mun-hye Baik's term describing the ways in which obscured remnants from the Korean War find themselves reframed as narratives of linear progress.[110] This is not to presume that Joanna's family understands her and Nan as conforming to celebrated narratives of migration or even that her mother experienced firsthand the crusades led by Billy Graham in South Korea in the 1970s. Her mother, in fact, was raised Buddhist, and her father was raised Catholic. Growing up, Joanna never attended Korean church, but she was raised and continues to be a practicing Christian. In *The Magnolia Story*, Chip and Joanna frequently distill life's problems, particularly financial hardships, within the trajectory of faith, revealing the promise of prayer in hard times.[111] This promise manifests in their fundraising for Restoration Gateway (RG), a nonprofit based in Waco that "exists to join Christ in restoring peace and healing wounds among the vulnerable children and war-torn people of Northern Uganda."[112] An episode of the original *Fixer Upper* is centered on finding a home away from Uganda for RG's white American founders, Dr. Tim and Janice McCall.[113] Dedicating *The Magnolia Story* to their children and the children of RG, the Gaineses came to learn of RG through their church. Longtime parishioners of Antioch Community Church, a nondenominational Christian church in Waco, the couple attends service with their children at a parish no stranger to controversy considering its pastor, Jimmy Seibert, has preached that homosexuality is a sin.[114] Controversy lingers, too, when considering the sides the Gaineses chose in the twenty-first-century culture wars, particularly in the case of the couple's monetary donation to Chip's sister whose successful run for a seat on the board of a school district in the greater Dallas–Fort Worth area was based on an "anti–critical race theory" platform.

Joanna has hinted that Chip might run for president of the United States one day, and she's not the only one; he was voted "Most Likely to Be the Next President" in high school.[115] If the image of Joanna as America's first lady reveals anything more than further evidence to support Asian America's *loyalty to empire*, it is that racial renovation ranges from the baseboards to the bloodline.[116] As I have shown through close attention to the Magnolia brand, it is neither only houses nor cities that can be refurbished but generations that can be reoriented. Let us not assume that Joanna's enactments of racial renovation began with Magnolia, for it is far more likely that the renovations began with her mother leaving Seoul to start a family with a white American. This angle of racial renovation, while utterly disturbed, understands an Asian woman marrying a white man as resulting in a better life for the child, a racial "remedy" so obviously rooted in racial science and white supremacy. It is telling, indeed, how the assumption of reproductive potential exists on gendered lines and is rarely branded onto Asian men partnering with white women, like in the case of Noguchi's parents. At its most racist, racial renovation sees the future as a site that can be whitened, and what a disaster that would be. Already in their own version of the White House, America's first family of renovation mirrors what we've long known about whiteness—that it is bound to the material benefits of land, property, and power. Through enactments of racial renovation, Joanna's Asian/white domesticity becomes representative of much more than the marketplace of American home and lifestyle but of the ways restoration courses through relations of closeness, like those between an author and the stories she does and does not tell.

INTERLUDE
A Rendering of Desire

Intimate theaters is an experiment in sex, space, and design. Vanilla Honey, the architect behind the practice, defines intimate theaters as "spaces rooted in explicit, continuous, and collaborative consent where bodies act as boundary projects."[1] Subverting the notion of queer belonging, intimate theaters infuse BDSM principles into the architecture of the suburban home, offering an interpretation of what it means to conceive of space not as a material or physical area but as a site of queer resistance. First and foremost a project about accessibility and consent in the built environment, intimate theaters is interested in an architectural practice capable of indulging a client's kinkiest fantasies.

Founder of intimate theaters, Vanilla Honey is an architectural designer and organizer with Korean Queer and Trans NYC (KQTxNYC). The philosophy behind the practice "centers the possibilities for queer futures, perverts the everyday, and reimagines design models rooted in consent protocols with a resistance to normativity."[2] The kinds of spaces imagined as intimate theaters first began to take shape in Vanilla Honey's architectural thesis, "Queertopias: Spaces of Belonging, Simulated Control, + Inclusive Pleasure."[3] In that

FIGURE 2A.1. Stoll's Queertopias, 2018. "Craving You" (*upper left*), "Down Low" (*upper right*), "Showroom" (*lower left*), "Center of Attention" (*lower right*).

thesis, various rooms of the suburban home—the kitchen, the bedroom, the closet, the attic, the basement—are imagined through the framing of the consensual and risk-aware codes of behavior practiced in BDSM sex and play parties. Cages, leather bondage gear, suspension equipment, X-crosses, pillories, spanking benches, and other BDSM paraphernalia are positioned into renderings of the suburban home, offering a blueprint for ways to bring what is relegated into the dungeon into the mundane arenas of everyday life. In mock-ups, human figures model how to interact with such spaces. In the kitchen, one woman lies bound and masked on the kitchen island as another woman gets set to spank her. They both don black leather lingerie. In the garage, what appears to be the same domme in the kitchen is now topless and seated on an ottoman placed atop a stage. In knee-high leather boots and elbow-length gloves and with a crop in hand, she makes eye contact with you, the viewer, as a masked man in all leather sits nearby and gazes upon her, an act of voyeurism that you, too, may find yourself partaking in. Meanwhile, two people in leather lock mouths behind the closed door of a stall. In the home gym, a wooden X-cross stands between two women, one whose arms are outstretched as her body is bound to the cross and another who ties a gag around her sub's mouth. In the living room, a man in bondage hangs horizontally on a triangular suspension frame.

Renderings of desire, the scenes portrayed in "Queertopias" withdraw the normativity from the heteronormative suburban home, but it is not as though this act of removal is inherently subversive, for the suburban house has long been a site where fetishists come out to play. In such scenes, the viewer bears witness to a philosophy of interior design that pulls the subcultural into the center of the home. It could be enticing or even instinctual for the viewer to focus on the enactments of erotic play on display. Intimate theaters, however, prove instructive in thinking beyond the lure of exhibitionism. Here, much more than sex and desire are worth remark. In flat architectural planes, we are presented with an opportunity to apply queer and Asian Americanist heuristics of "flatness," "unnameability," and "the two-dimensional" to think anew about belonging and Asian life.[4] On the one hand, we see the pursuit of belonging as resulting in an art of adaptability. The insistence of desire provokes one to adapt and remodel spaces in which normativity runs rampant. On the other hand, we might question the very presence of Asian life in Vanilla Honey's architectural renderings. In the scenes where people are present, the models are all light skinned, presumably white, or ambiguous at best. To me, this racial uncertainty is less a sign of the generalization of suburban whiteness than an invitation both to not take whiteness as the default and to think ambiguity outside the bounds of the human form. What I am insinuating here is to engage ambiguity beyond the surface of racial marking and to instead approach ambiguity as a prerequisite of embodied life in general, following mixed race Sri Lankan writer and activist Leah Lakshmi Piepzna-Samarasinha who has written, "I was happiest when I didn't have a body."[5] I could argue that intimate theaters ought to concern Asian/white life given that its creator, Vanilla Honey, is Korean and white American. To this point, as the architect's BDSM scene name, "Vanilla Honey" is a nickname that conjures an Asian/white aesthetic connotation insofar as *vanilla* most readily conveys the color white while *honey* ranges from an almost translucent white to a deep amber. But what I will argue for instead is a reading of art and culture that is not dependent on identitarian logics. The queer forms of adaptation made visible in Vanilla Honey's architectural scenes may come into being through an orientation to desire that places sex in the foreground, but it is not as though queer desire is the only thing happening here. What lies beyond that which is seemingly most indisputable? What gets dismissed in the midst of a sexually charged scene?

This book shifts to explore such questions. Moving from a study of the casual, tolerable, or even forgivable repercussions of empire, like cultural appropriation or racial renovation, *Torn* now turns toward exploring the more overt yet still ordinary violences of the imperial past. If the first two chapters considered the intimacy of imperial violence in the context of a photograph and domesticity, the next two chapters consider violence in more sexually explicit terms: Asian emasculation, sexual predation, misogyny, and fetishization. Setting contemporary cases of Asian/white notoriety alongside the feminist, queer, and liberatory work of Asian/white artists, the following pages examine race, gender, and sexuality as aesthetic experiences not fully intelligible, and thus the chapters fall within the tradition of minoritarian aesthetics, forwarding conversations in studies on the human condition, media, and performance. Sex and violence are major themes in the next two chapters, but as in intimate theaters, desire is only the beginning of the story.

3

THE HAPACALYPSE?
Gendered Anxieties and Paranoid Essentialism Before #MeToo

I am
paranoid
and
surrounded
by
evidence
—KAWIKA GUILLERMO, "Scat," *Nimrods: A Fake-Punk Self-Hurt Anti-Memoir*, 2023

I had to make something that fit to the shape of what I saw —ALEXANDER CHEE, "The Autobiography of My Novel," *How to Write an Autobiographical Novel*, 2018

Before the #MeToo movement went viral in late 2017, a series of cases emerged that would unsettle feminists and the public alike, prompting a shift in the ways sexual violence would be reckoned with for the following decade. Transnational feminist activism surrounding sexual assault had been prominent since at least the early 1990s, but from 2014 to 2015—when the American public learned of artist-activist Emma Sulkowicz, mass murderer Elliot Rodger, serial rapist Daniel Holtzclaw, and an "Emily Doe" we now know as Chanel Miller—the beginning of a culture war began to emerge as a battle between survivors and the accused.[1] To varying degrees, these cases populated headlines and cultural discourse. With Sulkowicz and Miller, conversations veered toward campus sexual assault, evidence, and accountability. With Rodger, debates unfolded regarding gun violence, mental health, and the growing incel movement. With Holtzclaw, the few but unceasing advocates, mostly Black feminists, pleaded for the public to consider the ceaseless violence and trepidation leveled against Black women by police officers. In classrooms, boardrooms, bedrooms, and community outreach centers, these cases opened up discussions about how pervasive sexual violence is as both an everyday reality and as a tool of systemic cisheteropatriarchy, but no space proved as generative as the internet in the parlaying of opinions surrounding debates on sexual violence. On either side of the culture war, the internet became a space where so many of us ventured to show solidarity, learn from open-access books and zines, and yes, eventually declare "me too" or "time's up." This chapter studies the four cases of Holtzclaw, Miller, Rodger, and Sulkowicz as exceptional not simply given the moment in which they occurred, just short of the precipice of movements like #TimesUp or #MeToo, but due to the moment in which they are thought to foreshadow: a mixed race apocalypse led by the offspring of Asian mothers and white fathers—Asian Americans, in other words, like Holtzclaw, Miller, Rodger, and Sulkowicz.

In each of the four cases, racial identity lingered on the fringes. Assumed white and thus mostly deracinated, the figures as well as the storylines and scholarship surrounding them tend not toward issues of race but of sexual violence and misogyny, or trauma and mental illness. There was, however, one instance where their mixedness became the focus of a rather staggering Asian American reckoning. It all began with a post made on Reddit by Eurasian Tiger, the once infamous moderator of the subreddit r/hapas. On that blog published in late 2015, Eurasian Tiger reflects on the uptick in violence committed by Asian men with white fathers, blaming "the hateful dynamic of White Men and Asian Women" for creating a growing demographic of hapa children who, in his eyes, are destined to incite the Hapacalypse, a joining of the words "apocalypse" and "hapa."[2] The portmanteau names a generational shift and by-product of interracial relationships in which more and more Asian people with white heritage and, in particular, sons of white men and Asian women, will commit abhorrent acts of violence. The son, in his words, of a Holocaust-denying white father and controlling Chinese mother,

Tenda Conrad Spencer, the user behind the username Eurasian Tiger, had developed a reputation for projecting his own experience onto all white male–Asian female (WMAF) couples. Once involved with white nationalism, Spencer has since spent time warning fellow mixed race readers to prepare for an impending onslaught of violence, from mass killings to suicide, basing his theory on a specific set of tensions he believes Asian/white children are exposed to at a developmental age: their Asian mother's emasculation of Asian men and their white father's fetishization of Asian women. According to Spencer, the Hapacalypse dawned in the mid-2010s, the same years when the public came to learn of Holtzclaw, Rodger, Sulkowicz, Miller as "Emily Doe," and others.[3] Needless to say, there are many assumptions that cloud the plausibility of his theory—not all mixed Asians have Asian mothers and white fathers, not all interracial couples are heterosexual—and yet, the theory amassed attention across Reddit in forums for mixed race people, interracial couples, MRAsians, incels, and others involved in the manosphere.

Two years after Eurasian Tiger's post, a fictionalized movie poster for *Hapocalypse Now Redux* began circulating on Reddit. In a rather riveting interpretation of the theory, the parody poster is a photoshopped version of Francis Ford Coppola's 2001 Vietnam War film *Apocalypse Now Redux*, the extended version of his 1979 film *Apocalypse Now*. On the pastiche poster, the font and background are mirror images of Coppola's cult classic, edited to suit the title with a slight change in spelling (H*apocalypse* as opposed to *Hapa*calypse), include a tagline, and incorporate the faces of Asian/white people who are thought to represent the Hapacalypse: Alex Buckner (a Phoenix man who killed his parents, two sisters, and set their house on fire), Matthew de Grood (killer of five students at a house party in Calgary), Daniel Derbyshire (the son of far-right journalist John Derbyshire who was fired from the *National Review* in 2012 after his racist response to Trayvon Martin's death), Daniel Holtzclaw (the former Oklahoma City police officer who is currently serving a 263-year prison sentence for assaulting more than one dozen Black women), Hanna Poison Ivy (a woman who allegedly used social media to lure men to degrade themselves and commit suicide), Krit McClean (a model and Columbia student who shut down Times Square when he publicly stripped and danced naked during a manic episode), Elliot Rodger (the racist misogynist whose 2014 killings in Isla Vista, California, made incel a household term), and Emma Sulkowicz (the artist and survivor who carried a mattress similar to the one they were raped on across Columbia's campus). Sulkowicz and Rodger are arguably the most known figures on the poster. Much has been written about Sulkowicz's performance art piece *Mattress Performance*

FIGURE 3.1. Hapacalypse Now, 2017.

(Carry That Weight) and Rodger's misogyny. Much has also been written about Chanel Miller, whose face, one can argue, would not have been left out of the poster if she had relinquished her anonymity by 2017, the year the poster was created.

With its relatively small sample size of not even ten cases of Asian/white life, the Hapacalypse poster and theory may look and sound hyperbolic. The inclusion of Sulkowicz, the lone survivor in a sea of perpetrators, may even cause readers to raise questions as to what counts as hapacalyptic. To this, it is worth noting that Eurasian Tiger posted the original blog on the Hapacalypse just four days after the Holtzclaw verdict went viral. Was a serial rapist the tipping point? Why is a survivor's endurance art included alongside examples of masculinist brute force? An adaptation of the original theory, the Hapacalypse poster underlines the nuances of gender for Asian/white life, capturing a paranoid essentialism that goes deeper than racial identity and interracial desire: masculinity is violent; femininity is not to be trusted. Clearly, these suspicions persist across time and context, but what is less clear is why gendered reductions remain so prevalent when gendered conduct is so vast. Existing in multitudes, Asian/white masculinity is seen as violent whether through Rodger's emasculation and incel incitement, McClean's muscular form, or Holtzclaw's predation. Existing in multitudes, Asian/white femininity is seen as untrustworthy whether through Sulkowicz's public allegations of sexual violence or the deceitful and death-dealing appeal of Hanna Poison Ivy. Emasculated and/or lecherous, submissive and/or domineering, Asian/white life confronts the limits imposed by colonial gender, setting in place an essentialist interpretation that all WMAF partnerships are enactments of racial fetish. By viewing the Hapacalypse in a larger context of American empire, one can begin to tease out the tensions of race, gender, and sexuality that undergird such paranoid reading.

More than the faces of Asian/white life, the most crucial detail on the poster is the tagline: "40 Years After the Vietnam War . . . It's a Different Kind of Apocalypse." Four decades "after" the supposed end of the Vietnam War is 2015, the twilight of the millennium, a transitional moment when there was in fact a critical mass of cases to support the theory. The Hapacalypse names a speculative present born from the not-so-distant past where hybrid vigor and hybrid degeneracy are not only racial metrics but gendered ones too. The tagline invokes malleability (a *different* kind of apocalypse) and the imperial temporality of permanence (40 years after the Vietnam War . . .). The ellipsis gestures to that which remains unfinished. If "40 years after" implies a decisive end to war, the concept of the Hapacalypse itself, a catastrophe emerging from histories of interracial encounter, pushes back on the idea of a finite end. That the theory encapsulates "a different kind of apocalypse" speaks to how the tension reverberating from the Vietnam War did not end but rather is transformed into something new.

The Hapacalypse is a phenomenon one could debate as real or exaggerated but that nonetheless encapsulates the approaching multiracial majority as well as the ongoing legacies of sexualized war crimes in Asia and the Pacific. If the Hapacalypse narrates a present rife with sexualized and gendered violence, then perhaps there is some cruel validity in Kip Fulbeck and Paul Spickard's sentiments in *Part Asian, 100% Hapa*: "Now is the Hapa time."[4] For all its insinuations about the mixed race child born from a white father and Asian mother, the theory opens up conceptual space to interrogate Asian American gender in general and specifically masculinity beyond the scope of its queer potentials.[5] Perceived as emasculated and feminized, Asian American masculinity indeed possesses a queer potential where masculinity may be dismantled and rescripted toward less cishet and patriarchal means.[6] In contrast to queer world-making, what the Hapacalypse suggests is that certain performances of Asian American gendered life may also function to uphold white supremacy through repeated acts of world-breaking or life-ending where the Asian/white subject doubles down on the racist and misogynistic logics of American subjectivity. Whether off-white or whitened, the Asian life that emerges as hapacalyptic conjures a future already underway.

Bringing racial mixture into the forefront of the study of Asian American masculinity, this chapter intervenes into Eurasian Tiger's theory, contending with the Hapacalypse to articulate how and to what end an assumed proximity to whitened masculinity disciplines the new face of the millennium. In titling this chapter in question form—The Hapacalypse?—I not only attempt to be explicit in my interrogation of such a theory, but I also mean to invoke two related questions: Is the Asian/white subject the harbinger of the end of the world? Or is empire's subject striking back? The answer relies, of course, on the details of each individual case and whether a feminist outlier—like Sulkowicz or Miller—is enough to counter the emerging forms of violence indicative of the Hapacalypse, liberating Asian/white life from the paranoid essentialism associated with it. Whereas the previous two chapters called forth an attention to the desire for wholeness and belonging, this chapter grapples with feelings of victimhood and unjust treatment. While chapter 1 examined photography and chapter 2 studied home decor, here I turn to the internet to delve into the ways prominent twenty-first-century mixed race figures have endeavored to contend with the afflictions surrounding rightful or wrongful grievance. In pursuit not of wholeness or belonging but of justice, Holtzclaw, Miller, Rodger, and Sulkowicz either actively resist or conspire with the white supremacist paradigms of anti-Blackness and heteropatriarchy. I am less interested in comparing the cases than I am in thinking them alongside one another. Through critical juxtaposition, Yến Lê Espiritu's method for bringing together seemingly different stories to reveal the forms of power that would otherwise remain unseen,[7] this chapter consists of two sections: one that situates Holtzclaw's serial violence alongside Sulkowicz's artistic engagement with sexual consent, and another that weaves Miller's 2019 memoir *Know My Name* with Rodger's manifesto and massacre in Isla Vista, California. Bringing the Hapacalypse into center frame, I seek neither to confirm nor contest the validity of such an idea but to listen to it, confronting the racialized anxiety that an intensifying Asian/white subculture is imminent. In doing so, I do not mean to suggest that the Hapacalypse christens some sort of irreversible shift branding all WMAF couples and their children as inherently dangerous, harmful, fetishistic, or beyond repair. Rather, I read the Hapacalypse as a manifestation of racial feeling, a racialized and sexualized antagonism that has recourse in the racial subjection of Asian Americans with white heritage. Confronting the Hapacalypse gives queer and feminist theorists and Asian Americanists a new vantage point for examining masculinity, complicity, and whiteness as an interlocking set of accommodating acts which form the basis of racialized and gendered anxieties like yellow peril and Asian emasculation, anxieties that reside at the heart of the Hapacalypse theory and its paranoid essentialism.

The Perpetrator at the Periphery: On Daniel Holtzclaw and Emma Sulkowicz

On his twenty-ninth birthday, Officer Holtzclaw is called into an Oklahoma County courtroom to hear the ruling of his case. The day is December 10, 2015, and over the past year and a half, thirteen Black women have come forward, accusing the police officer of rape, sexual battery, assault, forcible oral sodomy, and stalking. Having pleaded "not guilty" to all thirty-six charges, Holtzclaw is visibly nervous, fidgeting in his seat between his defense attorneys. Judge Timothy Henderson summons the courtroom and reads the first count. Holtzclaw's head immediately falls forward, shaking slowly from side to side. As the "guilty" counts accumulate, the shaking becomes more pronounced. His entire body begins to convulse. When he eventually raises his head, tears are streaming down his face. Intermittently, Holtzclaw glances toward the public seating area where members of his family sit just a short distance away; their sobs fill the courtroom. At the end, Holtzclaw is convicted on eighteen of thirty-six counts and ordered to serve 263 years in prison.

The verdict of *The State of Oklahoma v. Daniel K. Holtzclaw* is available online and the recording went viral. In it, not only does Holtzclaw's 263-year sentencing stand out, but so does the size of his body. Holtzclaw played football for most of his life and has the muscular build of a linebacker, appearing visibly larger than other police officers who the American public has grown to become quite familiar with, say, Darren Wilson, Daniel Pantaleo, and Derek Chauvin. Given that his trial occurred as #BlueLivesMatter emerged in response to #BlackLivesMatter, his case provokes one to make sense of how his anti-Black sexual violence fits within the context of an unremitting upsurge of publicly documented police brutality. However, while the recording of Holtzclaw's verdict circulated across the web, his case by and large received scattered media attention. Racial violence by all means is always already a tale about gender violence, but Black women are again and again relegated to the background. Black feminist scholarship on state and erotic violence has spearheaded our understanding of how Black women, femmes, and trans people are perpetually rendered as afterthoughts to the violence committed by cis men, such that they become quantifiable markers in discourse on sexual violence, subjects in dominant narratives of recovery, and vital to the construction of the carceral state.[8] Nonetheless, Black feminists remain at the center of the abolitionist charge even as cases of Black cis and trans women do not generate the amount of uprising reached in Ferguson, Cleveland, Baltimore, Oakland, New York, and Minneapolis.[9] An effect of misogynoir, Moya Bailey's revolutionary concept on the contempt directed toward Black women, the Holtzclaw case's relative lack of media attention speaks toward Aimee Cox's concern of "why a sympathetic liberal public will readily mobilize to protest the death or threat to life of Black boys, while the plight of Black girls fails to garner a comparable response."[10] It is without question that the sparse coverage on the Holtzclaw trial forestalled a national dialogue on what Black feminist theorists have been arguing for decades: that sexual violence functions as a central form of police brutality against Black people, particularly those in criminalized economies.[11] To this point, it is worth raising the issue that Holtzclaw more than likely targeted women with previous criminal records and/or current work as street-based sex workers because he wagered they would not come forward.[12]

Strikingly, when Holtzclaw's case did reach headlines, journalists correctly documented the race of the all-white jury and the thirteen Black women who came forward. Holtzclaw's race, like Andrew Cunanan's, escaped such visual accuracy. Rife with error, media coverage before, during, and after the conviction exposes an irregularity in which Holtzclaw was racialized including but not limited to "white cop," "technically half-white," "biracial," and the unraced "rapist cop."[13] Depending on the publication, writers described Holtzclaw as an "all-American good guy," "a monster," a "scapegoat," or the "poster child" for police brutality.[14] The flexibility of Holtzclaw's embodiment is striking indeed. He traverses the spectrum of race and decency. Does accuracy matter here? Some may argue that it does not. A rapist cop is a rapist cop. Others may refuse life details about a perpetrator altogether. To these points, feminist advocates and theorists have long shown how imperative it is to center the survivors or victims in cases of sexual assault. As aligned as I am with these commitments, I also wonder if there is anything we forfeit when we fail to acknowledge the perpetrator. Without humanizing, recovering, or exonerating a perpetrator like Holtzclaw, could there be value in pulling details of his case into the center of the conversation? By letting those details linger at the wayside of cultural discourse, have we lost an opportunity to further contextualize his anti-Black violence as paradigmatic of cisheteropatriachy and empire? By not confronting the rapist, in other words, are we relinquishing a deeper understanding of the expanse of sexual violence by simply staying true to our ethics of standing with and believing in survivors?

Let's consider the case at hand. Born in Guam, Holtzclaw is the son of a Japanese mother, Kumiko, and German American father, Eric. The two met in 1980 when Eric was stationed in Japan as a member of the US Air Force. At the time, Kumiko worked as a civilian police officer. After Kumiko immigrated to the United States, the Holtzclaws resettled in Enid, Oklahoma, a suburb one hundred miles north of Oklahoma City. Eric became a lieutenant with the Enid Police Department, and Kumiko stayed home with their son and two daughters. As a high school student, Daniel was a hometown hero, an All-State linebacker who received a full-ride scholarship to play Division 1A football at Eastern Michigan University where he graduated with a bachelor's of science in criminal justice. Eyes set on making it to the National Football League (NFL), his failure on draft day spurred an anticlimactic return to Oklahoma City where he put his degree to work and trained to become a cop. To confront a rapist like Holtzclaw necessitates an interrogation of the linkages between empire, whiteness, and American masculinity and the specificities of his association with the sexually violent histories of military occupation and policing. For a German American to be stationed in Japan, a former empire that forced women and girls into sexual slavery, for that man to marry a Japanese woman, conjuring an imperial history of war brides, and for the couple to give birth to their son in Guam, an unincorporated territory of the United States, there is no dearth of examples insinuating the Holtzclaw family's entanglements with empire's unceasing presence. Deepening a familial legacy of state-sponsored violence, Holtzclaw was well into his third year on the job when the accusations began in June 2014.

Beyond biography and ancestry, surely there are other ways to confront an abuser. Consider another event that same summer of 2014: Emma Sulkowicz's iconic yearlong endurance piece *Mattress Performance (Carry That Weight)* to which there is perhaps no more public confrontation with one's rapist in recent memory. From 2014 to 2015, the then–Columbia University undergraduate student committed to carrying a fifty-pound dorm mattress

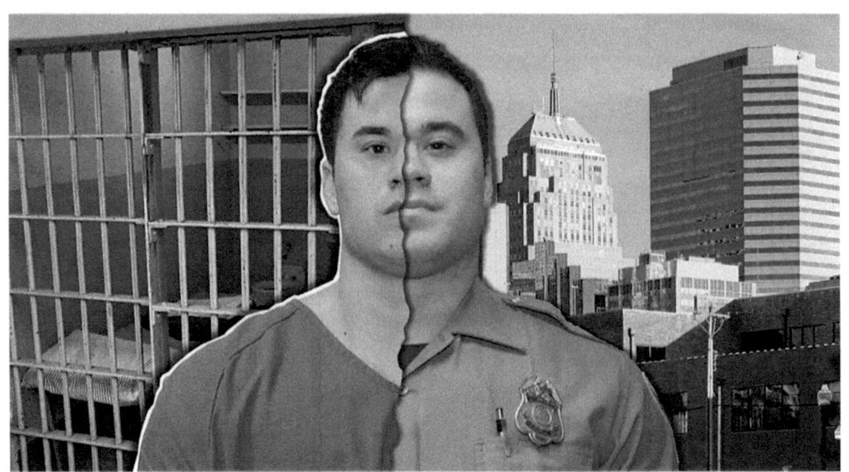

FIGURE 3.2. Daniel Holtzclaw, 2015.

similar to the one they were raped on across campus until their abuser, fellow Columbia undergraduate and German national Paul Nungesser, was either expelled or otherwise left the university. While the performance lasted for the entirety of their senior year, Sulkowicz had been carrying the weight of the assault since August 27, 2012, the night the rape occurred and the first day of Sulkowicz's and Nungesser's sophomore year. Eight months afterward, in April 2013, Sulkowicz filed a Title IX complaint with Columbia after they learned two other students were assaulted by Nungesser. Columbia dropped all three cases against Nungesser and denied Sulkowicz a request for appeal. In May 2014, Sulkowicz filed a complaint with the New York Police Department. After the district attorney's office found insufficient grounds for reasonable suspicion, Sulkowicz chose not to pursue further criminal charges. Doubling as Sulkowicz's senior thesis for the visual arts department, the performance began that summer of 2014 and came to an end at the Columbia commencement in May 2015 where both Sulkowicz and Nungesser walked across the stage, Sulkowicz with the mattress in hand aided by four other graduates. By then, Sulkowicz had earned international attention, winning the National Organization for Women's Woman of Courage Award (2016), the Susan B. Anthony Award (2014), the United States Student Association's National Student Movement Builder of the Year Award (2015), and the Feminist Majority Foundation and *Ms.* Magazine's Ms. Wonder Award (2015), and inspiring students at other colleges to carry mattresses or pillows in solidarity.[15] With *Mattress Performance*, Sulkowicz brought light not only to the widespread problem of campus sexual assault and the lack or inadequacies of institutional response, but they also made explicit the burden of bearing the physical, psychic, and emotional tolls of sexual assault. Given Sulkowicz's quick rise to feminist celebrity, reactions ranged from praise and admiration to slut-shaming, resentment, and hostility. The scope in public reception, not to mention the content of the work, caused many members of the press to brand the performance piece as a protest, but Sulkowicz had always been clear that the act of carrying a mattress was an act of endurance art, a specific form of performance art that requires stamina and entails sustaining a position or repeating an action for a long time, causing the artist to experience bodily pain, exhaustion, or hardship. In addition to the act of carrying the mattress, Sulkowicz supplemented the performance with a list of six "rules of engagement" detailing the parameters to which the performance would proceed including a guideline that they could accept help from others if it were to be offered.[16] While Sulkowicz had been clear about defining *Mattress Performance* as a performance and not a protest, some acts of endurance art—a tradition of performance where the audience is often transformed or moved by the artist—may especially incite activist reverberations.[17]

For all the attention Sulkowicz garnered, Nungesser, as written by the *New York Times*, "hovered in the background like a specter" until he shared his side of the story in said piece published in December 2014, just one semester before graduation and over two years after the rape occurred.[18] Viewing the performance as anything but a form of artistic expression, Nungesser accused Sulkowicz of attempting to bully him out of Columbia. In April 2015, Nungesser filed a Title IX lawsuit that would later be dismissed, alleging that the university, its trustees, its president, and Sulkowicz's senior thesis adviser exposed him to gender-based harassment and a hostile educational environment. He would also go on to discredit, deny, and diminish the experiences of the accusers while pointing out that his mother raised him to be a feminist. As written in that piece, "Mr. Nungesser said the charges against him, all filed within days of one another, were the result of collusion. The three women said in interviews with The New York Times that they decided to take action when they heard about one another's experiences."[19]

Like Nungesser, Holtzclaw also claimed innocence and believed the allegations against him came as a result of collaborative plotting. Within twenty-four hours after Jannie Ligons, a fifty-seven-year-old Black woman, and her family members reported her assault, Oklahoma City sex crimes detectives

FIGURE 3.3. Emma Sulkowicz, 2015.

Kim Davis and Rocky Gregory began the interrogation of Holtzclaw where he utilized a buffer non-Black people of color often exploit.

> DETECTIVE GREGORY: You ever slept with a Black woman?
> DANIEL HOLTZCLAW: I have. In high school I have.
> GREGORY: Okay.
> DETECTIVE DAVIS: Do you have a race that you prefer?
> HOLTZCLAW: I don't. I don't. I'm half Japanese so I'm not really . . .
> DAVIS: I was going to ask you if you were Asian.
> HOLTZCLAW: . . . preferential to anything. So, I'm not really . . . discriminating.[20]

Holtzclaw believes he is nonracist by association, using his Japanese identity as an alibi negating the possibility of him harboring racialized desires. Claiming that he is not "preferential to anything," Holtzclaw suggests that his mixed heritage prevents him from acting in discriminatory or racist ways. Just the opposite; what he demonstrates is *people-of-color blindness*, Jared Sexton's term detailing the consequence when one "misunderstands the specificity of antiblackness," furthering the lie that white supremacy harms people of color equally.[21] By unveiling his Asianness, Holtzclaw attempts to align himself with Blackness, a fraudulent intimacy that comes nowhere near the coalitional "love bonds" Seulghee Lee shows are possible in Afro-Asian America.[22] Holtzclaw's alibi, that he is Japanese, is as insufficient as his masculinist violence is racist.

Not once approaching the stand during his trial, Holtzclaw eventually broke his silence in May 2016 when ABC aired a *20/20* special on his case. Eager for the public to hear his side of the story, Holtzclaw phoned in to ABC from prison to proclaim his accusers' lack of credibility, presuming himself innocent by way of the women's incriminating pasts. As you read the following excerpt, ask yourself whether this is a man who seems to target people in vulnerable positions.

> ABC REPORTER: Let me ask you about Jannie Ligons. She immediately reported the event after it occurred. Why would she make that up?
> HOLTZCLAW: Let's get the factual facts out there. She's not innocent in the way people think she is. She had a bust in the '80s.
> ABC REPORTER: How does a 30-year-old drug bust relate to a rape case?
> HOLTZCLAW: It's credibility. It's her credibility. This is not a woman that is a soccer mom or someone who is credible in society. The detectives were approaching these women basically giving them a lottery ticket and all you had to do was say yes. All they had to do was go throughout the court case, cooperate, go on the stand, and now they're going to be billionaires for something that I didn't do.[23]

Holtzclaw's defense team had been keen on describing the survivors as women with "troubled pasts," casting the thirteen women as unreliable and accusing them of giving false testimony while Holtzclaw was constructed as a *good* cop, the type who would go out of his way to help women who use drugs or trade sex. In the ABC *20/20* special, Holtzclaw admits to coming into contact with each of the women but only to perform "good police work" by investigating the women's connections to crime in Oklahoma City's northeast quadrant. Several of the women who testified acknowledged that Holtzclaw stopped them not to offer assistance but to check for outstanding warrants and search for paraphernalia, threatening arrest unless they comply with his sexually violent demands.[24] Even after the conviction, when a panel of DNA experts concluded that the DNA of a seventeen-year-old girl found on Holtzclaw's pant zipper did not stem from vaginal fluids, the defense hunkered down on the "good cop" narrative, arguing the DNA stemmed from nonsexual touch like a routine body check. The DNA debacle was the basis of Holtzclaw's denied acquittal trial.[25] As for the women, not much more was disclosed other than their ages, they ranged from seventeen to fifty-seven years old, and their records—they were previously charged with either prostitution, drug use, or other criminalized activity. That these points so easily align with racist narratives of Blackness and criminality suggest Holtzclaw's defense felt propelled to base their case on the claim that the women's allegations would never stand in a court of law. Holtzclaw insisted that the Oklahoma City Police Department planted the idea of his arrest to the thirteen Black women. Little room was given to investigate the likelihood that he targeted his victims, those least likely to threaten his status, those least "credible." His lawful future is contingent on a police badge, while the women's perceived criminality is contingent on cultural readings of their Blackness.

From an anti-violence perspective, keeping survivors at the center of analysis is vital in understanding the links between militarism, colonialism, policing, and capitalism. By centering the perspectives and circumstances of women and women of color, feminists across activist, scholarly, legal, and policy circles have clarified the connections between domestic violence and economic violence, psychological intimidation and state surveillance, forwarding methods to acknowledge the pervasive nature of sexualized violence and organize against it. For all the impact this work has had, there remains a question of what to do with the one who wields the violence. While abolitionists have offered models of restorative and transformative justice, where accountability and repair are pursued in favor of criminalization and punishment, offenders overwhelmingly remain at the periphery of the public eye. In most cases, I can support this effect. The attention surrounding an offender more often than not lacks urgency compared with one focused on survivors; but in some cases, there exists a political potential and imperative in confronting the abuser. Grappling with the perpetrator may help us to imagine ways to anticipate and act against sexual violence at a structural level. The risk is that we momentarily decenter the very lives that dictate our political alliances. By focusing on the perpetrator, we shift attention away from the organizing led by survivors as well as their strategies of survival, but this may be a risk worth taking insofar as one investigates violence through an abolitionist practice that values liberation over mediation. There are risks involved when one heads into such dangerous territory. Liberation requires a systemic analysis, a careful dalliance between acknowledging violence without disavowing it. What results is not a sympathetic portrayal or a civilizing mission but a sustained confrontation with the intimacy of violence, which calls for an attention to the residual nature of harm and the way that violence transforms lives in differing ways.

In Holtzclaw's case, paying close attention to his transpacific history demonstrates the specific ways in which whiteness materializes and has recourse in the racial conditioning of racial capitalism's racialized labor force. Given the flexibility of his embodiment, it is fair to presume that the rapist's perceived race may change from white to "technically half-white" precisely because the meeting of whiteness and Asianness often results in an ambiguous racial presence.[26] Part and parcel of his work as a cop, Holtzclaw has been hailed and conditioned by policing's history in the establishment of slave patrols in addition to its continued function as a system of dehumanization. That he is the lone son in a proud family of armed and imperial service members only compels his violence to take on a reproductive and imperial logic. Targeting Black women, Holtzclaw "used whiteness" and "used race,"[27] his logic of humanity determined by "the cruel tension between property and humanity," which, as we've learned from Cheryl Harris, is "reflected in the law's legitimation of the use of Black women's bodies as a means of increasing property."[28] Through his enacting of violence as a member of law enforcement, Holtzclaw commits repeated racialized sexual violence and psychological manipulation to bolster his claim to power, a fragile and flawed power that began to slip away once his name was left uncalled on NFL draft day. There is indeed a cruel tension that links the fragility of masculinity and the drive for property. Claire Jean Kim writes, "Not-Blackness is a vital form of property in an anti-Black world. If Asian Americans don't possess whiteness, at least they have not-Blackness."[29] Asian and in possession of partial whiteness, Holtzclaw sought to secure his status by any means necessary.

To acknowledge and factor the history of Asian exclusion and Japanese incarceration into an analysis of Holtzclaw's anti-Black violence is to conduct an Asian Americanist study worthy of our moment, taking seriously what Justin Leroy describes as the field's insurgent and anti-imperialist potential in the aftermath of the protests surrounding Peter Liang's manslaughter conviction in his killing of Akai Gurley: "Asian American studies allows us to frame antiblackness as part of a conjoined history of domestic and imperial forms of racial governance."[30] Tethered to systems that profess the use of mass violence, sexual violence, and psychological terror against racially subjugated communities, Holtzclaw becomes an ideal actor to perform and augment whiteness even and especially as his racial ambiguity lingers out of frame.

In Sulkowicz's case, the artist and the public come into close contact with the abuser by way of a mattress. In *Mattress Performance*, the artist does not provide a biographical account of the abuser but offers insight into the literal and figurative weight of having to share space with one's attacker. As public, popular, and participatory as *Mattress Performance* was, however, one can argue that Sulkowicz's eight-minute film *Ceci N'est Pas Un Viol* (This is not a rape) invites an even more intimate encounter with the public's confrontation with the specter of an abuser. Directed by Ted Lawson and released on June 3, 2015, the video shows four angles of Sulkowicz and an anonymous actor with a blurred face entering a Columbia dorm room to have sex on a mattress not unlike the one they had just stopped carrying weeks prior once they crossed the graduation stage. What begins as consensual oral and vaginal sex quickly turns nonconsensual, and I detail that violent shift in the following sentences. Less than three minutes into the film, the viewer watches as the anonymous actor begins hitting and choking Sulkowicz as they cry for him to stop. He holds down their arms, removes his condom, and begins to penetrate Sulkowicz anally. Sulkowicz does not stop resisting and yelling for him to stop. At the 4:30 mark, the actor leaves the room and Sulkowicz lies on the blue mattress naked. The final two minutes of the film show Sulkowicz placing sheets and a pillow on the mattress before they go back into bed to lie down under the covers. On the film's website, which has since been deleted, the artist includes a trigger warning: "The following text contains allusions to rape. Everything that takes place in the following video is consensual but may resemble rape. It is not a reenactment but may seem like one. If at any point you are triggered or upset, please proceed with caution and/or exit this website. However, I do not mean to be prescriptive, for many people find pleasure in feeling upset."[31] The title is a reference to René Magritte's *The Treachery of Images*, a painting of a pipe with the caption "Ceci n'est pas une pipe" (This is not a pipe). Despite what one might consider similarities between the video and the assault—including a time stamp on the original film of "08/27/2012," the night of the rape—Sulkowicz is clear that the film is not a reenactment of Nungesser's rape.

Ceci N'est Pas Un Viol is not about one night in August, 2012. It's about your decisions, starting now. It's only a reenactment if you disregard my words. It's about you, not him.

Do not watch this video if your motives would upset me, my desires are unclear to you, or my nuances are indecipherable.

You might be wondering why I've made myself this vulnerable. Look—I want to change the world, and that begins with you, seeing yourself. If you watch this video without my consent, then I hope you reflect on your reasons for objectifying me and participating in my rape, for, in that case, you were the one who couldn't resist the urge to make *Ceci N'est Pas Un Viol* about what you wanted to make it about: rape.

Please, don't participate in my rape. Watch kindly.[32]

In *Ceci N'est Pas Un Viol*, the artist unleashes the potential of what psychoanalyst Avgi Saketopoulou calls *traumatophilia*, a concept less attentive to the healing of trauma than to the ways subjects interact with their trauma by revisiting it and allowing it to circulate while "maintaining a hospitable attitude to the revisitation of trauma."[33] Through a performance of "limit consent," Saketopoulou's related theory of relinquishing control, of "surrendering to the opacity in the other and to the opacity in ourselves,"[34] Sulkowicz enters into a scene of staged violation, giving up control without ever reentering a nonconsensual encounter. In doing so, the artist asks the viewer to reflect on their viewership. Does a voyeuristic pleasure set in? Or does one expect a performance of ideal survivorship? By giving viewers the critical information that the film is not a reenactment, the artist is straightforward and pedagogical, extending a series of invitations surrounding sexual consent, victimhood, and curiosity:

Here are a few questions to help you reflect.

- Searching:
  - Are you searching for proof? Proof of what?
  - Are you searching for ways to either hurt or help me?
  - What are you *looking* for?

- Desiring:
  - Do you desire pleasure?
  - Do you desire revulsion? Is this to counteract your unconscious enjoyment?
  - What do you *want* from this experience?

- Me:
  - How well do you think you know me? Have we ever met?
  - Do you think I'm the perfect victim or the world's worst victim?
  - Do you refuse to see me as either a human being or a victim? If so, why? Is it to deny me agency and thus further victimize me? If so, what do you think of the fact that you owe your ability to do so to me, since I'm the one who took a risk and made myself vulnerable in the first place?
  - Do you hate me? If so, how does it feel to hate me?[35]

In each bullet point, the artist urges the viewer to question the motives revolving their decision to press play. What could be read as accusation to me comes across as a distinctly feminist pedagogical tactic. With a trigger warning and guiding questions, the artist is attentive to the viewer's ability to access the film's content without relinquishing their own subjectivity. Of the above reflections, I take note of an undeniable urgency that arises in the three questions grouped under the category "Searching." More than simply asking *why*, Sulkowicz conducts a series of inquiries into the significance that evidence plays in accusations of sexual assault, offering a critique of the ways a lack of proof or data leads to public skepticism and victim-blaming.

By the time *Ceci N'est Pas Un Viol* was released, Sulkowicz had been branded a champion of the anti-sexual assault movement and similarly denigrated for bringing debates about nonconsensual sex into the public eye. After the video's release, the *Columbia Spectator* interviewed Lawson, the director of *Ceci N'est Pas Un Viol*, who sees the film as a meditation on art and media: [The film is] saying, "I'm not that interested in anyone's individual opinions on the Internet anymore. I'm interested in opinions as this kind of medium onto itself. . . . This work and a lot of Emma's work has been exploring that quite a bit."[36]

Much of the criticism of *Mattress Performance* surrounded the lack of evidence of Nungesser's assault. Years after the dust settled, the *New York Times* published "There Is Life After Campus Infamy," featuring Sulkowicz as one of five "average Janes" who went viral as undergraduate students. The feature seems to refuse Sulkowicz's description of the film as not a reenactment, writing that the "eight-minute explicit video, purports to recreate the night of Mx. Sulkowicz's assault in vivid, excruciating detail, offering up the 'proof' that so many commentators seemed to be demanding as 'Mattress Performance' went viral."[37]

In the realm of sexual assault allegations, where doubt shades the discourse surrounding a convicted perpetrator, evidence and the survivors' credibility recedes into the central framing of sexual violence reportage. The more prominent allegations against Harvey Weinstein, Brett Kavanaugh, Donald Trump, Bill Cosby, and Joe Biden exemplify the centrality of evidence in the context of sexual violence. A survivor's testimony remains inconsequential unless complemented with corroborating results of a rape kit or lie detector test, both of which contain barriers of access. While Nungesser's and Holtzclaw's assaults took place just before the #MeToo movement went viral, the survivors' disclosure motivated others to report, enacting the movement's central idea: encouraging survivors of sexual violence to disclose their experiences to offer the public a sense of how pervasive the problem is.[38]

To this day and in spite of all the virality and spotlight aimed toward Sulkowicz, their race is seldom mentioned. Vivian Huang has argued that the media's lack of attention toward Sulkowicz's biraciality is less an illustration of its color blindness and more a sign of "Asian racial inscrutability on a national stage, particularly when it does not rehearse familiar tropes of Asian submissive respectability."[39] With Chinese, Japanese, and Jewish ancestry, Sulkowicz's performance work falls within a long-standing tradition of Asian and Asian American feminist performance art, and as Huang proposes, this is not simply because of Sulkowicz's racial biography but more precisely because the work extends a radical tradition of operating against the majoritarian sphere, instilling a duty in the viewer to engage such work "with deference" to the genealogy of minoritarian aesthetics that is "the privileged domain of people of color, women, and gender nonconforming people."[40] So often deracinated by the public eye, the sensational cases of Sulkowicz and Holtzclaw demand an interrogation of how inscrutability quite literally looks different when the Asian body passes as white or racially ambiguous.

Just as we might consider Sulkowicz within a tradition of minoritarian art, whether their race is referenced by the public, we must also consider Holtzclaw in line with the traditions of whiteness in which he is located: the military industrial complex and police state. Despite his not being white, whiteness is an organizing structure that governs his logic of humanity. His police career and anti-Black sexual violence emerge in and through the social conditioning that is executed within institutions of policing and militarism, cumulatively modifying his *Asiatic racial form*.[41] What is important to note here is that the possibility for Holtzclaw to embody and augment whiteness takes place at the site of everyday enactments and embodied routines. In Holtzclaw's case, the repetitions he was tasked to perform as a police officer—surveillance, punishment, predation, promotion of racial terror, among many others—were as quotidian as they were bodily, animating whiteness. Just as Holtzclaw was trained to "serve and protect," he was *not* trained to thoroughly contend with his histories, particularly the social significance ascribed to his mixed race, including but not limited to the US imperial battleground within which his parents met.

Consider the following interaction during the interrogation. Once Detectives Davis and Gregory found out Holtzclaw was Asian, the subject of conversation took a strange turn:

> DETECTIVE DAVIS: Who's Japanese? Your mom or dad?
> HOLTZCLAW: My mom.
> DAVIS: Is your dad huge?
> HOLTZCLAW: No.
> DAVIS: How'd you get so big?
> HOLTZCLAW: That's what everyone asks me, and that's why I thought . . .
> DAVIS: Because, I mean, Asian genes are kind of small.
> HOLTZCLAW: That's why I thought I was adopted at first when I talked to them, but, uh, my dad's small, 5′ 9″. Japanese people are small in general, so . . . [42]

In the context of an interrogation for an alleged sexual assault, it is not outlandish to discuss a perpetrator's capacity for physical force. Davis's fixation on Holtzclaw's six-foot-two-inch stature and 260-pound weight is, however, in direct relation to his Asianness. Holtzclaw plays along; he acknowledges his mother's Asian heritage and his father's average height, constructing himself as an exceptional figure of transpacific encounter and Asian masculinity. His is an Asian masculinity that is as unemasculated as it is carceral and imperial, invoking the duality of model-minority masochism, which Takeo Rivera outlines as a self-subjugating embrace and a self-flagellating punishment.[43] Avoiding further discussion about his racialized gender, Holtzclaw retorts with a curious assertion—"Japanese people are small in general, so . . ."—begging the question, *so what?* "So . . . ," as uttered by Holtzclaw, is not simply a filler word but a conjunction revealing the speaker's own inability to chronicle the global and imperial ties that made his body. It is a racial ineptitude that Grace Kyungwon Hong might articulate as "the trace or residue of that which can never be fully erased, yet cannot speak."[44]

Although nowadays, interracial love and marriage signify, albeit falsely, a moving on from an earlier installment of American racism, a *multicultural whiteness* is an inevitable outcome of the contemporary politics of neoliberal multiculturalism, where the pressure to assimilate is threaded to the inability to acknowledge or, rather, the willfulness to deny the history into which whiteness entraps each of us.[45] Multiculturalism's longstanding prescriptions of racial progress not only remain embedded in its speculations of tomorrow, but they sustain whiteness's ability to reinvent itself through its acquisition of new racial subjects.[46] Contrary to statistics culled from US census data which proclaim the increased diversification of racial demographics, whiteness is deepening, capturing and accumulating nonwhite bodies who seem to reside in close proximity to its borders. On opposite corners of the *Hapocalypse Now* poster, the faces of Holtzclaw and Sulkowicz tell two very different stories. When read together, these stories can help distinguish the rather simple suspicion at the heart of the Hapacalypse theory: Something bad is happening. Whether one is a survivor or a perpetrator, a victim or a villain, there is an undeniable tension in being a person born in a moment where justice hinges on the contrast between evidence and believability. In the so-called Asian century, Holtzclaw and Sulkowicz provide further insight into the shifting forms of model-minority discourse, where Asianness is not always as explicit as it may seem. The larger point is this: If evidence is a requirement for believability in the context of sexual violence, it also plays a key role in the case of racial form—that is, whether one's race is believable or not. Like survivors, some people who live Asian/white lives never outrun the accusations that they are not really who they say they are.

Violence by Any Other Name: On Chanel Miller and Elliot Rodger

If one were to trace a genealogy of critical mixed race studies (CMRS), one would soon find themselves in Isla Vista, California, at the University of California at Santa Barbara (UCSB). Many of the field's most known scholars—Wei Ming Dariotis, G. Reginald Daniel, Paul Spickard—either teach, taught, or were trained there. The Department of Sociology houses the *Journal of Critical Mixed Race Studies*, one of the field's founders, Dariotis, earned her PhD in the Department of English, and in 2019, she founded the first degree-granting program in CMRS in the College of Ethnic Studies at San Francisco State University. Kip Fulbeck, the author of

Part Asian, 100% Hapa, is a distinguished professor of art. In the early 2010s, a UCSB literature student whose name many of us now know, enrolled in Professor Fulbeck's "Spoken Word" course her freshman year. By the time this student was preparing for graduation in 2014, the college town of Isla Vista became the site of a massacre, solidifying its legacy as a pivotal location in mining the neoliberal promises and cruel failures of multiracialism. The student is Chanel Miller and she's attending a vigil, listening to Richard Martinez give a speech about his "Not One More" campaign on gun violence. One month before graduation, Martinez's son was shot just off campus. He was one of seven victims in the killings perpetrated by Elliot Rodger.

For better and for worse, Chanel Miller and Elliot Rodger are well-known names in feminist and anti-violence circles. Miller is the award-winning author and artist whose memoir *Know My Name* was a *New York Times* best seller. The memoir revolves around her experience as the anonymous Emily Doe in the 2015 Brock Turner Stanford rape case.[47] Readers may recall this case for the public's response to Turner's outrageous sentencing. After Turner, a nineteen-year-old Stanford undergraduate swimmer, assaulted Miller when she was unconscious at a party she attended with her younger sister, Turner was convicted on three out of five felony sexual assault charges but had only been sentenced to serve six months. Even though a longer sentence or any other carceral response would neither have afforded Miller adequate justice nor solved the problem of campus sexual assault, Turner's sentence equated to a slap on the wrist, exemplifying how insignificant sexual violence is treated in the confines of the American legal system. Readers may also recall Miller's famed 7,138-word victim impact statement, which she read aloud one year after the assault, during the sentencing portion of the trial on June 2, 2016. The following day, Buzzfeed published the statement in full and it went viral. Miller relinquished her anonymity in September 2019, soon before the publication of *Know My Name*. One of the faces of the #MeToo movement, Miller remains a beacon for survivors of sexual violence. Rodger, on the other hand, is notorious for his violent misogyny. His case made incel a household term and his manifesto has influenced a generation of involuntary celibates. On incel forums, Rodger is referred to as a "saint" or the supreme gentlemen. It is common to see references to "E. R.," his initials, in these forums, and mass violence perpetrated by incels is regularly referred to as "going E. R."[48]

Both raised in California and born in the early 1990s to Chinese mothers and white fathers, Rodger and Miller are rarely, if ever, discussed together, yet their stories remain forever intertwined. In *Know My Name,* Miller details what happened that night in Isla Vista: "I was walking to a friend's house when two police cars tore past me."[49] By email, the campus community was notified that shots were fired. Miller rushed indoors just as Rodger's manifesto began circulating online. Tucked away in an off-campus apartment, Miller watched the killer's infamous YouTube videos. One line continues to haunt Miller: "I will punish all females for the crime of depriving me of sex." In Elliot's world, she writes, "the unspoken law was that women owed him sex, we existed only to receive him. . . . Sex was his right and our responsibility."[50] Miller makes a connection: "When headlines first broke after the assault, Brock's smiling photo accompanied every article. *Unfair that he is publicly shamed while she gets to hide,* commenters said."[51] She then quotes Rodger's manifesto: "*College is the time when everyone experiences those things such as sex and fun and pleasure. . . . In those years I've had to rot in loneliness, it's not fair.*"[52] Miller connects the commenters to Rodger, writing that "everyone needed someone to blame. He and I were both in some kind of pain, but what type of violence could his pain ignite?"[53]

Rodger's manifesto and final YouTube video document the killer's motive: to abolish sex and punish women, enacting revenge against humanity. The video shows Rodger sitting in the driver's seat of his BMW 3-series coupe, pompous and unwavering as he announces the imminent day of retribution. It is dusk and palm trees sway in the background. The setting sun shines onto Rodger's face as he laments the "torturous" life he's endured since puberty, one without "affection, and sex, and love."[54] A twenty-two-year-old, Rodger self-identifies as a kissless virgin who desperately desires sex and a blonde girlfriend. In Rodger's eyes, the objects of his desire view him as unworthy.

> It's not fair. You girls have never been attracted to me. I don't know why you girls aren't attracted to me, but I will punish you all for it. It's an injustice, a crime because . . . I don't know what you don't see in me. I'm the perfect guy, and, yet, you throw yourselves at these obnoxious men instead of me, the supreme gentleman. I will punish all of you for it.[55]

Rodger makes it known that the last eight years of his life were filled with unbearable loneliness. Facing social rejection and "unfilled desires," Rodger is giddy as he describes his plans to *annihilate, slaughter,* and *slay* women and his enemies, reducing them to "mountains of skulls and rivers of blood."[56] Resembling a mythical villain, his cackle is heard throughout the misogynistic diatribe unleashed toward young women and sexually active men. It

FIGURE 3.4. Chanel Miller, 2019.

is because "humanity is a disgusting, retched, depraved species" that Rodger views his retribution as proof of his status as *the true alpha male, the supreme gentlemen, the superior one,* and *a god.*[57] Throughout, Rodger asserts with conviction that "it's not fair," reminding the viewer that he "hate[s] all of you."[58]

The disturbing video runs just under seven minutes, but it is in the 137-page manifesto where it becomes clear that the life of Elliot Rodger is one of glaring hapacalyptic violence. Part manifesto, part memoir, "My Twisted World: The Story of Elliot Rodger" details the killer's life including his plans for May 23 as well as his lifelong struggles with isolation and bullying. "My Twisted World" is divided into six parts and is written chronologically, beginning with his birth on July 24, 1991, in London to his white British father, Peter, and Chinese Malaysian mother, Li Chin, and ending in Santa Barbara

FIGURE 3.5. Elliot Rodger, 2014.

where Rodger had been living since 2011. He immediately took a liking to the ocean-front city, admiring the presence of "hot blonde girls walking around *everywhere*."[59] The hope, for Rodger, was that by being immersed in the infamous Santa Barbara college party scene, he would meet his future girlfriend. The first evening offered no such luck. The nineteen-year-old overheard a couple having sex as parties roared outside his window. Anxious and alone, Rodger worried he would never be invited to join in on the fun. There would be a steady progression to Rodger's violence. At twenty, he began to consider carrying out mass violence. At twenty-one, he began to prepare. By then, he had stopped attending classes, spending his time sharpening radical views unveiled in the culminating pages of his manifesto:

> I concluded that women are flawed. There is something mentally wrong with the way their brains are wired, as if they haven't evolved from animal-like thinking. They are incapable of reason or thinking rationally. They are like animals, completely controlled by their primal, depraved emotions and impulses. That is why they are attracted to barbaric, wild, beast-like men. They are beasts themselves. Beasts

> should not be able to have any rights in a civilized society. . . . Women should not have the right to choose who they mate with. That choice should be made for them by civilized men of intelligence. . . . Women are like a plague that must be quarantined.[60]

For Miller to find Rodger's manifesto relatable to her own trauma of a highly publicized sexual assault incites a sharp assessment of how sexual assault and carcerality remain persistent problems of life and death on college campuses, what Jennifer Doyle has cogently named "campus sex, campus security."[61] But in a curious oversight, Miller fails to mention something the two of them share: racial identity. Their mothers are Chinese and their fathers are white. Why does this matter? One needs only to read the first few pages of Rodger's 137-page manifesto to realize that his hatred of women stemmed from the racial interior, where a revulsion of his Asianness engendered a deadly envy. Rodger could not fathom how other men seduced white women while he was "still suffering as a lonely virgin."[62] Being half-Asian, in Rodger's eyes, put him at a disadvantage of scoring the blonde women he desired. Still, Rodger positioned himself as superior to other men of color.

> I always felt as if white girls thought less of me because I was half-Asian, but then I see this white girl at the party talking to a full-blooded Asian. I never had that kind of attention from a white girl! And white girls are the only girls I'm attracted to, especially the blondes. *How could an ugly Asian attract the attention of a white girl, while a beautiful Eurasian like myself never had any attention from them?*[63]

Here, an internalized racial tension emerges within the empty space of unfulfilled sexual desire. Loathing the very thing that marks his Eurasian beauty, Rodger's aversion surrounding his biraciality is, on the one hand, not as harsh as the one targeting monoracial Asianness and, on the other hand, contradicts his self-fetishization. Understanding the racist "hierarchy" of race, Rodger places himself just underneath whiteness and above the rest. Speaking about one of his Latino roommates, Rodger ponders, "How could such an ugly animal have had sexual experiences with girls, and yet I haven't? . . . I am a beautiful, magnificent gentlemen and he is a low-class, pig-faced thug."[64] Boasting a masculinity at once insecure and resentful, Rodger self-soothed through punishment and retaliation. The mere sight of a young heterosexual couple inspired him to fantasize about killing them. Elevated, his rage became more pointed when the men were not white. "How," he asks, "could an inferior, ugly black boy be able to get a white girl and not me? I am beautiful, and I am half white myself. I am descended from British aristocracy. *He* is descended from slaves. I deserve it more."[65]

Rodger's attachments to British whiteness could be read as an attempt to offset his Asianness, making him, in his words, "different from the normal fully-white kids that [he] was trying to fit in with."[66] Born in London, Elliot spent the first five years of his life in the United Kingdom. During his early years, he embarked on a number of international trips and Hollywood premiers with his filmmaker father. He bragged about his luxurious taste and lifestyle; at age seven, his favorite food was lobster. He felt destined for, or at least deserving of, these pleasures. Like Holtzclaw's generational intimacy with US empire and state-sanctioned violence, Rodger also carries forth an ancestral familiarity with historical violence. Rodger was, after all, the grandson of renowned photojournalist George Rodger who is famous for his work in Africa and of capturing images of mass death during the Holocaust at the end of World War II. Like the genocidal motives behind the concentration camps his grandfather bore witness to, Elliot's massacre hinged on his deeper desire to become a dictator, enacting a war on women where—and this is his language—women would be quarantined into concentration camps, other than a few who would be spared for breeding through artificial insemination. In his world, sexuality would not exist. In our world, his presence continues to lurk in plain sight. His case was the impetus of the #NotAllMen and subsequent #YesAllWomen trends on Twitter, as well as the driving force behind his status as an incel hero. With his face plastered on the Hapacalypse poster, could Rodger have functioned as the opening act in a drawn-out Eurasian uprising? Could his massacre and its legacy foreshadow an intensifying subculture of those born to Asian mothers and white fathers?

Despite the amount of scholarship written about Rodger, not enough of it contends with this part of his story. This is a dangerous omission. Even in an episode of *Law and Order: SVU* based on Rodger's killings, the killer is played by a white actor.[67] Other than a few think pieces about his internalized anti-Asian racism, what we have to work with is mostly published in behavioral psychology or sociological journals, giving us much to explore regarding mental health, masculinity, and political violence. That these topics rise to the surface is unsurprising considering that once the public learned about Rodger, news outlets were quick to deem the murders a result of the shooter's mental health, tagging him as a "madman," "a lonely outcast," and a "rejected brat" with a "long-concealed mental illness."[68] Notably, Rodger's race was not deemed newsworthy, a privilege assigned to whiteness.

It gets worse. Weeks after the attacks, Elliot's father, Peter, spoke to Barbara Walters on ABC *20/20*. It was the first time a parent of a mass murderer spoke on television. Beyond expressing parental guilt, Peter had hoped to share the warning signs that he had missed as he advocated for improvements in the mental health-care system. Sharing that Elliot was in therapy since the age of seven, Peter confirmed public suspicion that his son was unwell despite not having a formal diagnosis. He describes his son as someone who might have had high-functioning Asperger's or autism. Peter insists, however, that his son, while a great liar, was "far from evil," suffering instead from an invisible mental illness.[69] Of course, the difference between mental illness and neuroatypicality or neurodivergence is an important one to remember, and although Peter fails to understand the distinction, he is convinced Elliot is sexist, which Peter discerns as "an inbred hatred": "This is the American horror story . . . when you have somebody who on the outside is one thing and on the inside is something completely different, and you don't see it."[70]

Can't the same be said about his mixed race? . . . *When you have somebody who on the outside is one thing and on the inside is something completely different, and you don't see it.* Peter's public appearance did little to appease the victims' families as it also evaded the contemporary public health crises that are men with guns and, more simply, *the average American male.*[71] Undiagnosed, Rodger's mental health remains to be the subject at fault even as the scholars who set forth to analyze the socialization of mass shooters are keen to note the killers' likelihood of being white men who harbor narcissistic, racist, xenophobic, and misogynistic views.[72] As we know, Rodger exhibits each of these attributes, his Asian heritage the only marker of difference, but it is this difference that demands my repeating that Rodger *loathed* being half-Asian, wishing he was like, in his words, "the fully-white kids" he was trying to fit in with.[73] His racial repulsion, however, did little to curb his ego, one manufactured from a place of insecurity. A bona fide narcissist, Rodger praised his "superior memory" while insisting he is "a superior gentleman" and "*the image of beauty and supremacy*," seeing in himself what others seemed to be missing.[74]

Within the span of an hour one night in May 2014, he killed seven people, including himself, injuring fourteen in the process. His violent attacks yielded nine different crime scenes, the first inside his apartment where he stabbed his two Asian roommates. He then drove toward UCSB. Armed, he knocked on the door of the Alpha Phi sorority house. After no one answered the door, Rodger turned around and fired eight bullets into two Delta Delta

Delta sorority sisters, who were pronounced dead at the scene. The killer then proceeded to drive into downtown Isla Vista, firing bullets into shops, fatally striking Chanel Miller's classmate in the chest. He struck cyclists with his BMW, injuring others until he crashed and turned the gun on himself.

"*Why do things have to be this way?*"[75] This question belongs to Rodger and is posed on the last page of his manifesto. Harsher gun control laws and a restructured mental health industry might offer momentary appeasement, but unless there is a systemic reckoning with racist desire on a personal level, legal reform stands no chance against the shifting and accruing powers of whitened masculinity. What do we do with the desires people like Rodger harbor? *Why* do things have to be this way? Is it enough to argue that Asian America is in thrall to imperial desire, engulfed in racist intimacies and liable to their extension? Rodger's case offers no redemptive narrative, but might that lack of recovery be the grounds, the canvas, the impulse for living out less racist relations?

Lessons may be gleaned from Miller and Sulkowicz, who turn to the arts as a way to take on the residue left by violent men. Their literary and performance labor produced a sense of collective empowerment in feminist circles. More menacing, Eurasian Tiger also exercises creative energy to express in words what he sees as imminent, but he is not the only person to use Rodger's case as inspiration. Consider the transfixing and unsettling performance *Art of Luv (Part 1): Elliot* by Royal Osiris Karaoke Ensemble (ROKE), a "musical priesthood" formed by artists Tei Blow and Sean McElroy.[76] A response to Rodger's killing spree, the performance begins with Blow and McElroy creating a meditative space through use of new age instrumentals and moving images on a screen set to the back of the two artists who kneel on the floor in white robes.[77] Within minutes, one of Rodger's videos appears on the screen. The video, "Why Do Girls Hate Me So Much?," shows Rodger walking toward the camera in the hills of Montecito, reflecting on the two and a half years of loneliness and misery he's been experiencing as a college student in Santa Barbara. One of many videos uploaded by Rodger in April 2014, this one shows him lamenting over what he finds to be an injustice: that women are repulsed by him despite the attention he gives to dress nicely, drive a BMW, and carry himself as a gentleman. For Rodger, the video extended an invitation for women to not only learn of his grievances but for them to explain themselves. The only woman to respond in any way, however, was his concerned mother, who called the police upon coming across the video, asking them to check on her son. Questioned by six police officers outside his apartment on April 30, Rodger managed to persuade the cops that it was all a "misunderstanding," and they proceeded to leave the premises. Woefully incompetent, the police did what they tend to do, missing out on an opportunity to do what they convince themselves they can do: serve and protect. If the police had run a background search, they would have seen that he had purchased three handguns. If the police had searched his room, they would have found the guns, an arsenal of other weapons, and a detailed description of his plan. Avoiding arrest, Rodger took down his videos only to reupload them again, minutes before the violence would transpire on May 23. Uploaded for the second time, "Why Do Girls Hate Me So Much?" carried the following description on YouTube: "Girls have never seemed to have any interest in me, and I want to know why. I'm such a perfect, beautiful, fabulous guy. I should never have had any problems with girls, but I do, and I find that ridiculous. This video is a reupload. I had to take the last one down because it gained to [*sic*] much negative attention. I'll keep uploading it until I get at least one honest answer from an actual girl."[78] In their performance, ROKE intersperses an excerpt from Rodger's video with other clips on dating and relationship advice, including ones targeted to men (mostly about how to get laid) and to women (about the need to take care in who they decide to date). Again, with the gendered anxieties. The two artists alternate in delivering the words from each clip as the video plays on the screen. With facial inexpression and an enigmatic tone, Blow recites Rodger's words in a deadpan manner, performing the inscrutability that Rodger, given his own words, so clearly experienced: "I feel so invisible as I walk through my college because none of the girls there pay attention to me."

For artist and science and technology scholar Ben Gansky, ROKE's *Art of Luv (Part 1): Elliot* reveals "the sinister potential of even the most seemingly absurd 'relationship advice.'"[79] The performance is a tremendous display of the life-and-death stakes of normative gender; and, yet again, the case of Rodger's violence is deracinated. What about male desire becomes apparent when reading Rodger's whitened masculinity as a form of Asian inscrutability? Consumed by misogynistic grievance and a steady-toned rage, Rodger's threat of violence was always inscrutable enough until it was not, but even when the public became outraged, there lacked a thorough reckoning on how his violence not only tells a story of gun violence, mental health, and masculinity but also of Asian masculinity and its whitened forms.

Beyond reading for inscrutability, the forms of violence that transpired across the cases of Rodger and Miller name a mode of contingent obscurity specific to the twenty-first century and the way the internet has become an increasingly quotidian part of life. As much as the internet has functioned to bring heightened awareness to the names of abusers and survivors, the attention that results is often short-lived. Cancel culture aside, those who are associated with sexual violence struggle to ever regain a sense of normalcy. Anticipating this, some like Miller see the value of obscurity. Consider her comments on an episode of *This American Life*. In response to a question posed by Ira Glass on Miller's decision to relinquish the anonymity of being Emily Doe, she shares, "In those four years, less than 10 people in my life knew, and at the time, it was cool that I had the power of invisibility. But long term, what's not cool is when you can't turn the invisibility off, because if you're always invisible, then you just start to slowly dissolve, and just to be in the world and leave such a big part of me at home every day led to such a fragmented experience by the end."[80] In addition to the impact of withholding one's identity, Miller's comments touch on a tension that describes why so many find comfort in racist, sexist, xenophobic, and other discriminatory rhetoric too common in online forums and gaming platforms. Whether users actively post or quietly lurk in these dark corners of the web, the "power of invisibility" is as big of an issue as it's contingency. For survivors like Miller, invisibility produced a mode of everyday life defined by fragmentation. For Rodger, perhaps invisibility translated both into a consequence for being Asian and male as well as a reason for turning to forums on PUAhate and Reddit, places where others felt invisible too, and through that sense of camaraderie, erasure transformed into a violent sociality where, like Miller, the invisibility eventually lifted.

Tensions emerge in the body and in the body politic. The Hapacalypse names a theory of paranoia and perhaps exaggeration. As is the case with such things, we do not always know the right way to react.[81] To do the risky thing and take seriously the individual cases of Holtzclaw, Miller, Rodger, and Sulkowicz as emblematic of the Hapacalypse is to question the twenty-first century paranoid essentialism surrounding Asian/white life. The value here is in coming closer to understanding why the mixed race figure continues to be such a source of anxiety. From the college campus to the back seat of a police car, this chapter has explored tension as it manifested through Rodger's narcissistic self-hatred and the inconclusion and lack of a systemic reckoning for Miller. For Holtzclaw and Sulkowicz, tensions emerge when assessing the parallels surrounding the perpetrators—both rapists are of German ancestry and continue to pronounce their innocence—as well as the cultural tensions that associated Holtzclaw with Blue and Black Lives Matter and Sulkowicz with art activism on campus sexual assault. Could such racial and sexual tensions, which are all gathered under the signifier of the Hapacalypse, become the basis for an urgent examination into the desires that produce such terrifying acts of violence? At the very least, they provide context for the problem that is "the monster minority,"[82] or Asian American masculinity post-multiculturalism, as it also allows for a comprehension of the ways Asian femininity lingers as a wedge in the production of the conditions that the Hapacalypse seeks to name. To be clear, despite the presence of Sulkowicz and Hanna Poison Ivy on the parody poster, the Hapacalypse, according to Eurasian Tiger, names a specific problem of Asian/white masculinity, bridging two lines of inquiry that emerged in back-to-back volumes of the *Journal of Asian American Studies*—namely, Angela Liu's 2021 article "MRAsians" and Lily Anne Welty Tamai's 2022 article "To Be Hybrid Anticipates the Future."[83] The former draws attention to the antifeminist views prevalent in the subculture of Asian American men's rights colloquially referred to as MRAsians, while the latter argues for the importance of studying mixed race history as Asian American history. Both articles model and endorse the reach of Asian American studies, making connections with feminist inquiry and CMRS. For Liu, this is done by linking MRAsians to Frank Chin and the mainstream men's rights movement. For Tamai, there is an offering of analytical framing: rather than claim that Asian America is increasingly mixed race, it has always been hybrid. To truly reckon with the Hapacalypse, I propose thinking Liu and Tamai together, an exercise that yields the following conclusions: MRAsians have always included mixed Asians, and the mixed future will include MRAsians. There is an irreparability here, a hopelessness and deidealization of the future, but there are other conclusions one may glean, ones that center the survivors. For example, Miller and Sulkowicz forward two different forms of creative expression—a memoir and endurance art—showing the ways feminist activism succeeds in its steadfast response to sexual violence, centering survivor narratives in a world largely inhospitable to Asian femininity. Why, then, have I discussed Holtzclaw alongside Sulkowicz and Rodger alongside Miller?

The answer lies in part with what remains constant throughout each of the four cases: deracination and grievance. More than a consequence of American color-blind racism, the contemporary deracination of Asian/white life could be said to serve white supremacy and its investment in obscuring a legacy of imperial violence. To this, one could wonder whether the Hapacalypse is a refutation or an extension of white supremacy. Clarity unveils through juxtaposition. By pairing a survivor with a perpetrator, I have hoped to reveal the opposing ways in which one orients to the affliction of grievance through the lens of gender. Miller and Sulkowicz survived harm by individual abusers and experienced that harm exacerbated by a lack of institutional accountability and redress. Like sexual violence, race is nonconsensual, by which I mean, race is a form of subjection that no one can consent to. Subjected by race and empire, Holtzclaw and Rodger felt wronged by their racial form in itself. Their victim mentality displays a masochistic and sadistic underside to their enactment of Asian/white masculinity. Unlike Eurasian Tiger, I know that nonviolent forms of Asian/white masculinity are possible, as seen, for example, in chapter 2's discussion of Isamu Noguchi. Insofar as the cases in this chapter force confrontation with sexual violence and misogyny, there is no hapacalyptic future without the Hapacalypse's essential couple form. Sourced from an anxiety surrounding the most judged if not hated couple form on Reddit (WMAFS), the Hapacalypse provokes a nefarious question, asked by Leslie Bow: "Racial feeling is a powerful tool; how will it continue to be wielded, by whom, and to what ends?"[84] As a way to unveil the political and affective complexities that underpin racial hierarchies, Bow's interest in the Asian fetish "lies not in its object or its practice, but in the alternative stories and perhaps discomfiting affective stances generated by its disavowal."[85] Drawn to such alternatives, I have sought to venture into the unsettling reverberations of racial feeling including but not limited to the violence presumed to be generated from racist love—that is, the Hapacalypse.[86]

The theory is only one manifestation of Spencer's views.[87] Notorious not only for his prolific posting on the hapa subreddit and Sluthate.com, Eurasian Tiger is also the creator of Redpill Comics/Blackpill Comics, a series of incel comics where his observations of racism and misogyny against Asian women take a more graphic turn.[88] Spencer has since retreated from his posting and his YouTube channel has been deleted, but there is no denying that Eurasian Tiger has left a mark.[89] Look no further than his username. To understand the ways animals operate as racial transitional objects, Bow asks, "What fissures arise in turning to nonhuman figures to express adult anxieties over Asian racial difference?"[90] "For Asian Americans," she continues, "it has not been childhood but parenting that has become animalized, as any 'Tiger Mother' can attest."[91] With the presence of Eurasian Tiger, there exists an abstraction within an abstraction, an extension of racialized anxiety resulting in an apprehension of a speculative future led by an infantry of those said to be the new face of the millennium. With the Hapacalypse, Asian/white life is again rendered exceptional but for very different reasons than the hybrid vigor present in mainstream representations of racial mixture. Here, the Asian/white body is an embodiment of violence's inevitability and war's permanence. The Hapacalypse is simply there to function as a warning call, and as with any warning, when one assesses its validity, one ought to contextualize the intent of its harbinger. How sound is the threat really? How credible is its source? Is the Hapacalypse merely paranoia? Or is it that Eurasian Tiger is actually onto something? Whether one heeds the warning, there is an argument to be made about how easy it is to find cases to support the theory. On the contrary, doubters may just as easily assemble a list of figures to dispel Eurasian Tiger, from beloved cultural icon Keanu Reeves and trans model-actor Chella Man to disability justice activist Stacey Park Milbern. As seen through this chapter's spotlight on Sulkowicz and Holtzclaw and then on Miller and Rodger, perhaps the only point of agreement between Hapacalypse believers and deniers is that intimacy, understood here as the very ways we come to see ourselves and our future through the fate of another, is under duress.

4

RACIST INTIMACIES

Racial Fetishization, the Femme Alter Ego and Her Retribution

Each tear waters some old pain,
Helping scars to form. —MICHIYO FUKAYA, "The Stone House," *A Fire Is Burning, It Is in Me*, 1996

Some call it coincidence
But I like to call it fate —LITTLE DRAGON, "Constant Surprises," *Little Dragon*, 2007

A crude and vexing question appears on a promotional image for the now-defunct HalfAsian.org: "Sweet n' Sour White Power: Why are there so many White Nationalists, alt-rightists, and racist [*sic*] with Asian wives and children?" Facetious, rash, and hastily thrown together, the image, like the Hapacalypse poster featured in chapter 3, seeks to provoke. Posted in 2017 by an account since deleted, the image is a collage including stills of far-right YouTube videos, Asian women raising their arms in the Nazi salute and wearing Trump's Make America Great Again red cap, and an interracial couple holding rifles with the flag of Nazi Germany displayed behind them. Pictured smiling alongside their Asian wives and mixed children,

John Derbyshire and Kyle Chapman epitomize the sentiment behind one commenter's response to the image: "wmaf, the official relationship of the altright." Derbyshire, a journalist whose son made an appearance on the Hapacalypse poster, is known for his anti-Black comments following the murder of Trayvon Martin in which he advised white and East Asian parents to protect themselves and their children by avoiding Black people.[1] Chapman is the founder of the Fraternal Order of the Alt Knights, a paramilitary group associated with the Proud Boys, and is also known as the Based Stickman, a nickname given to him after he rose to notoriety when he beat an anti-fascist protester with a stick at a March 2017 Trump rally in Berkeley, California.[2] Using such cases as evidence, the *Sweet n' Sour White Power* image makes a claim for assessing what seems to be an unusual romantic detour for a white nationalist: intimacy with Asian women. If white supremacy rests on white dominance, what do we make of a racist man's nonwhite racial preference and the Asian women who play along? From Mitch McConnell to J. D. Vance, one need not struggle to procure examples of such men. Are their wives, Elaine Chao and Usha Vance, simply objects to their husbands, willing and docile counterparts to the man-hating white feminist? Do they provide proof that McConnell and Vance are not as bad as they are made out to be, that their conservativism is antiracist? Or do we dare assign women agency, acknowledging their choices as conscious, proactive, and perhaps even comprehensible?[3] We know that some women of color, like Amy Chua, endorse and defend white men,[4] while others, like Michelle Malkin and Candace Owens, find home on the far right. We know also about the threat of the Hapacalypse and can imagine the unique challenges children like Ewan, Vivek, and Mirabel Vance face. Constructed as a saving grace, whiteness functions as a proxy for a life of security, safety, and fulfillment. Even though there are levels to white supremacy, there is nothing sui generis about its open arms, its penchant for dressing racism in interracial intimacy.

This final chapter offers an Asian American feminist theory to inspect such claims and, in so doing, lays bare a rather straightforward phenomenon: some intimacies are racist. When one thinks of *racist* intimacies, one may likely consider relations of racial fetish, sexualized racial desires, and even an unsavory but explicit racial preference in one's romantic history or sexual practice. Taking the idea at face value, intimacy acts as a euphemism for sex and desire. Within this train of thought, *racist* intimacies describe an event not unlike one that happened in March 2021, when a twenty-one-year-old white Southern Baptist man sought to destroy his sexual temptations,

FIGURE 4.1. Sweet n' Sour White Power, 2017.

murdering six Asian women and two others in three Atlanta-area massage parlors. Alternatively, if one were to engage intimacy as a heuristic, *racist intimacies* offer a means to observe the never-absent influence of empire's racial ideologies, specifically as they haunt the sexual and reproductive spheres of social life. As a framework, *racist intimacies* index an ideological dilemma in which race becomes both the problem to be solved and the solution to the problem. Within this train of thought, *racist intimacies* reflect on, for instance, how a white man's murderous desires illuminate a deeper history of how the sexualization of Asian women functions as an ongoing form of imperial warfare. Racism, like intimacy, can be taught, and when the attachment to race is so intertwined with desire—be it a desire to move beyond race, deny it, incorporate more races, solve the issue of race, or destroy one's racialized temptations—the very fact of race as a formation secured by empire is too easily disavowed or dismissed. In the context of Asian America, racist intimacies can be and have been traced through the hypersexuality of Asian women, a form of orientalist desire seen from the time spanning the Page Act of 1875, America's first restrictive federal immigration law targeting and branding all Chinese women as lewd and immoral, to the military's forced systems of sexual labor, to Robert Aaron Long's March 2021 murderous attempt to cure his sex addiction. *Racist intimacies,* as I seek to show through these pages, encapsulate a set of unfolding relations that unleash past forms of orientalist desire into the everyday dramas of human intimacy, which, among other things, complicates the pursuit of what is understood to be anti-racism.

By forwarding *racist intimacies* as a framework, I intervene into current debates on racialized desire and sexualized violence, drawing and departing from three distinct but related conceptual vocabularies: Leslie Bow's work on Asian fetishism and *racist love,* Sharon Holland's *the erotic life of racism,* and Lisa Lowe's use of intimacy as a heuristic in her formulation of *the intimacies of four continents.* In Lowe's *The Intimacies of Four Continents,* she distinguishes between two different but not completely unconnected humanistic approaches to intimacy.[5] Among the engagements of intimacy offered across American studies, critical ethnic studies, and queer and feminist theory is one approach that demonstrates how love, sex, marriage, and the family are woven into the very infrastructure of empire. A second strand views intimacy as a reading practice, a heuristic to assess the intimate links between empire, slavery, and liberalism. Devised by Lowe, this work thinks intimacy as a colonial calculus rather than only a quality of being close to one another. In *Racist Love,* Leslie Bow takes a temporal focus on the millennium, offering an extraordinarily timely reckoning with the murderous life and fraught pleasures of fetishistic desire in contemporary Asian America.[6] Bow observes the racialized pleasures humans experience through racialized things and nonhuman objects like robots and tchotchkes. Bow's approach to racial fetish through things provides an alternative entry point into Holland's theory of the erotic life of racism. A compelling and provocative intervention into queer and critical race theory, Holland's *The Erotic Life of Racism* returns to the Black/white color line to document how racism persists with an acute ordinariness, arguing that racism operates as a quotidian practice manifesting at the level of the erotic.[7]

Reading Bow, Holland, and Lowe alongside each other launches the study of racialized sexuality into a terrain of comparative critique, pointing toward the challenges of interpreting racism while abiding by the rubrics of liberal thought. I do not mean to suggest that this chapter offers a model to conduct work that is somehow uninhibited by Western epistemology. Rather, I seek to pool the arguments put forth by Bow, Holland, and Lowe to articulate how a seemingly straightforward phenomenon—some intimacies are racist—holds a fated dimension; that is, some intimacies are destined to be racist. Racist intimacies are none other than scattered instances of an enduring imperial closeness where racist desire traffics on the battlefield and in the colony as well as in the racial imagination, the archive, national sentiment, our homes, and our bodies.

Efforts to delve into the repudiating intimacies that link race to sexuality from the colonial era to the present abound. With an eyebrow raised to the concept of hybridity, Robert Young suggests that scholarship on race and coloniality reinvokes a Victorian *colonial desire*, "a covert but insistent obsession with transgressive, inter-racial sex, hybridity and miscegenation."[8] Notably, Young's formulation of the concept begins with an analysis of *South Pacific*, the 1958 film based on Rodgers and Hammerstein's 1949 Broadway musical of the same name. The musical is drawn from James A. Michener's Pulitzer-winning novel *Tales of the South Pacific* (1947), a collection of short stories inspired by and written while the author was stationed as a lieutenant commander in the US Navy on the island of Espiritu Santo in the New Hebrides Islands, an island country in the south Pacific Ocean now known as Vanuatu. The stories revolve around the interactions between Americans and a number of settler, immigrant, and indigenous characters during World War II. The plot of the musical and film focuses on two romances each imbued with colonial desire. The first involves a white American nurse who, after falling in love with a French expatriate plantation owner, finds difficulty accepting her lover's mixed race Polynesian children from a previous marriage. The second features a controversial romance between a young Tonkinese woman and an American lieutenant. As the lieutenant struggles to accept his love for a much younger woman of color, he sings a song that speaks to the white nurse's internal battle with racial difference. The song, "You've Got to Be Carefully Taught," intones the message that one is not born racist but rather is taught to be racist: "You've got to be taught, before it's too late. Before you are six, or seven, or eight, to hate all the people your relatives hate."

The musical and film are forthright about exploring issues of racial prejudice and interracial sex, but Young's argument that *South Pacific* is a story of colonial desire extends deeper than the story's mere inclusion of multiracial children and interracial romance. More than an obsession with interracial sex, colonial desire names an incessant temporal relation between people of color and the white people who desire them.[9] Colonial desire speaks to the ongoing nature, indeed the never-ending pull, that drives whiteness's desire of otherness. Contrary to the discourse that suggests that interracial sex indicates a moving away from racist history, colonial desire remains. The temporality of colonial desire therefore is of an enduring and perpetual nature. Whereas Young traces the emergence and disavowal of colonial desire through cultural studies and the British colonial condition, my engagement with race and intimacy is invested in theorizing the embodied remnants resulting from such insidious carnality. In other words, this chapter locates, addresses, and problematizes that which comes after the event of colonial desire: racist intimacies as they are confronted by that which is regarded as their very reproductive product, the mixed race subject.

In what follows, I begin with an overview of colonial desire in the context of orientalism. Here, I elaborate on the cultural work that earlier feminist narratives of white and Asian miscegenation perform, addressing how this chapter builds on yet also departs from work that considers Asian and Asian American women as objects of desire. The following sections can be read as case studies in which I employ racist intimacies as a lens, turning to the work of contemporary mixed race artists Chanel Matsunami Govreau and Maya Mackrandilal to observe the ways twenty-first-century feminist cultural production has sought to contend with the tangled relations of orientalist desire through the vantage point of the performance alter ego. Throughout, I emphasize how my formulation of racist intimacies is situated in relation to the theories of racist love, the erotic life of racism, and the intimacies of four continents, teasing out the paradigmatic distinctions across each concept and discerning the ways racism and intimacy arise through their respective angles. To this end, I should be clear that although what I am calling racist intimacies is not beholden to any specific time or space, the analysis offered in this chapter is informed by a multiracial diasporic critique of US empire. Writing in the decade after Barack Obama's so-called post-racial America, I am (as I believe we all are) confronted with the delicate task of reconceiving racism and anti-racism in the wake of the Black Lives Matter uprisings in the summer of 2020, the subsequent wave of global solidarity against anti-Black racism and reckoning with anti-Asian violence, as well as corporate and institutional commitments to *be* anti-racist, only to then retract their Diversity, Equity, and Inclusion initiatives soon after. There is something about this moment that necessitates returning to that which seems straightforward (i.e., racism and, to a certain extent, anti-racism), questioning how these relations endure and shift across global political rifts. It goes beyond asking those who pledged to be anti-racist, *How have we measured up?*, though it is a question that ought to be asked frequently. Instead, I am interested in apprehending the ways neoliberal multiculturalism has further embedded itself within the infrastructure of everyday encounters, transforming to resemble something we might simply call the erotic life of anti-racism.

Orientalist Desire and the Object of Study: From Assimilation to Minoritarian Retribution

Cultural depictions of Asian/white miscegenation have long been a fascination for scholars within Asian American and sexuality studies. Such a long-standing interest has not only provided key insights into the orientalist structure of racialized sexuality but also kept our sights set, perhaps too set, on deciphering the Asian woman both in the context of romance and as an object of desire. One need not spend much time with the literature on Asian/white sexuality to notice that the most prevalent narrative structure concerns the romance plot between the white man and the Asian woman. For Gina Marchetti, Celine Parreñas Shimizu, and Laura Hyun Yi Kang, these narratives perform cultural work, often upholding and sometimes contesting notions ranging from American exceptionalism to the stereotypes of submissive or hypersexual Asian femininity.[10] Whereas Marchetti and Shimizu turn to cinematic representations of Asian and white interracial sexuality to show, respectively, how orientalism forms the basis of American cultural identity and how Asian women on screen reject normative understandings of race, gender, and sexuality, Kang thinks across form and discipline, teaching us how the bodies of Asian women "bear a promiscuous range of afflictions" that impact the epistemological and methodological tensions in various disciplines, which then enable and constrain the composition of Asian and Asian American women as objects of study.[11] Other scholars have endeavored to show how the white man–Asian woman dyad has historically helped to signify the assimilability of Asian Americans. As Susan Koshy's study on Asian-white miscegenation from the late nineteenth to the late twentieth century argues, interracial sex between white men and Asian women has and continues to conflate sex acts into race acts, transforming the meanings of desire in the United States and its colonial territories. "The unique features of Asian American racialization," Koshy writes, "were shaped by and helped reformulate white and nonwhite racial meanings," a point that supports Kumiko Nemoto's argument that Asian/white relationships can function to serve both progressive ideals and patriarchal ones.[12] Interesting affinities also exist between transnational feminist scholars, who argue that the personal scales of intimacy and sex are fundamental to the infrastructure of colonization and imperialism,[13] and critical mixed race scholars, who trace how the mixed body both shifts and is shifted by cultural understandings of race and intimacy.[14]

There are, of course, other narratives beyond the white man–Asian woman dyad that ground studies of Asian/white interracial sexuality. Scholars have drawn attention to the historically charged "colonial dyad" between the white man and the native boy, the dangers of sexual racism that exist for gay men of color, and the ways the rape of white women by Asian men becomes a metaphor for yellow peril.[15] No matter the composition of the dyad, however, it is the romance plot and the specter of sexual encounter between Asian and white bodies that charge scholarly and cultural fascination. When regarded in the context of romance, Asian/white sex acts become assimilatory acts, or "race acts" to keep with Koshy's language. To instead regard Asian/white encounter through the lens of racist intimacies, which is to say in the context of ongoing imperial warfare, merits closer examination into the ways interracial sexuality not only endures as a forbidden relation but may pose problems for the reproduction of empire only insofar as the figure of the hybrid were to engage in an anti-imperialist critique, thus transforming the equation of *sex act = race act* into *sex act = revenge act*. With this possibility in mind, I recast the narrative of Asian/white encounter as one not of romance or desire but of minoritarian retribution.

Heeding the studies outlined above, the romance plot undoubtably *shapes* the ways the artists this chapter focuses on come to understand themselves and thus may motivate their gestures of retribution. However, it is not romance that *commands* their performance but a different kind of racist intimacy I interpret as a playfulness, a fantasy of avengement. In contesting and contending with the romance narrative, the artists I engage in the following pages devise of minoritarian retribution through two distinct affective stances. For Brooklyn-based sculptor and performance artist Chanel Matsunami Govreau, interracial desire inspires a performance-based undercover investigation into white men's attraction to Asian women where humiliation emerges as the artist's raison d'être. Performed twice, once in

2010 at the Art Lofts Gallery in Madison, Wisconsin and again in 2011 at the Raandesk Gallery in New York City, *Requesting Access* is a live photo shoot and movement-based audio performance. As in much of the artist's early work, this performance features an embodiment of Govreau's monstrous femme alter ego, Queen Gidrea, a character the artist first created as a college student working on air for the University of Wisconsin's late-night radio station.[16] For Los Angeles–based artist and writer Maya Mackrandilal and her performance alter ego the Goddess Lakshmi the Global Matriarch, it is the affect of boredom, specifically a boredom with whiteness, that emerges through racist intimacy. In her 2015 transmedia project *How to Be a Monster*, Mackrandilal compiles a series of pigment print collages on bamboo paper with Mackrandilal performing as the Hindu goddesses Kali, Saraswati, Lakshmi, and Durga. In each print, Mackrandilal is seen dominating, objectifying, and punishing white men. If "monsters are meaning machines," then Govreau's and Mackrandilal's monstrous reincarnations display minor aesthetics of insurgency as they reanimate the historical interpretation of mixed race monstrosity where the racial hybrid's individualized experience of degeneracy is linked to the structural threat racial mixture poses for the nation's endorsement in white supremacy.[17]

Given their mixed race and the sexual nature of their performances, Govreau and Mackrandilal could be classified within the same archive of feminist art activism as Chanel Miller and Emma Sulkowicz—the cultural workers featured in chapter 3—as well as contemporary artists Laurel Nakadate and Gina Osterloh. For these reasons, the artists exist in opposition to the more popular and less controversial representations of the Asian/white femme, a racialized gendered figure who is more often than not heralded as the product of the assimilatory act, which is to say, a symbol of post-raciality. Think of Joanna Gaines, the Texas-based TV personality discussed in chapter 2, or Lara Jean Song-Covey, the Asian/white heroine of Jenny Han's young adult romance trilogy *To All the Boys*, later adapted into three Netflix films. One might also consider Emily Mariko, the food and lifestyle influencer whose simple, Asian-inspired meal preps helped her gain over 12.5 million followers on TikTok. If one were wondering about the ways this figure arises in literary form, one might turn to critic Andrea Long Chu, whose 2022 essay "The Mixed Metaphor" encapsulates how Asian American novelists construct the Asian/white protagonist as a metaphor, a figure representing Asian America as both trope and reality.[18] What focusing on these more common or canonical narratives prevents us from observing, however, are the ways the prevalence of the romance narrative, even as it may retreat into the background, makes explicit how the entangled relations that construct racism's erotic life can change under and in the wake of empire. For our intents and purposes, let us venture into the ways the femme alter ego serves as *ressentiment* to racist intimacy. Contrary to narratives of romance and post-race, we see that Govreau and Mackrandilal are adamantly race conscious. Setting and entering into the scene of Asian/white encounter, the artists direct the narrative toward one of resentment and feminist rage. As an analytic, racist intimacies unfold the ways Asian racialized femininity in particular forms both *the object of* orientalist desire and, through the performance of an alter ego, *the basis of* retribution for orientalist desire. The remainder of this chapter follows in the direction of the two artists who confront racist intimacies in a way that generates possibilities of pleasure and power for bodies who remain tethered to the scene of racist intimacy. By staging an encounter between the white man and the femme of color, the two contemporary artists mobilize the femme alter ego as a method for contending with racist intimacy, rehearsing the unique limits of consent and bodily autonomy in the aftermath of colonial desire.

Access and Anticipation: A Date with Asian Barbie

In collaboration with photographer Martin Solheim, *Requesting Access* begins with an artist barefoot in the center of an enclosed gallery space. Solheim is always just a few feet away, photographing the performer's every move. The artist, Chanel Matsunami Govreau, wears a rose-tinted *shitagi*, an undergarment traditionally worn underneath a kimono, and their hair is entwined with dozens of soft screen-printed sculptures.[19] Audience members line the opposite wall, sitting at a distance. Throughout, an audio track fills the sound waves, telling a story of the time the artist went undercover to investigate whether their mixed race Asian-and-white body was Asian enough to satisfy the fetish some white men harbor for Asian women. As spectators watch, Govreau's hands cross their chest, grasping the kimono to cover as much skin as possible while their voice travels through the gallery speakers: "There is power in vulnerability. As women you learn how to cultivate that power in very specific ways and I've learned to cultivate that power as well, but it really scares me what that can do because it really doesn't feel like power at all."[20] Govreau's voice breaks and they begin to weep: "I don't know, when I was struggling before high school, at the end of middle school, that's when the racial thing started surfacing . . . about how people view me. How people all of a sudden really wanted to start classifying me as Asian when I've been treated white my entire life. Then all of sudden with my womanhood came also this Asian identity as well."[21] A tension emerges between assimilation and the fetishization of otherness. Their rhythmic posing feels natural, exuding an ease of being watched; it is as though they have been trained to seize the attention of a crowd.

Never not photographing their movements, Solheim, with his white, male, and fully clothed body, offers a stark contrast to the artist, who now begins to slowly unwrap the kimono and strip. Bare and baring secrets, Govreau, through the speakers, returns us to the past; not long ago, they made a profile on a sugar daddy–sugar baby (SD/SB) website. With "Asian Barbie" as the account name, Govreau created a mild-mannered version of themself renamed as Shizuka, a Japanese word meaning "silence" or "a gentle, quiet child." As is the case with much internet-based sex work, this website featured two main players: older, wealthy gentlemen and younger, attractive women and femmes. Upon finding a person of interest, the men are asked to "request access" in order to receive more of their potential date's photographs and to begin negotiating an arrangement. Within minutes of the post going live, the requests came flowing in.

When I first sat down to interview Govreau in April 2019, I learned that the artist's Japanese mother worked as a set builder for a number of *Godzilla* motion pictures filmed in Tokyo during the '60s and '70s.[22] When their mother moved to the United States, their father's white family discarded her as a visa-seeking, green-card gold digger. I learned other things too, like how the artist had been searching on Craigslist for freelance work when they came across an advertisement for the sugaring website. At the time, Govreau had been working as an intern, and upon telling their manager that they were looking for side gigs, he proposed they put their young Asian and femme body to work in the clubs or on the street.[23] Offended but curious, Govreau sought out to investigate whether their body aligned with the racialized and sexualized overtones in many underground economies.

Performing as Shizuka, they bought a temporary pay-as-you-go GoPhone and began talking with men who ranged from wanting to schedule and pay for weekly sex, casually date, and fall in love. When they met up with men for dinner, the performances never lasted long. Their Asian femme body fit the script. At this point in the photo shoot, Govreau's long dark hair flows against one side of their chest, meeting a now-exposed white strapless bra and slip shorts. With care, they wrap their wrists in a satin fabric, mimicking both the pre-match ritual Muay Thai boxers engage in to prepare for battle

FIGURE 4.2. Chanel Matsunami Govreau, *Requesting Access*, 2010.

and the post-fight practice of bandaging the hands to facilitate healing. This is a symbol not just of ritual and protection but of offense; Govreau anticipates conflict. Minutes pass.

"[Censored name] almost committed suicide," the artist cries on the voice-over, speaking on behalf of a friend, a mixed race Asian woman who worked as an escort.[24] By now, the kimono which lay wrinkled on the ground untouched for some time, is gently spread out flat on the floor. The woman whose chosen name means silence kneels on the kimono as the voice-over intermixes sobbing with words on suicidal misery. Still kneeling, the artist rests bare hands across their stomach, moving outward and back again. In a reference to Japanese ritual suicide—hara-kiri or seppuku—the right palm grips an invisible dagger, stabbing the abdomen and slowly pulling the phantom weapon across. The left hand quivers, mirroring the right to move outward and back again, always touching the area near the imagined wound. This synchrony repeats six or seven times until the body collapses in a child's pose. Both hands begin unraveling the silk sculptures still interlaced in the artist's hair, many the size of an egg and some resembling a miniature throw pillow. Ripped from their hair, the screen-printed pieces wait to be taken home by audience members as a keepsake for those who witnessed what the artist rates as their most challenging performance.

Piece by piece, the small sculptures fall onto the kimono. Piece by piece, Govreau unloads a secret, the motive:

> I wanted to know why people told me that that's why I needed to do it. That that's what was expected of me. I wanted to know why people think that Asian women date white men—because of the money, I wanted to know is there any part of that that is true for myself. I wanted to know why is it that Asian women date older white men. . . . I have a line in a poem, "I am only human in theory, and woman in practice." I think that's what it is about. I'm only human in theory, woman in practice. I can only figure stuff out when I put them into practice.[25]

By going undercover to explore firsthand the orientalist desire some white men harbor and the resulting impact on the Asian femme's psyche, Govreau puts a different meaning to what LeiLani Nishime has referred to as "undercover Asians."[26] In her study on multiracial Asian Americans in contemporary visual culture, Nishime examines the limits of "our visual vocabulary" to demonstrate how multiracial Asian Americans fail to register as multiracial due to an overwhelming tendency to view multiraciality as an exception to racial formation and the politics of representation.[27] Beyond a fixation on their specific racial mixture, "undercover" Asian Americans only further display the complex construction of racial categories. As Nishime suggests, "Rather than exceptions to racial rules, multiracial bodies help us decipher the playbook."[28] *Requesting Access* pushes this interpretation into deeper terrain; we not only come to behold the unique experience of Govreau's being an undercover Asian (treated as white as a child and Asian as a woman), but through their going undercover in the fetish scene, we become witness to the undercover Asian's casting as "only human in theory, and woman in practice."

The words of Sylvia Wynter reverberate in Govreau's culminating words. "Being human," writes Katherine McKittrick who offers a critical genealogy of Wynter's work, "signals not a noun but a verb."[29] By testing this theory, Govreau shows through action that their body, like so many others, fails to bear the privileges afforded to those deemed fully human: white, male. McKittrick continues, "Being human is a praxis of humanness that does not dwell on the static empiricism of the unfittest and the downtrodden and situate the most marginalized within the incarcerated colonial categorization of oppression; being human as praxis is . . . 'the realization of the living.'"[30] Wynter's oeuvre shows how humanness is shaped by differentiating relations to race, space, and temporality, illuminating the joy and tragedy present in the act of living. Speaking not from critical theory but at the level of diligent self-reflection, Govreau distills what a critical theorist might reference as the human into the affective sites that animate the racist intimacies that unravel through the artist's racialized femininity.

While we can presume that not all white and Asian couples are an enactment of racial fetish, such erotic relations, as with all relations, remain informed by the ubiquity of racism. It is no wonder, then, that the very vexed desires that spurred Govreau to enter the racially charged date were informed by a suspicion, or rather an *anticipation*, that their body, like their mother's, is embedded in a form of racial hailing known in slang as yellow fever and more insidiously as orientalist desire.

To reread anticipation onto *Requesting Access* is to attempt to decipher the fraught relation between bodily autonomy, pleasure, and work. To anticipate is to expect, predict, and in some cases, to prepare for what is likely to commence. Failure is always a possibility. As a state of action and an affective relation, anticipation is a mode of listening to one's surroundings, remembering enough of the past to assume an event and count on its repetition. Anticipation also characterizes the way many of us play. To tease, to bottom, to top is to be cast in a script the other has likely rehearsed or even memorized. Whether one successfully anticipates the other's next move, we tend to know our roles. This is not at all to suggest that erotic exchange conforms to a predetermined role-play or lineup of events but to reference the historical weight in many codes of sexual behavior. As much as *Requesting Access* is about the artist's affective response to their dabbling in SD/SB arrangements, it is also about the agency activated in the Asian sugar baby's often assumed submissive position. When I spoke with Govreau, they disclosed their intention to scam white men, tricking them into believing that their fantasy was actualized. The artist fixates on the figure of the white man, anticipating his intentions in order to navigate the ensuing traumatic event and the suicidal misery they failed to anticipate.

It is without question, then, that anticipation is not foolproof. In the pursuit of pleasure, anticipation is often the least of our concerns. Like in the case of Jun Lin—the Chinese international student murdered by Luka Magnotta, the white Montreal gay cannibal killer who performed acts of necrophilia and cannibalism on Lin's dismembered body—sexual desire obstructs the ability to anticipate the worst possible outcome. In his engagement with Lin and Magnotta, Bobby Benedicto brings queer theory's death drive to bear on death's racist preferences, demonstrating the challenge to "disavow the potentially suicidal nature of homosexual desire" if "one were to see oneself not in Magnotta but in Lin."[31] With a searing response to the erotics of death associated with gay male pleasure, Benedicto pushes what Leo Bersani has called homosexuality's "suicidal urge" into the case of the queer of color who is always marked as a heightened risk for annihilation and whose pursuit of pleasure already awaits the racist targets of desire. Like Magnotta, where enough evidence suggests his murderous acts were figments of a "racist imagination," and Lin, whose body was lured by an "unanticipated death," those who enter the scene of racist desire, unbeknownst or not, risk annihilation.[32] And as Benedicto shows, "a refusal to adopt the defensive posture demanded by knowledge of the horrors that await and that will always have already taken place," a refusal thus of anticipation, may not only derail the continuation of life but may also facilitate one's very desire to self-shatter.[33] To refuse anticipation is to perhaps embody the condition of abjection where the queer of color succumbs to the dangers of difference only to arrive at the nothingness that already traffics in the queer body.

Needless to say, Govreau's performance fails to compare to Lin's death. On the one hand, the artist approached the fetish scene not to pursue pleasure but to fool the white man seated in front of them, mocking his orientalist desire. On the other hand, Govreau, too, is queer, and while their nonbinary queer femininity exists in opposition to Lin, the fetish scene repeatedly binds their Asian bodies to white masculinity. And although different, Govreau's mixed-raceness still garners a relation to racialized flesh that positions suicidal misery, like Lin's suicidal urge, in perilous proximity to racism's erotic life. It is to this point that Bow's engagement with racial abstraction offers a frame of reference for Govreau's account name "Asian Barbie." Transforming this version of their performance alter ego into a racialized doll, Govreau invites men to access orientalist desire through a nonhuman representation of the Asiatic body. This process of abstracting race, as we have learned from Bow, elicits feelings of anxiety and desire in non-Asians and Asians alike, feelings that provoke pleasures of fetishistic attachment which become the condition of possibility for anti-Asian violence. Racist love, in other words, encapsulates the curious process in which attraction functions as a form of racial resentment whether one consents to the request for access.

In spite of the persuasive work of radical sexual politics that challenge sex practices like BDSM and race play as either inherently transgressive or problematic, the emancipatory pleasures made possible in such acts depend on those involved and exist outside the bounds of consent. This is to say that the very feeling of erotic desire throws into question the concept of consent insofar as our desires escape the ways we in the post-#MeToo moment have come to understand consent: an active, vocal, and enthusiastic agreement. If we cannot control what turns us on, how might those bodies who host the most ravenous desires—often feminized and of color—truly consent to or not to provide access? Whereas Holland insists "the autonomy usually attached to erotic choices should be reevaluated to think through these attachments," psychoanalyst Avgi Saketopoulou asks, "How meaningful of a concept can [consent] be really when it comes to people who have been historically denied the prerogative of withholding it?"[34] While negotiating boundaries and communicating consent is central to sex work, Govreau entered the workplace with little orientation and heavy historical baggage. Does the mere "request to access" signal a course of action leading toward informed consent? What precisely are the gentlemen requesting access to? These questions concern consent but fail to register whether Govreau consented to being an Asian Barbie in the first place. The character simply was a perfect fit, a form of Asian abstraction molded outside of Govreau's choosing—molded, that is, out of racist self-love. If, however, we read Govreau's character choice as an anticipatory one, the question of bodily autonomy is overshadowed by a desire to take part in the racial stereotype or rather to weaponize it to satisfy their own curiosity that, in fact, they are not an Asian Barbie. And while it is fair to doubt whether the gentlemen felt deceived or ashamed, Queen Gidrea's revenge was never really about the men. For Govreau's alter ego, retribution was as matter of fact as a refusal to continue the performance, resisting pleasure in the scene of racist intimacy and turning inward to contend with the grief disguised as disgust.

Interlude: The Femme Alter Ego

In 2018, Los Angeles–based artist Phung Huynh transformed rapper Rocky Rivera into Kali-Ma, the Hindu goddess of time, creation, and destruction. In a series of drawings, paintings, and silkscreen prints, Huynh depicted the Filipina Bay Area emcee as the feminine destroyer of evil. With piercing eyes and large hoop earrings and her tongue sticking out, Rocky Rivera inhabits the ferocity of the goddess. Like Kali, Rocky has multiple arms, many holding weapons to kill—fire, a machete, a bow, and sage to cleanse. One hand grips the blond hair of a white man's severed head; the man bears an uncanny resemblance to Proud Boys founder Gavin McInnes. Twelve other heads dangle from the Bay Area rapper's neck.[35] We learn from an interview with Huynh that each severed head does in fact represent a member of the Proud Boys, the far-right, neofascist, and all-male organization that has been promoting white supremacist violence since its inception in 2016.[36] Similar to many depictions of Kali, the men's heads are strung together to form a garland the goddess wears around her neck. Around her waist hangs a girdle of their severed arms. Her skin, a midnight blue, alludes to the sky and to the sea as representations of the goddess's infinite nature. It is worth noting that *Kali* comes from the Sanskrit root word *kala* which means "time." Rocky Rivera as Kali-Ma speaks to the temporality of the intimacy of violence and the timeless and timely pursuit femmes of color have continuously enacted in hopes to destroy, as they endure, the violent forces wielded by white supremacy.

Huynh's image of Rocky as Kali has been printed onto tote bags, clothing, candles, skateboard decks, stickers, and most famously, on the cover for the rapper's 2018 album *Rocky's Revenge*. Engineered in collaboration with Women's Audio Mission, a nonprofit invested in bringing women and girls into audio engineering, the eleven-track album builds on the artist's genre of militant feminist hip-hop, embracing the feminist affect of anger and evoking the figure Sara Ahmed has introduced as the *feminist killjoy*.[37] Its title track shows the artist unapologetic about her rage: "Yes I'm angry, I have a lot to be angry about" and "I kill white supremacists, white feminists, white apologists."[38] Rocky's searing declarations position her alongside a legacy of femmes of color enraged by the ongoing need for minoritarian subjects to survive what Joshua Chambers-Letson has articulated as "conditions of negation and annihilation."[39] From their vantage points on American soil, Huynh and Rivera speak to the particular manifestation of white supremacist violence enacted against the indigenous, refugee, and diasporic populations of Southeast Asia. Their collaboration offers a momentary refuge for Asian women whose comportment embodies rage only insofar as it also holds the exhaustion felt when one continues to orient toward life through the frame of survival. That the Filipina rapper is transformed into a South Asian deity signals a weaving of *proximate racial histories* angry feminists of color have been dying for.[40]

Theories of queer and racialized femininity bring an affective register to bear on racist intimacies. Like Macarena Gómez-Barris, whose theorizing on decolonial queer femme epistemes shows the value of embodying non-normative femininity "as sources of knowing and perceiving," Amber Musser carries this sentiment further when she argues for a transformative form of "femme aggression."[41] Women's anger and rage are more than affects that describe intense feelings of hostility. Often targets of institutional, patriarchal, and white rage, contemporary feminists of color encounter anger as

FIGURE 4.3. Phung Huynh and Rocky Rivera, *Rocky's Revenge*, 2018.

an affective surplus, an excess they deploy as a tactic to incite, provoke, and generate redress. Femmes of color are following in the spirit of Audre Lorde's keynote at the 1981 National Women's Studies Association, "The Uses of Anger: Women Responding to Racism," where she details anger as a source "loaded with information and energy."[42] Through a framework invested in the transmission of sensorial knowledges and politics, queer femininity becomes a vital means through which refuge, resistance, and revival are mobilized in the realms of the everyday and the aesthetic. Feminist rage therefore is a *queer gesture*.[43] The mobilization of femme rage not only unravels the social fabric differentiating between what Judith Butler has called "real" and "artificial" femininity, but it extends the femme across time, building queer kinship through intergenerational lineages of femme uprising.[44] As seen in Rivera's *Rocky's Revenge*, rage is an invaluable weapon; it is the condition of possibility for which her targeted revenge against white supremacy is manifested through sound. Here, revenge is less about inflicting physical harm or injury but an exercise in provocation that rethinks the very principles governing a feminist politics of transformative justice.

To rage to the point of imagining or exacting revenge is to encounter the breaking point between respectability and fury. Less an outcome of a "hysterical" outburst, revenge is a performance mobilized by the subject's abundance of distress and fatigue. For one to be compelled toward revenge, one likely has endured for too long a state of irreparability, perhaps even insatiability, whereby the process of healing or making amends has proven unsatisfying, let alone incomplete. When women and femmes harness this excess, they are often subject to imposed slander; think here of the "feminazi."

How, then, might the feeling of rage inspire the production of a new identity altogether? Insofar as vengeance requires a methodical scheme, the naming of revenge through an embrace of an alter ego Rocky Rivera enacting her revenge as Kali-Ma, for instance—represents a lure to embody anger's excess differently, detached from pure personhood and compounded by abjection. The femme alter ego becomes the very site through which abject embodiment, femme affect, and racist intimacies coalesce. To this we might ask, what forms of transformative justice are made possible through the performance of an alter ego? Through Musser, we find reference in thinking the femme alter ego not as a performance of becoming but as a citational practice. In *Sensual Excess*, Musser begins at the flesh to think through Black and brown epistemologies of sensuality and the senses of selfhood, arguing that "citation can alter the boundaries of the self."[45] Indeed, Rocky Rivera does not *become* Kali, but her acts of citation illustrate a racialized and gendered form of knowing, a queer gesture of what it means to be femme, brown, and angry in our ever-precarious present.[46]

The femme alter ego, then, emerges not only as an agent of retribution but as a kind of ressentiment to racist intimacy.[47] By reassigning the sense of hostility produced by orientalist desire so that the frustration is endured by the femme alter ego, an artist can acknowledge racialized femininity's presumed inferiority without ever succumbing to it. Furthermore, the artist can maintain a spotlight on the figure of the white man, reversing the value system and power dynamic that favors white masculinity while staging and directing an erotic scene with an encounter less to do with the erotic than with the affective valiances of revenge. The Asian American spectatorship made possible through the femme alter ego becomes yet another method for contending with the fraught terrain of racial stereotyping.

To this point, as readers may note, the brownness of Rivera (Filipina) and Kali-Ma (Hindu goddess) are different and it is the fact of this difference that brings to mind José Esteban Muñoz's theory of brown feeling, which, while rooted in a Latinx brownness, manages to enliven "a certain ethics of the self that is utilized and deployed by people of color and other minoritarian subjects who don't feel quite right within the protocols of normative affect and comportment."[48] The different brownnesses of the Asian diasporic figures discussed in this chapter exist in relation to (but not undifferentiated from) other forms of brownness. Varied and not all encompassing, brownness can stem from the depressive stance, as it does for Muñoz, as well as it might yield a form of femme aggression, as Musser has shown. It is thus not in spite of brownness's varied forms but because of them that the racist intimacies illuminated by Rivera's alter ego fall within a rather expansive tradition of minoritarian retribution, existing again in relation to (but not undifferentiated from) other forms of racialized desire while maintaining a distinct Asian Americanist bend.[49] As an Asian American feminist epistemology, racist intimacies is concerned less with a reconciliation between various forms of minoritarian life than it is in holding racial affect and imperial desires in tension.

That said, it is worth emphasizing that the act of femme aggression unleashed by the femme alter ego exists in clear distinction from the masculinist anger and envy that structure the dichotomy of racist love and racist hate, the two models of racial stereotyping as surmised by Frank Chin and Jeffrey Paul Chan in their 1972 essay "Racist Love," which is the title Bow adapts to encapsulate the curious process in which sexual attraction functions as a form of racial resentment.[50] The aesthetic dimension of the femme alter ego's aggression is cut from an entirely different cloth than the macho outrage that lines the pages of Chin and Chan's essay, a toxicity that surfaces again in the 1974 introduction to the anthology *Aiiieeeee!*, edited by Chin, Chan, Lawson Fusao Inada, and Shawn Wong in which they rely on misogyny and anti-Blackness to stake their claim that "racist love" emasculates Asian American men.[51] Daniel Y. Kim has argued that the *Aiiieeeee!* group express a profound sense of racial and masculine envy toward Black masculinity in particular, pointing to the serious problem of how an Asian American fetishization of Blackness becomes the group's creative force in resisting racist hate.[52] On the other hand, for the femme alter ego to enact femme aggression against racist intimacy, it is not that she automatically avoids racial fetishization, but through acting in the tradition of brownness as a form of political power more aligned with what Shimizu has shown with the Asian American femme fatale, she contends with racial affect in a way that counters and critiques the fetishization of Blackness present in the formulation extended by Chin et al.

Readers of Bow will note that her engagement with racist love does not address the *Aiiieeeee!* group's racial envy, opting instead to study the fetishistic life of racist love as it emerges in nonhuman representations of the Asiatic body. Bow's interest in the Asian fetish, importantly, "lies not in its object or its practice, but in the alternative stories and perhaps discomfiting affective stances generated by its disavowal."[53] An alternative in its own right, the alter ego as secondary personality invites reflection into the intimacies of femme aggression. Following Lowe, who observes residual and emergent intimacies as "the implied but less visible forms of alliance, affinity, and society among variously colonized peoples," I want to steer attention onto the intimacies that unravel between both an artist and an alter ego as well as the various alter egos mentioned in this chapter.[54] More visible, the dominant intimacies that emerge when one reads the Asian/white encounter as a scene of romance or sexual contact are the same intimacies that inform Bow's proposition that "Asian women's creative practice is institutionally celebrated in the world of high art when they embrace exhibitionism, adhere to racial-sexual exoticism."[55] There are, to be sure, other forms of intimacy that flicker in the scenes directed by Govreau and by Mackrandilal, as the next section elaborates on. Less visible than the provocative image between the white man and the Asian woman are the more unsettling intimacies of multiracial solidarity that motivate the femme alter ego toward minoritarian retribution. Let us not forget that *intimate* in its noun form denotes a very close friend, not unlike an alter ego, or even the possibility for a radical alliance between an Asian Barbie and the Hindu Goddess.

Aesthetic Motives of the #NEWGLOBALMATRIARCHY

In her 2015 transmedia project *How to Be a Monster*, Mackrandilal invites us to toy with the notion of revenge through her own reincarnation as Kali. Wearing all black and sitting on a makeshift gold throne, Mackrandilal as Kali holds the body of a dead white man in her lap, a specter of Michelangelo's *Pietà*. The corpse dons Confederate flag underwear, which is only one reason why the print may not automatically register as an incarnation of Kali. Adapted after Michelangelo's late-fifteenth-century sculpture of the Virgin Mary and Jesus, Mackrandilal's performance of Kali finds the goddess sitting and not standing. She has only two arms. There are no weapons in sight. The only clear resemblance to Kali is the protruding tongue, but even that is made different—what juts out from the femme's mouth is not a tongue but a red dildo. The choice to alter Kali in this way is intentional. Mackrandilal explains,

> Kali comes to us, not as her fearsome incarnation (garlanded with skulls, wearing a skirt of severed arms, clutching a scythe in one hand and a severed head in the other) but as the Pietà. When Michelangelo was criticized for the youthful features of Mary in his iconic take on this archetype, he responded by saying: Do you not know that chaste women stay fresh much more than those who are not chaste? How much more in the case of the Virgin, who had never experienced the least lascivious desire that might change her body? Kali is no "chaste" virgin. She is the idea at the root of "virgin" related to "virile"—to feminine sexual agency. She holds the dead body of white supremacy gently in her arms, her tongue-phallus protruding. She is the monstrous body, the queer body, asserting its eternal beauty.[56]

In the absence of Kali's more distinguishable features, the viewer bears witness to a queer critique not only of Western art history but of two fundamental psychoanalytic concepts: the ego and the mother. The ego—Freud's notion of the self that mediates desire and reality—traffics in Mackrandilal's work as the white supremacist and in Michelangelo's as the post-crucifixion Christ. Known in the West as a personification of the Divine Mother Mary, Kali destroys the ego through a maternally informed act of labor. If the mother cradles the son of God, then the monster discards the remains of the Confederacy. If Michelangelo's Virgin Mary is seen in mourning, delivering the world its savior, Mackrandilal's Kali, on the other hand, delivers the viewer an escape from the confines of normative femininity which binds the femme of color to a perpetual caregiving position. The femme alter ego presents a mother who destroys the ego only insofar as she becomes a monster.

How to Be a Monster is a part of #NEWGLOBALMATRIARCHY (hereafter #NGM), a series of solo works and collaborative projects with FEMelanin, a collective of multidisciplinary femme artists of color. #NGM is led by Mackrandilal whose performance alter ego, the Goddess Lakshmi the Global Matriarch, acts as the spokesperson for the furious goddesses who, as written by Mackrandilal, "find themselves in a world that has forgotten the radical abundance of women."[57] By situating the series within the twenty-first-century political scene of Islamophobia and the growing publicity of sexual violence, and by acknowledging the present's enduring relation to histories

FIGURE 4.4. Maya Mackrandilal, *The Goddess Kali as Pietà*, 2015.

of racialization, Mackrandilal imbues femme rage with the aesthetics of redress. It is then perhaps more than serendipitous that *How to Be a Monster* debuted in Chicago in June 2015, just days before Bree Newsome climbed the South Carolina capitol building's flagpole and took down its Confederate flag.[58] This chance rencontre of women of color clashing with white supremacy illustrates the feminist reach of what L. H. Stallings has described as the "neoteric sex wars" in "the New South."[59] On the one hand, *How to Be a Monster* enables us to visualize the retribution femmes of color have historically enacted as a result of racialized and gendered attacks on their bodies. On the other hand, it tempts the viewer to locate themselves within such fraught terrain that demarcates justice from violence, the femme top from the white and masculine degradee.

For all its focus on orientalist desire, there is a potential for radical politics in the femme alter ego's pursuit of retribution. Consider Mackrandilal's performance as Saraswati. The artist holds open Cedric Robinson's *Black Marxism* as a white man goes down on her, a playful citation of Mia Khalifa—the "pro-am" (pro-amateur) porn star notorious for being the first woman to perform oral sex on camera while wearing a hijab. The Confederate flag is at the center, covering the man's ass. Saraswati seems disinterested, bored even, by the sex. Legs spread, it is *Black Marxism* (not a white man's tongue) that captures the attention of the goddess of knowledge, music, and art. Reading Robinson, the artist gleans from the Black radical tradition, charting a way forward for the femme of color whose body is never not entangled within white supremacy's racist desires. For this reason, the book is a compelling choice. On the surface, the title on its cover matches the blue and red of the Confederate flag underwear, while the black background contrasts with the white man and the stars on his trunks. More viscerally, its message produces a stark contrast in the artist's comportment. Utterly indifferent to the man going down on her, Saraswati is fully immersed in *Black Marxism*. By rejecting Asian/white sexual intimacy in this way, Saraswati's attentiveness shows her in favor of Black study, a prerequisite for multiracial solidarity and, in particular, an Asian and Black radical politics. I imagine Saraswati reading the first page of the final section of *Black Marxism* in which Robinson writes, "For the unaware, nothing was amiss."[60] These words refer to Eurocentric models of history and their deficiencies for which Marxist theory is not immune. They also capture the kind of world in which racist intimacies traffic. Committed to becoming aware, the goddess becomes a student of Robinson's germinal text without resorting to the type of fetishization Chin et al. perform in their discussion of Blackness in "Racist Love." Unresponsive to the racist love happening below the belt, Saraswati mobilizes Robinson's insights to make visible the titillating intimacies refracted through the orientalist equation, which places the femme of color in the same frame as the white man. What gets lost in European historiography is a sweeping story of race and resistance, and it is Robinson who urges a shift toward studying the traditions of the African diaspora. This matters not only for the Black radical tradition but also for what it offers our understanding of racist intimacies as an Asian American epistemology that, again, is in relation to (but not undifferentiated from) other forms of difference and desire including a minoritarian diligence in studying the history of race and resistance.

Race, we know, is historically contingent, entrenched in debates about representability, and intimately linked to the modern political regime. If we have been taught to fear in color, how have we been taught to desire? How have we been taught to think? And how might an attention to minoritarian retribution allow us to think anew about forms of fetishization that traffic in racist love and racist intimacy? Racial fetish, it seems, leaves little room for recuperation, even as there is work in queer and feminist studies, particularly on Black female sexuality that illuminates the potential within racially informed desire whereby bodies historically exploited and withheld from protection creatively redefine pleasure and agency.[61] While Anne McClintock's feminist intervention into fetishism creates productive distance from psychoanalysis's insistence on the phallus and its emphasis on the scene of castration, her work in *Imperial Leather* sought not to redeem past narratives of fetishism, domesticity, and empire but laid bare their "historical force" and "their continuing implication for our time."[62] For Kadji Amin, "racial fetishism is the paradigmatic bad relation."[63] Its erotic charge is a temporal operation, one both kindled and upheld by a long colonial history of sociocultural practices. Indeed, it is often through racial fetish that we are reminded of how historical racial injury lives on in the throes of the present. Racial fetish, in other words, is one scene where racist love and racist intimacy traffic. And although some may willingly, eagerly, and ethically enter into scenes of race play (kink or not) and experience pleasure,[64] individual desires cycle back to racial subjection. Some intimacies, as a result, are destined to be racist.

In this light, with Saraswati caught in the middle of Black and white, further context may be drawn from Holland's *The Erotic Life of Racism*, which returns to the Black/white color line to document how racism persists with an acute ordinariness, arguing that racism operates as a quotidian practice manifesting at the level of the erotic. Insisting that a critical engagement with racism must occur where Black meets white, Holland asks a series of

FIGURE 4.5. Maya Mackrandilal, *Saraswati, Goddess of Knowledge and Art (Black Marxism)*, 2015.

difficult questions: "Can work on 'desire' be antiracist work? Can antiracist work *think* 'desire'? What would happen if we opened up the erotic to a scene of racist hailing?"[65] In posing questions that link race and sexuality, Holland emphasizes "that when we see and say 'race,' regardless of how much we intend to understand race as being had by everyone, our examples of racial being and racist targets are often grounded in *black matter(s)*."[66] She continues, "In this instance, the black body is the quintessential sign for subjection, for a particular experience that it must inhabit and own *all by itself*."[67]

While some have shown the way Indigenous and non-Black people of color fit into the color line, there is value in following Holland and resisting any urge to factor in other forms of racialized otherness into the space where Black resides, particularly when thinking at the level of the erotic.[68] However, following Holland again in mining "the interstice between the insistence of critical race theory upon the 'ordinary' in racist practice and the call by queer theory for us to take care of the *feeling* that escapes or releases when bodies collide in pleasure and pain," I raise a different question: What happens when whiteness collides with Asianness not only in orientalist desire but in racial mixture?[69] To this point, Bow would assert that "racist love is particularly illuminated where 'Asian' intersects with the veiled discourses of white supremacy."[70] Thinking with Holland on the erotic life of racism and its repetitive collision of bodies "in pleasure and pain," how might we contend with racism's erotic life when whiteness has in some capacity crashed into Asianness, as it has in Mackrandilal's prints of the Hindu goddess as well as her own mixed race? This question asks less how Asianness and mixed-raceness trouble Holland's insistence on Black matters but how whiteness collapses color into itself, forming a new and augmented version of what Holland names "the 'white' side of the equation."[71]

Born to a white father and an Indian Guyanese mother with Black and Chinese heritage, Mackrandilal lingers within the touch between white and color, creating transdisciplinary installations that force confrontation with the desires that are kindled from living a life always in close proximity to racist intimacy. In perpetual positions of submission, the white men don Confederate flag underwear, pig masks, and an array of bondage. Failing to adhere to positions of dominance, the frames of whiteness featured in Mackrandilal's project encounter the alter ego and the threat she poses. Provocative, the intent is in fact not to provoke but to disarticulate the project of looking from the construct of whiteness, that color without color. Mackrandilal's aesthetic motives hinge on the minor details in the print. A stack of books compile what the artist has told me is her dream syllabus, including

Framer Framed by Trinh T. Minh-ha, *White Girls* by Hilton Als, *Citizen* by Claudia Rankine, and *Much Maligned Monsters: A History of European Reactions to Indian Art* by Partha Mitter. Rather than a Saraswati veena, resting within the goddess's grip is an acoustic guitar. Tribal images of the Goddess Kali adorn the background, plastered in repetition. That the South Asian deity chooses to study Black political thought, during oral sex no less, presents an epistemological invitation to ruminate on the convergence of multiple racial histories rubbing up against each other. This is not only grounds for multiracial solidarity. Rather, it is an aesthetic gesture of minoritarian retribution for orientalist desire—a dislodging of whiteness from power through playful punishment.

As the Goddess Durga, Mackrandilal wears a red headscarf and holds a rifle in her left hand, each a signpost to the "Bandit Queen" Phoolan Devi (1963–2001).[72] Behind the goddess are photographs of Bush administration officials involved in the illegal torture of US detainees. Each official has a rifle crosshair plastered across their face. Here, Durga rides a white man rather than her customary tiger. The juxtaposition of South Asian femininity and white imperialist masculinity is twofold: on the one hand, it is an explicit contrast between the Bandit Queen and the Bush officials; on the other hand, it is an ancestral rendition of the artist's mixed race. To carry white ancestry is to remain bound to the intimate contours of imperialism which repeatedly place different bodies in close proximity, so close, in fact, that they touch, and through that touching, they may mix.

In *The Goddess Durga as Phoolan Devi*, the artist's face is assured and resolute as her hand is raised in *Abhaya mudra*, a gesture of sanctuary, care, and protection. It is as though the artist extends an explicit warning to white men and a gesture of safety to femmes of color. In fact, when I spoke with Mackrandilal about the audience's reactions to the piece, she confirmed that most white men felt uncomfortable, criticized even, while women of color rejoiced, often embracing the artist for her offering of momentary bliss in a world not gentle on bodies both feminine and nonwhite. Mackrandilal's expression, then, functions as a sign of *brown jouissance*, Musser's term describing the "fleshy mixture of self-production, insatiability, joy, and pain," which allows for a reimagining of "the possibilities of resignifying that affective fleshiness, by showing us that which is not encumbered by discourses of sexuality, but that which traffics in sensuality."[73] Brown jouissance offers insight into the potential embedded in racialized feeling's excessive nature and offers instruction on how that excess translates onto the surface of a pigment print. Mackrandilal's performance as

FIGURE 4.6. Maya Mackrandilal, *The Goddess Durga as Phoolan Devi*, 2015.

the Bandit Queen yields the excess of racialized and gendered rage, a rage that makes accessible the speculative potentials of a revolutionary, intergenerational, and minoritarian world building and world breaking.

To more fully understand Mackrandilal's aesthetic motives for retribution, it is essential to situate her work within the broader scope of minoritarian performance for which Muñoz has been a guiding voice, instructing scholars and practitioners to engage the concept of disidentification. For Muñoz, to disidentify as a minoritarian subject is to neither assimilate within nor completely resist dominant structures. Instead, "disidentification is a strategy that works on and against dominant ideology."[74] This working on and against blurs the binary demarcating resistance from assimilation and encourages a strategy that takes seriously anti-assimilationist thought while also valuing the ways assimilation may offer strategic and methodological survival tactics. Disidentification is, on the one hand, a theory on the survival strategies that minoritarian subjects employ in a majoritarian public sphere; on the other hand, it is a form of world making. Through disidentification, change is enacted within. It imagines a queer world for the future while also staging new political possibilities in the present. This disidentifying method of survival and resistance disrupts linear time via the minor aesthetic, simultaneously tearing down the values of the majoritarian public and recycling these dominant structures to make something better.

What Muñoz wants us to understand is how queer and racialized people adapt and shift within structures of power, an enduring lesson that appears in *The Sense of Brown*, his final work before his untimely death. There, Muñoz turns to Nao Bustamente's *Indigurrito* (1992), a staged performance in which Bustamente embodies an Aztec princess turned dominatrix.[75] She wears a harness, but rather than strapping a dildo, a burrito protrudes from her crotch. Inviting white men in the audience to absolve their white guilt, Bustamente enacts a ritual, cleansing the white man who stuffs his mouth with the artist's cock-burrito. Such satire is not devoid of radical potential; rather, it is the means for contending with the historical weight of colonization. Like Bustamente's portrayal of the Aztec princess, Mackrandilal's performance as a Hindu goddess engages queer sexuality, humiliation, and parody for the purpose of addressing the harms of colonialism and imperial warfare without assuming aesthetics alone can lead to redress.

In each print of *How to Be a Monster*, Mackrandilal mobilizes the minor position to make visible the disturbing intimacies that govern the orientalist equation, which places white masculinity alongside the brown femme. This juxtaposition emerges again in a collaboration with FEMelanin, a femme collective led by Mackrandilal, in their performance *Bedtime Stories of White Supremacy* (hereafter *Bedtime Stories*).[76] Performed just months after *How to Be a Monster*, *Bedtime Stories* debuted at the Mana Contemporary in Chicago in November 2015. Starring the Goddess Lakshmi, her pet whiteboy, and the members of FEMelanin, *Bedtime Stories* stages a storytelling session where the lead puts white supremacy to bed. The performance features the Devis (the Sanskrit word for goddesses) stationed across the exhibition room while Mackrandilal as Lakshmi sits on a throne in the center of the room. Her pet whiteboy lies motionless at her feet, wearing only thin black briefs and wrist cuffs. They await the audience members who are checked at the door by pseudo-guards. The guards are femme, donned in black leather, and play a key role in the performance. Whenever a white man enters the space, they ask a series of penetrating questions usually reserved for people of color: "What's your name? Who are you with? Can they vouch for you? Why are you here? Can I see some ID, please? What's your occupation? Where were you born? Are you sure? What is in your pockets? You're going to need to submit to a pat-down. Step over here, please. Wait, please."[77] After, the guards direct the audience to their seats on the floor. Lakshmi stays sitting throughout the interrogations, her body unconscious. All other Devis close the exhibition doors and proceed to walk throughout the space, weaving through the audience members as they read text written on their bodies. The bedtime stories commence.

Convening as a multiracial femme collective, the group pushes their recharting of the genealogy of Hindu deities to the juncture where rage and comparative race meet. Speaking on behalf of the goddesses, the Global Matriarch elaborates, "They will raze the earth with the righteous fire of their anger and build a new one from the ruins: a culture of abundance, radical justice, and balance."[78] Placing anger at the center of their artistic practice, the goddesses utilize rage as a form of sustenance, nourishing a community of multiracial femmes in vengeful pursuit of a more just world. Mackrandilal explains, "If art is the liminal space where fantasy touches reality, #NGM demands that this space be utilized to free oppressed people."[79]

Through dominance, submission, bondage, and interracial encounter, FEMelanin brings racialized anger to bear on a longer history of racialized violence against Black women, referencing what Christina Sharpe has theorized as a set of "monstrous intimacies."[80] When Mackrandilal asks, "Is it possible to seduce the oppressor into relinquishing his power?," we are confronted with a reworking of what Sharpe, quoting Frederick Douglass, has described as "the violence, often sexual, by which one is 'made a subject, subjected by others,' and the other 'is a subject but . . . the author of his own subjection.'"[81] Responding to Douglass's memories of his witnessing his Aunt Hester's beatings, Sharpe notes that these transactions "are often registered by conditions of violation, narrative, and other confinement, of produced and reproduced shame refused and/or transmitted from one generation to the next."[82] At base, there is a repetitive nature to monstrous intimacies. It is, in other words, not simply a passive endurance but an active passing-on of conditions of violation that gives such intimacies life: "Thinking about monstrous intimacies post-slavery means examining those subjectivities constituted from transatlantic slavery onward and connected, then as now, by the everyday mundane horrors that aren't acknowledged to be horrors."[83] Mundane horrors not recognized as horrors range from interracial sex to any number of acts featuring forced yet well-disguised submission, including a request for access or a pet whiteboy. In citing Sharpe, I mean not to dismiss the specificity of Black life and its perpetual and distinct condition of racialized subjugation but to linger on the quality of repetition that permeates any scene of racist intimacy and its inheritances. Whereas Sharpe tracks "the romantic residue of slavery" to "examine and account for a series of repetitions of master narratives of violence," I have opted to shift away from the romance narrative, seeking neither to condone nor condemn interracial sex but to call attention to the reprisal moments of racist intimacy that have less to do with romance than they do with minoritarian refusal, including its promise and its fantasies.[84] Twisted together, the erotic life of racism and orientalist desire can motivate gestures toward their own demise, such as an Asian Barbie suspending access or a Hindu goddess seducing the oppressor into relinquishing his power even if only through a performance. The femme alter ego joins a chorus of artists and scholars who remind us that racism is a sexual affair, but it is the work of the femme alter ego's retribution that exposes the tensions that arise when anti-racism becomes a badge of honor, a rehearsal, or a repetition of empty promises in an era that features a steady uptick in discourse on anti-racism just as there too exists no such decline in racist violence.

Earlier, I mentioned the erotic life of anti-racism, and it is on that note that I wish to conclude. Insofar as racist intimacies interpret a set of unfolding relations that should leave us feeling angry and eager for change, I wonder how our very desires to be anti-racist find themselves living on occasion a racist life. To be anti-racist is, as is generally understood, to actively commit to changing behaviors, policies, and ideas that perpetuate racism. The problem with defining and structuring racial politics in opposition to racism is that the reverberations fall way to the more explicit scenes of racism, assuming also that we all mean the same thing when we say *racism*. Moreover, empty promises abound in a moment in which the desire to brand oneself or one's institution as anti-racist is in itself a racist desire. What do we make of anti-racism's neoliberal turn? Consider Ibram X. Kendi's *How to Be an Antiracist* (2019) and its surge in sales following the summer of 2020 or the widespread citation in racial equity tool kits of Angela Davis's earlier declaration that "in a racist society, it is not enough to be non-racist, we must be anti-racist."[85] With an overwhelming desire to *be* anti-racist, have people and organizations actively participated in the work of anti-racism beyond the fervor or pressures of the moment? Too much of anti-racism has become an identity devoid of a politics of critical resistance. Could it be that the celebratory tones of inclusion, belonging, and progress, each a cornerstone of multicultural American discourse, find themselves festering within the colonial and imperial logics governing much of the discourse on anti-racism? How are these shortcomings or well-meaning complicities related to the more disturbing and perceptible forms of racist desire, such as Sharpe's monstrous intimacies or the staggering list of white men affiliated with the alt-right who have dated or married Asian women?[86] One answer is that racist desire has no preference in party or affiliation. If a white supremacist partners with a woman of color, is his racism less racist? Of course not, but are his desires indicative of a more modern and multiracial white supremacy? That is the question. We need only to recall bell hooks's always insightful text "Eating the Other: Desire and Resistance" to note the importance of a "mutual recognition of racism" as "the only standpoint that makes possible an encounter between races that is not based on denial and fantasy."[87] This matters not only for the ways desire touches the interracial couple form but also for those of us who claim a desire for an anti-racist world.

Anti-racism is seductive. Its radical intentions can incite an alluring promise—to *be* anti-racist—which is an ontological desire, and like other forms of desire, there is often something left unfulfilled. When the moment passes and the passion wanes, what happens then? Was once enough? Does the desire swell, or does it whither? Does it lie dormant, in longing? Do you find yourself slowly becoming less moved by the seduction, less interested, or simply satisfied and perhaps ready to move on, removing the Black Lives Matter signs from your yards and falling back into a kind of normalcy? Does the desire expire? Or do you simply forget?

The anti-racism I am speaking of is a neoliberal one with neofascist tendencies. To factor an erotic life into that interpretation of anti-racism is to trouble if not renounce our understandings of racism and anti-racism as known and recognizable entities. If we want anti-racism to do what we want it to do, we ought to be careful in how we proceed. What we may glean from the Asian/white hybrid, that subject entrenched in racist intimacy, are the ways anti-racism forces one to become quite intimate both with the scenes in which racism's residue festers and with efforts to anticipate racism's emergent forms. What matters is not whether the anticipation is correct but the submission and surrender that transpire after the fact, which are lessons the femme alter ego can bestow. Giving in to the Asian/white dyad from the affective positions of humiliation and boredom, her confrontation and contestation of racist intimacies catalyze an urgent examination into the desires that produce the terrifying acts of violence too common in Asian/white encounter. Insofar as Asian femininity forms the object of racist intimacies, it can also function as the basis of a desire for some different kind of world where intimacies without racism may reside. To move in that direction, the femme alter ego must surrender to the fact of white supremacy's sexual undercurrents. Here, surrender takes the shape not of acquiescence but of permission. Becoming one with one's objecthood, the hybrid's femme alter ego leaves behind a wish that things did not have to be this way and a suspicion that retribution is already underway.

CODA
Torn Together

A feeling and an affliction, *torn* provokes a sense of woundedness and oscillation. It can describe a literal splitting of one thing into two. It can speak to a state of hesitation or indecision. Fragmented, broken, incomplete. Unsure, in doubt, ambivalent. These are words too often used to characterize mixed race life, and it has been my aim in this book neither to refuse these clichés nor to look beyond them but to confront the conditions of their possibility. In doing so, I set out to locate how the legacies of imperial expansion and America's colonial mission produce affective, psychic, and quotidian tensions. I gathered these tensions as signs of the *intimacy of violence*, a theoretical framework for locating and naming the residual effects of empire and colonialism as forms of violence that manifest in the intimate spheres of Asian/white life ranging from a fragmented sense of self and feelings of racialized isolation to the sexualized domains of emasculation, predation, and fetishization. To think with Asian/white life is to sit with tension, accepting that some things cannot be healed and to suggest otherwise is only to reproduce harm.

First and foremost, *Torn* has searched for deeper clarity on the ways empire refuses neat conclusion, which may seem obvious in the era in which I write, one of resurgent fascism and ongoing genocide. We are indeed bearing witness to the perpetual *imperial boomerang* of governments and administrations who are extending the militaristic techniques they developed in war and in their colonies only to then deploy them onto their own citizens and students.[1] These violences tear at us, but we too can tear away from the structures of settler colonialism, empire, and racial capitalism that make these forms of violence seem ordinary, normal, necessary.

In a poem titled "Torn Map," Palestinian American poet Naomi Shihab Nye encapsulates this interpretation of torn: a tearing we endure, a tearing we enact. Here, the accidental tearing of a map is a welcomed departure from reality, doubling as an act of wishful thinking and speculation.

Once
by mistake
she tore a map
in half.
She taped it back,
but crookedly.
Now all the roads
ended in water.
There were mountains
right next to her hometown.
Wouldn't that be nice
if it were true?
I'd tear a map
and be right next
to you.[2]

A tear is not a break. To that which is torn in half, there remains a potential for reconnection. Taped back together, the map, though ripped, is better now. All roads lead to water; a home near mountains. The distance between the two no longer exists. A tear is not a break but an opportunity. I sense longing and agency, two positions that define the past conditional temporality: a productive attention to the scene of loss.[3] *Wouldn't that be nice if it were true?*

The poem does not beckon one to presume change is so simple. It does, however, drag the structural threat of division into center frame insofar as the yearning that appears on the last line is at the fault of empire and colonialism. These are the reasons a separation takes place. As is the case of occupation, borders, partition, displacement, and even defection, a war-torn map is a matter of life and death.[4]

In another poem, "No Explosions," Nye again gestures to the residual life of empire and the colonial present. Some signs of independence only underscore how inaccessible, contingent, and withholding freedom is.

To enjoy
fireworks
you would have
to have lived
a different kind
of life[5]

The American tradition of shooting lights into the night sky produces noise, smoke, screams, and reminders of drone warfare and, to a certain extent, gunfire. An explosion of pyrotechnic stars is less an occasion to gather and celebrate but simply an explosion, a reason for fright.

Poetry can function as grief management. Memories rise to the surface; words inch as close as possible to ephemera. Naming grief and the pain it incites is pivotal to any healing regimen. Jennifer Mullan concludes as much: "When a wound goes unnamed and untended, it will grow and fester—eventually infecting everything around it."[6] A leader in the movement to decolonize therapy, Mullan bases her clinical practice on the premise that colonization is one of humanity's core wounds. For Mullan, healing from colonialism is impossible unless one were to work to acknowledge the wounds it leaves within. For mixed race life, an experience she lives, these wounds speak toward an embodied inheritance where two or more racial histories have collided within one body. Mixed-raceness also describes the context Nye writes from as a daughter of a white American mother and a Palestinian father who became a refugee during the 1948 Nakba. A prolific poet and writer of children's books, Nye draws on her mixed-raceness as a means to write toward our shared humanity. Racial mixture again seems primed to dabble in cultural exchange, connection, and commonality. In *Borderlands/La Frontera*, Anzaldúa goes so far as to delineate mixed race life in psychic terms, designating *la mestiza* in "a constant state of mental nepantilism, an Aztec word meaning torn between ways . . . a product of the transfer of the cultural and spiritual values of one group to another."[7] In speaking of being torn, I am not suggesting mixed race life is inherently injured, tragic, or partial, nor am I convinced that it is somehow a privileged domain of empathic living. I am, however, adamant that US imperialism and colonization have produced irreparable harms. Asian/white life has merely functioned as my representative case study for illuminating what festers when one fails to face the conditions that tear us away from one another.

In no uncertain terms, this book took shape from a suspicion that we have been fooled into thinking that healing is imperative, that it is something other than a departure from the truth that we are fine as we are. Some may claim a naivety to such a thought. How could we possibly be *fine*? Injury happens, violence leaves its mark, and those traumas can be painful, damaging, and deadly if left untreated. We seek ways to recover, ease the pain, or return to a moment when the hurt hurt less. Healing, to me, feels like succumbing to a Marxian false consciousness or even a relation of cruel optimism, Lauren Berlant's observation of the historical present, "when something you desire is actually an obstacle to your flourishing."[8] Healing suggests a successful return to some version of health and normal functioning that never quite matches up with how I see the world and the people around me, let alone myself. Am I missing something? Am I being pedantic, taking "healing" too seriously? Is this the depressive position José Esteban Muñoz refers to?[9] Must I better hone Eve Kosofsky Sedgwick's reparative reading practice?[10]

Studies have shown how communities and people learn to live with violence, finding joy and recovery but also finding no other way to proceed but to surrender to the pain. If we consider violence as a given in the world as we know it, how might that baseline act as the grounds to test the theory of healing with all of its restorative connotations? Yes, there is violence and there is survival, but if healing means restoration, then perhaps there is no healing to be done because we are—and this is my suspicion—good enough as we are. It is okay to be torn apart.

To be torn is, in my understanding, not to live a life of constant suffering but to have collected and implemented strategies of preservation more aligned with sustenance than repair. On this premise, *Torn* has inquired into the moments of relief that keep us here and alive in spite of it all. My curiosity has lain less in how humans have sought to heal or lessen pain and more in the efforts to reenergize or refuel with the purpose not to make better but to continue to make time. Such a study would be incomplete if I did not also record what transpires in the lack of such solace, and thus what I have assembled is a record for how one does or does not find relief from the hold of violence. Although the feeling of relief is not enough to undo violence, just as it is, in many ways, not enough to be *just* fine, I have found that practices of recurrent tending can alleviate the strain of violence if only enough to provide us with the tools and energy to keep doing what we are doing, finding a means to continue, to stay carrying the weight, and perhaps that is a tension worth sustaining.

In the chapters that precede this conclusion, I have taken up the case of Asian/white life in an effort to be accountable to one's one, which is to say, I am writing to those with whom I identify, and this identification, though presumably based on race, is more pointedly directed elsewhere, to a place of shared struggle. Let me explain. Maria P. P. Root, a psychologist who spearheaded the study of multiracial life, created a resource in the early 1990s, the Bill of Rights for People of Mixed Heritage, which sought to empower mixed race people through a list of rights, such as "I have the right not to keep the races separate within me" and "I have the right to identify myself differently than strangers expect me to identify."[11] In 2019, educator Emi Ito took inspiration from Root's interest in affirmative personhood and conceived of the Bill of Responsibilities for Multiracial People of Color with Light Skin and White Passing Privilege, including the need for people such as myself "to actively fight against racism and dismantle white supremacy," "combat colorism," and "call out racism and discrimination."[12] Like Ito's reworking of Root, I have argued for an engagement with multiracial subjectivity that views the self not as a focal point but as the starting point for pursuing deeper knowledge of one's embeddedness in history, a prerequisite for resistance and solidarity. This book's pages chronicle cases and cultural work of people who, like me, are "off-white" or Asian with "winter skin," as Teresa Williams-León and Seni Seneviratne respectfully put it.[13] The purpose, at least on the surface, is to offer a sustained critique of how Asian/white life is folded into the infrastructure of American empire and colonization. I have endeavored to show how the intimacy of violence infiltrates our lives, tempting us to conform to the logics of progress and disavowal which have long fueled the US war machine. In addressing empire's subtle impressions, I have provided examples of how one may refuse or rework those logics. I have also illuminated the dangers of assimilation and complicity. *Torn* aligns questions of personhood with demands for social transformation, exposing shared struggle as one solution to our world's most pressing challenges.

Insofar as this book concerns Asian/white life, it ultimately seeks comprehension of something that concerns all of us: the shifting terrains of white supremacy and American empire. I have not sought to essentialize Asian/white life but to lift Asian/white life as a lens with which to understand how gender and sexuality are inseparable from the intertwined projects of America's nation building and its imperial expansion in Asia and the Pacific. Tracing the sexual and psychic life of US empire leads one to reckon with the whiteness inside Asian America, a consuming and pervasive presence but one that is also feeble and able to be discontinued. Asian/white life, as I have shown through cases where one is mistaken as white or chooses to pass as white, is particularly primed to function as a lens to assess this dynamic. For some, whiteness is an option, and I ask why some enactments of Asian/white life understand whiteness as a means of survival (e.g., Daniel Holtzclaw or Joanna Gaines) while others have creatively attempted to destroy or destabilize its grip on us (e.g., Chanel Matsunami Govreau or Maya Mackrandilal).

Empire is insecure, instable, and incoherent.[14] I understand whiteness in the same vein. Like empire, whiteness festers within Asian America. It is at once a rubric, a racial standard, and a residual marker of interracial intimacy. Tracing the whiteness inside Asian America, even more so, functions as a lens to expose the fundamental illogics of whiteness itself. For Asian/white life to conform to whiteness is not simply an aesthetic choice but a political one. I am not speaking about ancestry or heritage here. I am speaking on the white supremacist structures of anti-Blackness and Indigenous dispossession that America stands on and to which some forms of Asian/white life prove awfully complicit with. More than decentering white people, more than celebrating mixed race being, a critical reckoning with racial mixture means prioritizing shared struggle as the motive for mixed race knowledge, activism, and community. If a study on mixed-raceness can offer anything in this moment—by which I mean any moment impaired by imperial and colonial presence—it hinges on a commitment and enactment of shared struggle. Rather than explore mixed-raceness as an understudied identity or experience, *Torn* has shown how a sustained confrontation with empire's irreparable harms, especially those most ordinary and subtle, becomes the premise for anti-imperial solidarity, as seen, for example, with the retributive desires carried out by the femme alter ego.

Further clarity can be gleaned from the mass mobilization for a free Palestine. Across the world, people have acted in urgent solidarity to stop Israel's unfolding genocide in Gaza through fundraising, joining political demonstrations, calling representatives, attending city council meetings, forming encampments, and participating in targeted campaigns to boycott and divest from state, corporate, and institutional complicity with Israel. In these spaces, people show up from a place of pain, desperation, helplessness, fortitude. In the midst of devastation, a kind of joy, though brief, can take place. Being with others likewise undone has, at least for me, produced a momentary solace from the kinds of pain that witnessing a genocide produces. Sights and sounds are enough to incite a reassurance—you are not alone in wanting an end to the bombs and killing—that, though fleeting, is lasting too: smiling children at the protest, city streets filled to the brim with families, friends, and strangers marching together, student walkouts at graduation, chants that ring true. Free, free, Palestine. There is only one solution. Intifada, revolution. The people united will never be defeated. Palestine will be free.

Although recentering and worthwhile, feelings of collectivity and acts of solidarity are not an indication that the violence has waned. Israel's decades-long genocidal campaign against the Palestinian people cannot possibly be relieved through the organizing efforts taking place across the world, particularly following October 7, 2023. Israel's genocidal harms, from the martyrs to the destruction of bloodlines, trees, homes, hospitals, and schools, cannot possibly be restored.

And yet, what does emerge as a possibility, it seems to me, is a willingness to confront the violence as well as an acceptance that repair is not always in the cards. Doing so is a vital step in any relation of anti-imperial solidarity. The transient yet impactful moments of connection that arise in pro-Palestine rallies and demonstrations, in other words, may signal a different interpretation of what it means to be *torn together*. Unlike the description offered in the introduction to this book, where *torn, together* is split by the punctuation mark of a comma, *torn together* is not disjoined through pause, separation, or distinction but rather indicative of what it means to exist alongside or next to. Set apart only by a single space, like Nye's torn map, *torn together* encapsulates the pulse of what it means to orient toward life through the lens of shared struggle. Without the comma, *torn together* offers a meditation showing the ways genocide and ethnic cleansing, crimes against humanity too often minimized as global tensions, are resisted and challenged through mass mobilization and community organizing. These tensions are met with a momentary relief that may not undo the excruciating levels of death and destruction but still point toward the enduring promises of multiracial solidarity and the antiwar movement.

The fields with which this book is in direct conversation—women of color feminism, Asian Americanist critique, American studies—have ethical and political obligations to keep their eyes on genocide, and in some ways they can be said to have answered those calls. The more emergent field of critical mixed race studies can learn from their successes and shortcomings.

A critical study of racial mixture becomes thwarted when its focus centers on identity and experience. A turn toward shared struggle could help unhinge the field's tendencies to view mixed-raceness as an intrinsic bridge across difference. Doing so may incite an insurgent reading of the timeless lyrics *my kind's your kind*, words sung by Karen O, the mixed race Korean lead singer of the Yeah Yeah Yeahs in the 2003 indie rock song "Maps."[15] Beyond romantic love, universality, and an assumed sameness, this line activates the pulse of shared struggle, of being *torn together*, a reckoning with our embeddedness with one another, pointing toward a call to "think alongside the unthought."[16] Living together in critical interrelationship means practicing a form of interdisciplinarity rooted in a relational analytic, which seeks to explore interrelations of difference that emerge for racialized and dispossessed subjects. It is a relation of "colonial unknowing" and "insurgent proliferation," which can be described as "the politics of knowledge," "critical promiscuity," and "comparative global humanities after man."[17] For mixed race life, a recognition of being *torn together* offers a way to conceptualize the never-absent presence of imperial ideologies and colonial practice in our contemporary moment. Bianca Nozaki-Nasser, a Japanese-Lebanese-Syrian interdisciplinary artist, makes this clear in her writing: "Instead of more photo essays documenting mixed kids with white features, as a multiracial person I'm interested in mapping thresholds as a means for navigating one other. Histories we are asked to forget on purpose. Gaps in understanding. Liminal thresholds for new ways of relating to one another."[18]

The intimacy of violence is persistent. Survival, therefore, is not easy, but it is made possible insofar as it is pursued as a collective affair. In the introduction to this book, I cited Viet Thanh Nguyen: "All wars are fought twice, the first time on the battlefield, the second time in memory."[19] In January 2024, Wael Al Dahdouh, Al Jazeera's bureau chief in Gaza brought new meaning to Nguyen's words: "Many Palestinian journalists feel that we were let down, left alone to face this massacre and this carnage and the world did not look at the bigger picture, did not really stand by us as we would have liked. . . . We feel that we are being killed twice: once by the bombs, and once by this silence, this shy way of expressing support."[20] Asian American studies has long noted the connections between the War on Terror, the "question of Palestine," and the US Cold War interventions across Asia, settler colonialism in Hawai'i, and Japanese internment.[21] The field's growing interest in Muslim Americans, Arab America, and Palestinian rights, as Rajini Srikanth has shown, draws out a question every scholar ought to sit with: "Can we move beyond the rhetoric of our aspirational commitments to antiracist, anti-imperialist, antiwar, and anticolonialist struggles, and can we be bold enough to condemn the Apartheid Wall, both at our border with Mexico and in Israel, reject Islamophobia, demand an end to police violence, oppressive settler colonialism, and militarism?"[22] Putting action behind our words, condemning the intimacy of violence necessitates an acknowledgment that that which we purport to denounce may not only outlast us, but it will in fact change us. Do not all bodies fail to retain their original shape? Call it growth, time, or wear and tear, but change is natural, a constant, so they say. Strange, then, this obsession with wholeness, repair, and returning to a past form. If being torn brings to the fore our unbounded relation to something larger than ourselves, then perhaps surrendering to our being *torn together* is enough to fashion a mode of living capable of tending to a world more deserving of us all.

Notes

PREFACE

1 Hall, "Eating Salt," 241.

2 Moraga, "Breakdown of the Bicultural Mind," 231.

3 Hall, "Eating Salt," 251.

INTRODUCTION

1 An earlier version of my writing on Datchuk's *Half* appears in "Half and Both: On Color and Subject/Object Tactility," *Women and Performance: a journal of feminist theory* 30, no. 1 (2020): 104–12.

2 Cheng, *Ornamentalism.*

3 See Abu-Lughod, Hammami, and Shalhoub-Kevorkian, *Cunning of Gender Violence*; Choy, *Empire of Care*; Gonzalez, *Securing Paradise*; Hasso, *Buried in the Red Dirt*; Hochberg, *Becoming Palestine* and *Visual Occupations*; Kapadia, *Insurgent Aesthetics*; Kelly, *Invited to Witness*; Jinah Kim, *Postcolonial Grief*; Jodi Kim, *Settler Garrison*; Maira, *Missing*; Maurer, *Ocean on Fire*; Ngô, *Imperial Blues*; Puar, *Right to Maim*; Rafael, *White Love*; Said, *Orientalism*; Saranillio, *Unsustainable Empire*; and Stoler, *Imperial Debris* and *Duress.*

4 Here, I am referencing language from Joan Scott's "The Evidence of Experience" (1991) and the book series *Difference Incorporated* published by the University of Minnesota Press.

5 Vuong, *On Earth We're Briefly Gorgeous*, 33.

6 Vuong, *On Earth We're Briefly Gorgeous*, 33.

7 Vuong, *On Earth We're Briefly Gorgeous*, 33.

8 Vuong, *On Earth We're Briefly Gorgeous*, 33.

9 Vuong, *On Earth We're Briefly Gorgeous*, 33; emphasis in original.

10 See Saketopoulou, *Sexuality Beyond Consent*; Ninh and Roshanravan, "#WeToo"; and Buggs and Hoppe, *Unsafe Words.*

11 Trask, "Color of Violence."

12 Vuong, *On Earth We're Briefly Gorgeous*, 61.

13 Vuong, *On Earth We're Briefly Gorgeous*, 61; emphasis in original.

14 Vuong, *On Earth We're Briefly Gorgeous*, 12.

15 V. Nguyen, *Nothing Ever Dies*, 4.

16 Vuong, *On Earth We're Briefly Gorgeous*, 13; emphasis in original.

17 On violence folded into narratives of freedom, see C. Reddy, *Freedom with Violence*; Lowe, *Intimacies of Four Continents*; and Butler, *Force of Nonviolence*. On lessons from the transformative justice movement, see Chen, Dulani, and Piepzna-Samarasinha, *Revolution Starts at Home*; INCITE! Women of Color Against Violence, *Color of Violence*; Mullan, *Decolonizing Therapy*; Spade, *Normal Life*; Kaba and Hassan, *Fumbling Towards Repair*; and Dixon and Piepzna-Samarasinha, *Beyond Survival*.

18 See Lowe, *Intimacies of Four Continents*; Ruiz, *Ricanness*; Sharpe, *In the Wake*; and Tadiar, *Remaindered Life*.

19 R. Williams, *Marxism and Literature*; Hong and Ferguson, *Strange Affinities*; Gordon, *Ghostly Matters*; and Gilmore, *Golden Gulag*.

20 Vuong, *On Earth We're Briefly Gorgeous*, 23.

21 I credit Boram Jeong for bringing me to this point during a writing workshop with the Asian American Feminisms section at the 2022 Association of Asian American Studies conference.

22 Fanon, *Wretched of the Earth*, 181.

23 Fanon, *Wretched of the Earth*, 181.

24 Think of Neferti Tadiar, who has examined how permanent imperial war produces modes of living outside the binary of productivity and disposability, and Josen Masangkay Diaz, who reimagines the racial and gendered possibilities of Filipino American subjectivity that arise within a diaspora contending both with postcoloniality and authoritarian rule. Especially relevant to my study, Vernadette Vicuña Gonzalez's archival reckoning with the life of mixed race vaudevillian and actress Isabel Rosario Cooper offers an intimate portrayal of how beauty and desire inform the soft power of imperialism through the lens of transpacific femininity, a point elaborated at length by Denise Cruz, illuminating how sexuality is critical to understanding the inner workings of imperial masculinity and its role in the more "hard" power of militaristic presence. See Tadiar, *Remaindered Life*; Diaz, *Postcolonial Configurations*; Gonzalez, *Empire's Mistress*; and D. Cruz, *Transpacific Femininities*.

25 Cho, *Haunting the Korean Diaspora*; Haritaworn, *Biopolitics of Mixing*.

26 Brina, *Speak, Okinawa*; Cho, *Tastes like War*; Saraswati, *Scarred*; and Troeung, *Landbridge*.

27 Kang, *Compositional Subjects*, 71.

28 Kang, *Traffic in Asian Women*.

29 See Bow, *Asian American Feminisms*; Bow, *Betrayal and Other Acts of Subversion*; Cheng, *Ornamentalism*; Chuh, *Imagine Otherwise*; and Lowe, *Immigrant Acts*.

30 See Scott, "Evidence of Experience"; and Mani, "Multiple Mediations."

31 Gordon, *Ghostly Matters*, xvi.

32 Gordon, *Ghostly Matters*, 7.

33 Gordon, *Ghostly Matters*, 6.

34 P. Williams, *Alchemy of Race*, 19.

35 Gordon, *Ghostly Matters*, 22.

36 Amin, *Disturbing Attachments*, 11.

37 See Eng, "Colonial Object Relations"; and Eng, "Reparations and the Human."

38 Berlant, "Intimacy," 283.
39 Lowe, *The Intimacies of Four Continents*, 17–18.
40 Lowe, *The Intimacies of Four Continents*, 18.
41 Berlant, "Intimacy," 284.
42 Not only is this an overt and racist preference toward those with white ancestry, but it is also erroneous in that the future, to be clear, is not anticipated to get cooler but warmer with climate change and environmental disaster. I credit Kimberly Skye for helping me see this latter point during the Performance Studies summer workshop on ecologies at Northwestern University in 2018.
43 Unlike hybrid degeneracy, hybrid vigor implies a racially mixed offspring is genetically superior to both or one of their parents. Hybrid vigor, otherwise known as heterosis, is a genetic phenomenon where outbreeding yields improved functionality or increased growth in a hybrid offspring. A hybrid is heterotic, then, if it exhibits more enhanced biological traits than either of its parents. The concept has been applied to organisms across the plant and animal kingdoms, yet its influence on human breeding is most contentious. Human beings are genetically very similar, so when the notion of hybridity is extracted from its genetic context and applied to the sociality of race, the racist pillars upholding racial difference broaden and strengthen. As a systemic tool of racial control, the notion of hybrid vigor exists in a peculiar relationship to hypodescent and the one-drop rule, which classifies a person with one Black ancestor as legally Black. A curious reversal of hypodescent occurs when hybrid vigor is thought to remove traces of inferiority in people of color, regenerating the ideology of white supremacy.
44 Anthropologist Jayne O. Ifekwunigwe has called attention to the ways *Time*'s 1993 cover represents "the dangerous ways in which confused media . . . induce fantasies about a future replete with 'interracial' cyborgs" (2). Deeming mixed race people "artefacts of the past and beacons of the future" (1), Ifekwunigwe situates the problematic origins of miscegenation alongside contemporary discourse which celebrates mixed race as a new racial category primed to beget an answer to racial conflict. See Ifekwunigwe, *"Mixed Race" Studies*, 1–2.
45 Berlant and Warner, "Sex in Public."
46 Funderburg, "Changing Face of America."
47 See Roh, Huang, and Niu, *Techno-Orientalism*.
48 Nancy Kwan, personal interview, March 18, 2022.
49 Tauber and Singh, *Blended Nation*.
50 Lyndon B. Johnson, "The Immigration and Nationality Act," October 3, 1965.
51 See Teng, *Eurasian*.
52 American writer Pearl S. Buck coined the term "Amerasian" before the Department of Justice and Immigration and Naturalization Service formalized it as "an alien who was born in Korea, Kampuchea, Laos, Thailand or Vietnam after December 31, 1950, and before October 22, 1982, and was fathered by a U.S. citizen." See INS Form 360, *Petition for Amerasian Widow(er) or Special Immigrant*. For a history of Amerasians, see Doolan, *First Amerasians*; and Doolan, "Cold War Construction of the Amerasian."

53 Hapa haole linguist R. Keao NeSmith has shown how the term originated in the early nineteenth century to describe the growing presence of hapa haoles, half-white or half-foreigner Hawaiians who were born after the European and American colonial occupation of Hawai'i. See Porzuki, "How the Hawaiian Word 'Hapa.'"

54 King-O'Riain, "#Wasian Check."

55 Palumbo-Lio, *Asian/American*, 1; emphasis in original.

56 Root, *Racially Mixed People in America.*

57 Rico, Jacobs, and Coritz, "2020 Census."

58 See DaCosta, *Making Multiracials*; Dalmage, *Politics of Multiracialism*; and Sundstrom, *Browning of America.*

59 The US Census Bureau began collecting detailed data on multiracial people in 2000. In that first year, 6.8 million people checked more than one box. By 2010, that number jumped by 32 percent making multiracials the fastest growing racial group in the nation.

60 Nakashima, "Servants of Culture," 271, 272.

61 Kina and Dariotis, *War Baby/Love Child*, 13.

62 See Saldanha, "Reontologising Race"; and Althusser, "Ideology and Ideological State Apparatuses."

63 See "The New Face of America"; Berlant and Warner, "Sex in Public"; Sexton, *Amalgamation Schemes*; Nyong'o, *Amalgamation Waltz*; Anzaldúa, *Borderlands/La Frontera*; Vasconcelos, *The Cosmic Race/La raza cósmica*; Root, *Racially Mixed People in America*; and Elam, *Souls of Mixed Folk.*

64 See Shiao, "Meaning of Honorary Whiteness"; and Yip, "Biracial Asians Viewed More Favorable."

65 For a different, *stranger* interpretation of interracial encounter, see Mannur, "Matter Out of Place."

66 Omi and Winant, *Racial Formation in the United States*, 55.

67 Harris, "Whiteness as Property."

68 See C. Anderson, *White Rage*; DiAngelo, *White Fragility*; Hamad, *White Tears/Brown Scars*; and Matias, *Feeling White.*

69 Ju Yon Kim, *Racial Mundane*, 3; emphasis in original.

70 See Ahmed, "A Phenomenology of Whiteness"; and Muñoz, *Sense of Brown*, 10.

71 For a convincing analysis on racist science in the context of Indigenous dispossession in the Pacific, see Arvin, *Possessing Polynesians.*

72 See Koshy, *Sexual Naturalization*; Coráñez Bolton, *Crip Colony*; and Sexton, *Amalgamation Schemes*, 9–10; emphasis in original.

73 See Bow, *Racist Love*; Bui, "Eugenic Ecologies" and "Objects of Warfare"; M. Chen, *Animacies* and *Intoxicated*; Cheng, *Ornamentalism*; Choudhury, "Making of the American Calorie"; R. Lee, *Exquisite Corpse of Asian America*; Spillers, "Mama's Baby, Papa's Maybe"; Musser, *Sensational Flesh*; Tompkins, *Racial Indigestion*; and Weheliye, *Habeas Viscus.*

74 Since its formation, the journal has published a total of three issues. The inaugural issue, "Emerging Paradigms in Critical Mixed Race Studies," was published in 2014. Since then, a second issue of the first volume was published in 2022, and a second

volume was published in 2023. Quite a significant gap in publication years, the journal has struggled to find consistency. G. Reginald Daniel, the longtime editor of the *Journal of Critical Mixed Race Studies* and founding member of CMRS, expressed an editorial interest in forming issues around mixed-raceness in a regional context, with the second issue titled "Mixed Race in Nordic Europe" and the third "Mixedness and Indigeneity in the Pacific." Daniel passed away in 2022. During the 2024 CMRS conference, it was announced that the journal would undergo a revamping.

75 See Critical Mixed Race Studies web page, https://criticalmixedracestudies.com/.

76 Three queer women of color, all Asian and white, founded CMRS: artist-scholar Laura Kina, literary scholar Wei Ming Dariotis, and American studies scholar Camilla Fojas. Since their founding, the association has leaned social scientific with a focus on education and identity, retreating from the kinds of queer and insurgent intentions Kina, Dariotis, and Fojas embodied in their leadership.

77 On racial mixture beyond US borders, see King-O'Riain et al., *Global Mixed Race*. For a history of racial mixture in the Americas, see Bost, *Mulattas and Mestizas*.

78 See Rondilla, Guevarra, and Spickard, *Red and Yellow, Black and Brown*; Guevarra, *Becoming Mexipino*; M. Washington, *Blasian Invasion*.

79 Wiegman, *Object Lessons*.

80 See Cvetkovich, *Depression*; Love, *Feeling Backward*; Freeman, *Time Binds*; and Wiegman, "Times We're In." See Saketopoulou, *Sexuality Beyond Consent*; Singh, *No Archive Will Restore You*; and Stuelke, *Ruse of Repair*.

81 Pauline Gumbs, "Foreword," 4; emphasis in original.

82 A few studies that come to mind: Balance, *Tropical Renditions*; Bruce, *How to Go Mad*; Chambers-Letson, *After the Party*; J. Chen, *Trans Exploits*; Dolan, *Utopia in Performance*; V. Huang, *Surface Relations*; Kina and Bernabe, *Queering Contemporary Asian American Art*; N. King, *Queer and Trans Artists of Color*; T. King, *Black Shoals*; Kondo, *Worldmaking*; Khubchandani, *Decolonize Drag* and *Ishtyle*; Muñoz, *Cruising Utopia*, and *Disidentifications*, and *Sense of Brown*; Lothian, *Old Futures*; McMillan, *Embodied Avatars*; L. Pérez, *Chicana Art*; Ponce De León, *Another Aesthetics Is Possible*; Ramos, *Unbelonging*; Reed, *Art of Protest*; Shomali, *Between Banat*; Tsing et al., *Arts of Living*.

83 See Nopper and Zelickson, "Wellness Capitalism"; and Ehlers and Krupar, *Deadly Biocultures*.

84 See Grosz, *Volatile Bodies*. Think also of the Cartesian mind-body split, the Spinozian notion that the body is an extension of the mind, the Butlerian theory of performativity, Foucauldian biopower, Valerie Fournier's attention to how gender is performed through pain, violence, and other inscriptions on the "hurting flesh," and Thomas Laqueur's work on hierarchy, dichotomy, and the social life of scientific models of gender and sex. Let us also recall Grosz's intervention for a Deleuzian rejection of dichotomy.

85 While many scholars have found it difficult to materialize affect, affect theorists argue that studying viscerally charged attachments is crucial to the dialectic between individual embodiment and contemporary sociocultural analyses. In

particular, Patricia Clough suggests that "the turn to affect is a harbinger of and a discursive accompaniment to the forging of a new body," what she calls the "biomediated body." Thus, the affective turn symbolizes the creation of a new body, a biomediated body that challenges the late nineteenth-century notion of body-as-organism. See Clough and Halley, *Affective Turn*, 2.

86 Clough and Halley, *Affective Turn*, 5.

87 Examples of recent work include Cheung-Miaw, "Fate of 'Shared Interests Among People of Color'"; Cuéllar, "Waterproofing the State"; Edwards, *Other Side of Terror*; Hobart, *Cooling the Tropics*; Hu Pegues, *Space-Time Colonialism*; M. Huang, *Reconfiguring Racial Capitalism*; Karuka, *Empire's Tracks*; Lowe and Manjapra, "Comparative Global Humanities After Man"; and Vimalassery, Pegues, and Goldstein, "Colonial Unknowing and Relations of Study." One can also think of the intellectual labor behind moves to departmentalize studies at the intersection of race, colonialism, migration, and sexuality. For example, the Department of Race, Diaspora, and Indigeneity (University of Chicago), the Consortium of Studies in Race, Migration, and Sexuality (Dartmouth College), the Department of Studies in Race, Colonialism, and Diaspora (Tufts University), and the Program in Ethnicity, Race, and Migration (Yale University).

88 See Bascara, *Model-Minority Imperialism*; Chong, *Oriental Obscene*; Chuh, *Difference Aesthetics Makes*; Collins, "Some Group Matters"; De Lauretis, *Alice Doesn't*; Eng and Han, *Racial Melancholia, Racial Dissociation*; Ferguson, *Aberrations in Black*; Freeman, "Queer Temporalities" and *Time Binds*; Halberstam, *In a Queer Time and Place*; Haraway, "Situated Knowledges"; Hartsock, "Feminist Standpoint"; Love, *Feeling Backward*; Mani, "Multiple Mediations"; Muñoz, *Cruising Utopia*; Scott, "Evidence of Experience"; Shimakawa, *National Abjection*; Son, *Embodied Reckonings*; and Yao, *Disaffected*.

89 See Ahmed, *Cultural Politics of Emotion* and *Promise of Happiness*; P. Anderson, *So Much Wasted*; Balce, *Body Parts of Empire*; Berlant, *Female Complaint*; Butler, *Bodies that Matter*; Crosby, *A Body Undone*; Cvetkovich, *An Archive of Feelings*; Espiritu, *Body Counts*; Fleetwood, *Troubling Vision*; Hall, "Eating Salt"; Hennessy, *Profit and Pleasure*; Love, *Feeling Backward*; McSorley, *War and the Body*; McCormack, *Queer Postcolonial Narratives*; Melamed, *Represent and Destroy*; Pascoe, *What Comes Naturally*; H. Pérez, *A Taste for Brown Bodies*; Schalk, *Bodyminds Reimagined*; Sedgwick, *Touching Feeling*; Singh, *Unthinking Mastery*; Somerville, *Queering the Color Line*; and Stoler, *Haunted By Empire*.

90 See Eng, *Feeling of Kinship*; Ferguson, *Aberrations in Black*; Gopinath, *Impossible Desires*; Manalansan, *Global Divas*; Ponce, *Beyond the Nation*; and Puar, *Terrorist Assemblages*.

91 See Amin, Musser, and Pérez, "Queer Form"; Brooks, *Bodies in Dissent*; Chambers-Letson and Son, "Performed Otherwise"; Chung, "Defiant Still Worker"; Huang and Lee, "Contingency Plans"; S. K. Lee, "Staying In"; León, "Forms of Opacity"; McMaster, "Revolting Self Care"; Mengesha and Padmanabhan, "Performing Refusal/Refusing to Perform"; R. Pérez, "Proximity"; and Ruiz, "Waiting in the Seat of Sensation" and "El Caribe on the Horizon."

92 Muñoz, *Cruising Utopia*, 71.
93 Vuong, *On Earth We're Briefly Gorgeous*, 76–77; emphasis in original.
94 Vuong, *On Earth We're Briefly Gorgeous*, 231.
95 Vuong, *On Earth We're Briefly Gorgeous*, 85; emphasis in original.
96 Singh, *No Archive Will Restore You*, 29.
97 Gramsci, *Selections from the Prison Notebooks*, 324.
98 Singh, *No Archive Will Restore You*, 27.

CHAPTER 1. SEDUCED WHOLE

1 For more on how the narrator's self-reflexivity is situated within the novel's political project, see Wolfson, "Man of Two Faces."
2 V. Nguyen, *Sympathizer*, 63.
3 This notion, that white masculinity and Asian femininity form the perfect match, is discussed in Teng's 2013 study, *Eurasian*. It also plays a part in Nguyen's *The Sympathizer* when the narrator discusses Asian/white interracial sexuality and that it is, for the white man, "impossible not to nibble on dark chocolate." In chapter 3 of *The Sympathizer*, there is a blurring of lines between "us and them," with a connection made between yellow fever and the white men it ails.
4 See Saldaña-Portillo, *Revolutionary Imagination*.
5 Such narratives also transpire in popular children's books. See Oz and Annisa, *I Am Whole*; and Diggs and Evans, *Mixed Me!*
6 I credit Livia Maguire, a Duke University undergraduate student in my "New Directions in Asian American Studies" class, for bringing this latter point to my attention during a conversation on April 8, 2024.
7 There is also a collection of books that feature portraits of interracial couples and families. See Kaeser and Gillespie, *Of Many Colors*; Kalman, *No Difference Between Them*; and Pfluger, *Holding Space*.
8 This passage appears inside the front cover of Zimmern's *Eurasian Face*.
9 These are words used in the blurbs on the back of Fulbeck's *Part Asian, 100% Hapa*.
10 "Pushed to the Limit" is one of the titles of porn films investigators found while searching through Cunanan's possessions, as noted in a July 1997 *Newsweek* article "Facing Death" by Evan Thomas.
11 For more on Loving Day, see the organization's web page, https://lovingday.org/.
12 FBI, "Andrew Phillip Cunanan."
13 Perry and Pasternak, "Cunanan Doesn't Fit."
14 *Oprah Winfrey Show*, April 24, 1997.
15 In 2009, Tiger Woods fell from grace after several women reported having affairs with him.
16 See Blanco Borelli, *She Is Cuba*; Carter, *United States of the United Races*; Daniher, "Yella Gal"; Mitchell, *Imagining the Mulatta*; M. Washington, *Blasian Invasion*.
17 Orth, "Killer's Trail."
18 See Isaac, *American Tropics*; Balance, "Notorious Kin"; Lim, *Brown Boys and Rice Queens*.

19 Orth, *Vulgar Favors*, 52–53.
20 David, "Sexual Fields of Empire."
21 Isaac, *American Tropics*, xvii, xvi.
22 Isaac, *American Tropics*, xvi.
23 Isaac, *American Tropics*, xxv.
24 Isaac, *American Tropics*, xvii–xviii.
25 Lim, *Brown Boys and Rice Queens*, 8.
26 Lim, *Brown Boys and Rice Queens*, 22.
27 Lim, *Brown Boys and Rice Queens*, 13.
28 Lim, *Brown Boys and Rice Queens*, 18.
29 See episode 2, "Manhunt," in *The Assassination of Gianni Versace*.
30 Musser, *Sensational Flesh*.
31 Yao, *Disaffected*, 173, 175.
32 *TURA!*, the long-awaited documentary on Satana, was released in select theaters in August 2025. Directed by Cody Jarrett and narrated by Margaret Cho, the film features archival footage and interviews with family, friends, and colleagues, including John Waters and Dita Von Teese.
33 Balance, "Notorious Kin," 89.
34 Mendoza, *Metroimperial Intimacies*, 11.
35 Mendoza, *Metroimperial Intimacies*, 6.
36 Mendoza, *Metroimperial Intimacies*, 5, 6.
37 Mendoza, *Metroimperial Intimacies*.
38 Mendoza, *Metroimperial Intimacies*.
39 D. Rodríguez, *Suspended Apocalypse*, 11.
40 Appadurai, "Grassroots Globalization and the Research Imagination."
41 Cabico, "Love Letter from Andrew Cunanan," 35.
42 A history of the HIF is described as follows: "Hapa Issues Forum (HIF), a nonprofit community organization, was founded in 1992 by three University of California, Berkeley students; Eric Akira Tate, Steven Masami Ropp, and Greg Mayeda. It was formed to address the mixed race Asian experience in America by providing a voice for people of partial Asian or Pacific Islander ancestry, creating a nonexclusive multiracial community, providing a forum for reasoned dialogue, working with other community organizations to broaden awareness of Hapas, and challenging this nation's rigid notion of race. After fifteen years of community activities and achievements and continually gaining numbers in the Asian multiracial population, the organization disbanded because of the correlating increase in divergent interests and goals." See "Hapa Issues Forum Records."
43 Dariotis, "Hapa."
44 Indigenous and allied critics have been forthright about how the broader deployment of the word disregards its colonial roots. See Arvin, *Possessing Polynesians*; Chang, *Hapa Tales and Other Lies*; Dariotis, "Hapa" and "To Be 'Hapa'"; Rabin, "Excursus on 'Hapa'"; and for a general overview of the issue, see Johnson, "Who Gets to Be 'Hapa'?"

45 A full list detailing the exhibition history is available at https://kipfulbeck.com/the-hapa-project/exhibitions/.
46 Fulbeck, *Part Asian, 100% Hapa*, 24.
47 Fulbeck, *Part Asian, 100% Hapa*, 158.
48 Fulbeck, *Part Asian, 100% Hapa*, 17.
49 Fulbeck, *Part Asian, 100% Hapa*, 17.
50 Fulbeck, *Part Asian, 100% Hapa*, 259–60; emphasis in original.
51 Fulbeck, *Part Asian, 100% Hapa*, 262.
52 I am therefore at odds with Henry Louis Gates whose belief that "we are all mixed" underlies *Finding Your Roots*, the PBS show he hosts, and that relies exclusively on DNA testing and genealogical research as a way to chart human connection, normalizing racial mixture without accounting for why it has been normalized. See Hirsch, "'We Are All Mixed.'"
53 Ruiz, *Ricanness*, 3.
54 Mahtani, *Mixed Race Amnesia*, 3.
55 Eng, *Feeling of Kinship*.
56 Hong, *Death Beyond Disavowal*, 26.
57 Teng, *Eurasian*.
58 Teng, *Eurasian*, 131.
59 Teng, *Eurasian*, 129.
60 Teng, *Eurasian*, 120.
61 I borrow the term "model majority" from Rebecca Chiyoko King-O'Riain whose study on multiracial Japanese Americans addresses the impact the Black/white binary in the multiracial movement has had on the identity formation for those in the Japanese American community. See King-O'Riain, "Model Majority?"
62 Muñoz, *Cruising Utopia*, 27–28.
63 Muñoz, *Cruising Utopia*, 27.
64 Muñoz, *Cruising Utopia*, 28.
65 *Hyphen*, no. 13 (Winter 2007).
66 Muñoz, *Cruising Utopia*, 28.
67 Kristeva, *Powers of Horror*, 4.
68 Kristeva, *Powers of Horror*, 8.
69 Kristeva, *Powers of Horror*, 9.
70 Shimakawa, *National Abjection*, 3, 2; emphasis in original.
71 Shimakawa, *National Abjection*, 2.
72 Shimakawa, *National Abjection*, 3; emphasis in original.
73 Shimakawa, *National Abjection*, 15.
74 Bhabha, "Other Question" 66; Shimakawa, *National Abjection*, 15; emphasis in original.
75 Fulbeck, *Part Asian, 100% Hapa*, 262.
76 For a critical mixed race study relevant to this history, see Villanueva, "Photographing Mixed-Raced Bodies."
77 See K. Brown, *Mortevivum*; and Campt, *Listening to Images*.
78 Barthes, *Camera Lucida*; Sontag, *On Photography*.

79 McClintock, *Imperial Leather*, 123.
80 Rekdal, *Appropriate*, 85.
81 Rekdal, *Appropriate*, 88.
82 See novels Chou, *Disorientation*; and Kuang, *Yellowface*. In film, consider representation from Fu Manchu's character and his daughter being played by white actors to Emma Stone and Scarlett Johansson playing Asian American and Pacific Islander characters. In poetry, see Waldman, "White Poet."
83 Rekdal, *Appropriate*, 190.
84 Rekdal, *Appropriate*, 40; emphasis in original.
85 For example, Michael Warner articulates the concept of heteronormativity as the belief that heterosexuality is natural, normal, and expected. By critiquing the assumed normality of heterosexuality, Warner offers a queer analytic that challenges the presumed authenticity of heterosexuality. Concurrently, in *The Twilight of Equality?* Lisa Duggan queers the concept of heteronormativity with a theorization of homonormativity, "a politics that does not contest dominant heteronormative assumptions and institutions, but upholds and sustains them" (50). Duggan argues that with the emergence of this "new homonormativity," lesbians and gays do not so much resist dominant heteronormative institutions as defend them through their social and neoliberal economic assimilating actions. By recognizing that prerequisites of normality are dependent on rigid understandings of gender and sexuality, queer theorists such as Warner and Duggan reveal the instability of such seemingly authentic institutional formations. Another major hallmark of queer theory is its attention to the disciplinary and performative nature of identities. To this, Judith Butler's work on performativity challenges feminism's assertion that the identity of "women" is a natural given and argues that gender is discursively constructed. Butler argues that any understanding of gender as natural will continue to dish out disciplinary consequences to those who do not abide by a hegemonic and thus authentic gender model. In conversation with French feminist and poststructuralist thought, Butler works to deconstruct gender to show that the very notion of gender is a "repeated stylization of the body, a set of repeated acts . . . that congeal over time" (45). Gender therefore should neither be seen as something we are nor as a construct defined by authentic masculine or feminine performance but instead as a practice we do repeatedly. See Butler, *Gender Trouble*; Duggan, *The Twilight of Equality?*; and Warner, "Introduction."
86 Halberstam, *In a Queer Time and Place*, 52.
87 Marlon Bailey, "Gender/Racial Realness," 377–78.
88 Halberstam, *In a Queer Time and Place*, 45.
89 See Somerville, *Queering the Color Line*.
90 Shohat and Sham, *Unthinking Eurocentrism*, 285.
91 Shohat and Sham, *Unthinking Eurocentrism*, 215.
92 For a discussion of the cult of authenticity, see Brydon, "White Inuit Speaks." For a discussion of the fetishization of authentic speech and the violence of that fetishization, see Griffiths, "Myth of Authenticity."
93 Arrizón, *Queering Mestizaje*, 1.

94 Arrizón, *Queering Mestizaje*, 63; emphasis in original.

95 For Stefani, this stems from her deep love of Japanese culture, an affection born from her father's work travels to and from Japan when Stefani was growing up. She also identifies with Latinx culture because of her upbringing in Anaheim, California. See Calador, "Gwen Stefani." On the racial and sexual politics of kawaii, see Kanesaka, "Mixed-Race Fantasy Behind Kawaii Aesthetics."

96 Rekdal, *Appropriate*, 90–91.

97 Prins, "Coming to Light."

98 Shah, *Stranger Intimacy*.

99 Rekdal, *Intimate*, vii; emphasis in original.

100 Rekdal, *Intimate*, 94.

101 Rekdal, *Intimate*, 196.

102 Rekdal, *Intimate*, 198; emphasis in original.

103 Rekdal, *Intimate*, 201.

104 Rekdal, *Intimate*, 200.

105 Rekdal, *Intimate*, 94; emphasis in original.

106 Rekdal, *Intimate*, 196.

107 Rekdal, *Intimate*, 120; emphasis in original.

108 Rekdal, *Intimate*, 136.

109 Rekdal, *Intimate*, 142, 143.

110 See Garza, *Restless Dead*.

111 Rekdal, "Intimacy."

112 Min, *Unnamable*, 3.

113 Scrimgeour, "Inside Mark Zuckerberg's Top-Secret Hawaii Compound."

114 Sharma, *Hawaiʻi Is My Haven*.

CHAPTER 2. RACIAL RENOVATIONS

1 Third culture kids refer to children living in a culture different from one or both of their parents. See Pollock and Van Reken, *Third Culture Kids*; Mayberry, "Third Culture Kids"; Brara, "Finding a Place for Third-Culture Kids." For a study on multiracial Asian childhood, see Chang, *Raising Mixed Race*.

2 Cited by Alan Fern, in the foreword of Grove, *Isamu Noguchi*, viii.

3 Sueyoshi, *Queer Compulsions*, 13.

4 Ashton, *Noguchi*, 11.

5 Ashton, *Noguchi*, 11.

6 Noguchi, "Guggenheim Proposal," 17.

7 Housing and preserving his work, the museum and gardens stand on land first purchased by the artist in 1974. For more than a decade, beginning in 1961, Noguchi had been living and working in a studio across the street from that land.

8 Noguchi, *Isamu Noguchi Garden Museum*, 12.

9 Indeed, Asian/white and East/West are not the only dichotomies associated with the artist. The Smithsonian American Art Museum curated *Isamu Noguchi, Archaic/Modern (2016–2017)*. See Hart and Lemmey, *Isamu Noguchi*.

10 Meillier, "History of the Noguchi Museum," 2:34–2:41.
11 Meillier, "History of the Noguchi Museum," 2:45–3:28.
12 Herrera, *Listening to Stone*, 7–8.
13 Ghanayem, "Proactive Grief."
14 Ashton, *Noguchi*, 288.
15 Ashton, *Noguchi*, 288.
16 Altshuler, "Introduction," 59.
17 Ramos, *Unbelonging*, 2.
18 See Ceizyk and Adams, "Fixer-Upper Loans"; Giovanetti, "How to Finance a Fixer-Upper Home"; Warden, "6 Fixer-Upper Loans"; Wood, "Fixer-Upper Houses."
19 See Cummins, "Fast Furniture Is an Environmental Fiasco."
20 Outside of HGTV, in the early 1990s, the sitcom *Home Improvement* debuted starring Tim Allen, a father and "toolman" who was the host of the show *Tool Time*.
21 Tongson, *Normporn*.
22 Matthews, "These 'Fixer Upper' Features."
23 Overdeep, "Chip and Joanna's $10.4 Million."
24 His response is as follows: "Hi there Anna, Thanks so much for reaching out! Joanna is honored you thought of her. Unfortunately, the Gaines are not able to accommodate any additional requests during this time. Thanks again for thinking of her. Have a great rest of your week." Brock Murphy, "Request to Interview Joanna Gaines," email message to author, January 9, 2023. As it turns out, the days I was in Waco conducting research overlapped with when Joanna Gaines took herself and twenty-five members of her family to Seoul for a week. It was the first time Joanna had visited the country of her mother's birth, and she described the trip as feeling like being home: "For years, my mother talked about taking her three daughters to Seoul, South Korea, when the cherry blossoms are in full bloom." Remnants from Japanese imperial rule, the cherry blossoms may not have been in full bloom while the Gaineses visited Korea, as gathered from the photographs shared on social media, but their smiling faces are enough to convince any viewer that the trip proved meaningful in each family member's journey into the past. See Gaines, "From the Journal."
25 The first time Joanna's Korean heritage is alluded to was in the first season of the original *Fixer Upper*, at the 35:30 mark of episode 7, "Family Returning to Waco Craves Cowboy Charm for Fixer Upper," when Chip brings home a Little Caesars pizza for dinner and tells the kids to remove their shoes, "a Korean custom."
26 Gaines, *Stories We Tell*, 2.
27 Gaines, *Stories We Tell*, 3.
28 Gaines, *Stories We Tell*, 8.
29 Gaines, *Stories We Tell*, 20.
30 Examples abound of word "decor" in the Magnolia universe. One example takes place in season 1, episode 8, of the original *Fixer Upper*, when a sign with the words "Today is a good day to be a good day" appears at the 37:48 mark.
31 Gaines, *Stories We Tell*, 4.
32 Gaines, *Stories We Tell*, 5.

33 Gaines, *Stories We Tell*, 110.
34 Gaines, *Stories We Tell*, 43–44.
35 Gaines, *Stories We Tell*, 9.
36 Gaines, *Stories We Tell*, 15; emphasis in original; Barthes, *Mythologies*, 39; emphasis in original.
37 R. Brown, *For a "Christian America,"* 241.
38 Gaines, *Stories We Tell*, 171, 55.
39 Gaines, *Stories We Tell*, 65.
40 Storti, "Scenes of Hope, Acts of Despair."
41 Lorde, "Age, Race, Class and Sex," 114–23, 115.
42 Gaines, *Stories We Tell*, 174–75.
43 Gaines, *Stories We Tell*, 173–74.
44 Hemmings, *Why Stories Matter*.
45 Barthes, *Mythologies*, 39; emphasis in original.
46 Ho, *Racial Ambiguity*.
47 Gaines, *Stories We Tell*, 119.
48 Khokha and Lagos, "Writer and Activist Cherríe Moraga."
49 As of 2024, there are three volumes of the Magnolia cookbooks. Recipes include mostly American meals, with a steady diet of Mexican food, presumably due to Texas's proximity to Mexico, and some Asian dishes: summer rolls, chicken pho, kimchi, japchae, bibimbap, chicken fried rice, Mongolian beef. Some dishes are paired with short stories giving insight into Joanna's connection with the meal.
50 A notable case in opposition to this trend is Brina, *Speak, Okinawa*.
51 The dedication reads, "For my dad, You have always been one of my favorite people to cook for. Growing up, I loved making your lunches for work every day. You always brought home an empty lunch pail and praise for every last bite. Nowadays, it's a warm dinner or pan of fresh cinnamon rolls that I enjoy surprising you with, and then that picture you send when you've cleared the plate. My love for cooking has always been about the moments that unfold after the meal is made—the connection, the gift it is to nourish the people I care for—and that love took root with you. It will always be a great joy of mine to cook for you, Dad." See Gaines, *Magnolia Table*, vol. 3.
52 Perhaps Jerry is left to the margins because he was under investigation due to an alleged connection to a prostitution ring inside of a massage parlor Jerry had been said to frequent. See Giacomazzo, "Who Is Joanna Gaines' Father?"
53 A desire to look wasian is trending. Monoracial Asians and non-Asians alike are using makeup trends such as bold brows, colored contacts, and enhancing the undereye area, to appear visibly wasian. See General, "Growing Makeup Trend."
54 On April 27, 2024, Tom posted the following on Twitter: "you can tell when someone's gay? I can tell when they're wasian. that's wadar."
55 To many, including convicted former and, alas, second-termed President Donald Trump, whiteness stands in for knowledge and superiority. See a 2022 article by Taylor Ardrey in *Business Insider*, "Trump Once Told His Biracial Ex-Girlfriend that Her Intelligence Came 'from Her Dad, the White Side,' Book Claims."

56 See Kang, *Traffic in Asian Women*; and Bow, *Racist Love.*
57 Gaines, *Stories We Tell*, 6.
58 Belew, *Bring the War Home.*
59 Belew, *Bring the War Home*, 3.
60 According to the Waco, Texas Population, *World Population Review.*
61 Gaines, Gaines, and Dagostino, *Magnolia Story*, 54; emphasis in original.
62 Chaney, "Touring the Spectacle of Slavery," 138.
63 Chaney, "Touring the Spectacle of Slavery," 138.
64 Gaines, *Stories We Tell*, 13.
65 Gaines, *Stories We Tell.*
66 Gaines, *Stories We Tell*, 151.
67 For more on race and the home in reality TV, see Hageman, "Debt by Design."
68 Hageman, "Shiplap."
69 Hageman, "Creator's Statement—Shiplap"; emphasis in original.
70 Hageman, "Creator's Statement—Shiplap."
71 Frances, "Review of 'Shiplap.'"
72 Gaines, *Stories We Tell*, 181.
73 "The Cottonland Castle," Historical Landmark Marker, 1977.
74 "Castle Heights," Historical Landmark Marker, 2008.
75 See "Cottonland Castle."
76 Horton, "Do Chip and Joanna Gaines?"
77 Gaines, "The Castle."
78 Mehta, *Racism of People Who Love You*, 115.
79 Gaines, Gaines, and Dagostino, *Magnolia Story*, 8.
80 *Fixer Upper: The Castle*, "Episode 3: Story of Color," 4:17–4:42.
81 Bow, *Partly Colored*, 1–22.
82 E. Anderson, "White Space."
83 Iyamah, "Interior Race Theory," 13; emphasis mine.
84 hooks, "Homeplace (a Site of Resistance)"; Heneghan, *Whitewashing America*; Iyamah, "Interior Race Theory," 12.
85 Iyamah, "Interior Race Theory," 15.
86 Winfrey, "Chip and Joanna Gaines," 15:26–15:30.
87 Gaines, *Stories We Tell*, 49.
88 Brent, *Ideas of Order*, "Joanna Gaines," 18:34–19:00.
89 I borrow this phrasing from Ross, "Colonialism in the Décor."
90 Bennett, *Vibrant Matter.*
91 Stein, "Joanna Gaines Reveals."
92 B. Brown, *Sense of Things.*
93 B. Brown, "Thing Theory."
94 B. Brown, "Thing Theory," 4.
95 Magnolia, "History of the Old Church."
96 "The Old Church," Magnolia Silos Marker, September 2023.
97 Saegert, "Magnolia 'Deconstruction.'"
98 B. Brown, "Thing Theory," 3.

99 Magnolia, "History of the Old Church."
100 Hartman, "Venus in Two Acts." For a poignant engagement with the shadows of Jesse Washington's lynching, read the photo essay on Andscape written by a journalist who shares his name. See J. Washington, "Waco Horror."
101 Carrigan, *Making of a Lynching Culture.*
102 Mockett, *American Harvest*, 151.
103 Mockett, *American Harvest*, 23, 24.
104 Mockett, *American Harvest*, 367.
105 As described on his profile on the Center for Christian Counseling and Relationship Development's website.
106 Mockett, *American Harvest*, 29.
107 Mackinder, "Geographical Pivot of History."
108 Rundstrom, "Heartland."
109 H. Kim, *Race for Revival*, 4.
110 Baik, *Reencounters.*
111 See "Chapter 12: Getting to the Bottom" in Gaines, Gaines, and Dagostino, *Magnolia Story.*
112 Description taken from the "Restoration Gateway" page on Idealist.
113 "Missionaries Enlist Kids," season 1, episode 9, *Fixer Upper.*
114 Spargo, "Pastor Who Heads Church."
115 Gaines, Gaines, and Dagostino, *Magnolia Story*, 179, 101.
116 Jung, "Loyalty to Empire."

INTERLUDE. A RENDERING OF DESIRE

1 Honey, "Work."
2 Honey, "Architect."
3 Stoll, "Queertopias."
4 See V. Huang, *Surface Relations*; Min, *Unnamable*; and Storti, "Case for the Two-Dimensional."
5 Piepzna-Samarasinha, *Dirty River*, 143.

CHAPTER 3. THE HAPACALYPSE?

1 For more on rape as war crime and the legal definitions of sexual violence, see Jaleel, *Work of Rape.*
2 On December 14, 2015, Eurasian Tiger shared these thoughts on a post in the Hapa subreddit titled, "Why More and More Hapa/Half-Asian/Eurasian Criminals Is Inevitable; The Coming Hapacalypse."
3 One of Spencer's videos, "10 Things All Half Asians Know to Be True but Don't Want to Admit," is dedicated to Thomas Wagoner, a student at Arizona State University who took his own life on the first day of the spring 2016 semester, citing racial bullying in suicide notes.
4 Fulbeck, *Part Asian, 100% Hapa*, 262.

5 See Eng, *Racial Castration*; and T. Nguyen, *View from the Bottom*.

6 See J. Chen, *Trans Exploits*; and Fung, "Looking for My Penis."

7 Espiritu, *Body Counts*.

8 See Haley, *No Mercy Here*; and A. Ritchie, "Law Enforcement Violence." On the higher rates of police violence against Black women, see B. Ritchie, *Arrested Justice*. For an engagement with dominant narratives of exploitation, the connections between injury and pleasure, and Black female sexual expression, see Fleetwood, "The Case of Rihanna," 421.

9 On anti-carceral feminism, see Davis et al., *Abolition. Feminism. Now*.

10 See Moya Bailey, "They Aren't Talking About Me" and *Misogynoir Transformed*; and Cox, *Shapeshifters*, 6–7.

11 Perhaps one of the most successful acts of resistance against this trend is #SayHerName, developed by the African American Policy Forum. One of the founders of #SayHerName is Kimberlé Crenshaw, whose work on intersectionality structures the framework for the Say Her Name movement.

12 For a discussion of Holtzclaw's pattern of sexual assault and intimidation, see A. Ritchie, *Invisible No More*, 104–26. For a discussion of the relationship between criminalized sex work, police violence, and the risk of disclosing assault, including its relevance in the Holtzclaw case, see J. Rodríguez, "Pornographic Encounters and Interpretive Interventions."

13 See Taylor, "White Cop Convicted" and "Cop Used Whiteness"; Schmitz, "Daniel Holtzclaw Used Race"; and Wolf, "Daniel Holtzclaw."

14 See Patterson, "Oklahoma Cop Convicted"; Diaz et al., "Ex-Oklahoma City Cop"; Cross, "Daniel Holtzclaw"; and Arnold, "Who Is Daniel Holtzclaw?"

15 A group of students across more than one hundred college campuses organized and participated in a National Day of Action to Carry That Weight on October 29, 2014, where students carried mattresses in solidarity with Sulkowicz.

16 See Vivian Huang's discussion of Mattress Performance in chapter 2 of *Surface Relations*.

17 For work on the tradition of endurance art and art activism, see Madison, *Acts of Activism*; Rice, *Long Suffering*; Ruiz, *Ricanness*; and Shalson, *Performing Endurance*.

18 Kaminer, "Accusers and the Accused."

19 Kaminer, "Accusers and the Accused."

20 Holtzclaw Trial, "Daniel Holtzclaw Interrogation," 1:03:02–1:03:19.

21 Sexton, "People-of-Color-Blindness," 48.

22 Seulghee Lee, *Other Lovings*.

23 "What the Dash Cam Never Saw," *ABC 20/20*, May 6, 2016.

24 More than speculating, I would bet that the number of women Holtzclaw assaulted is higher than thirteen. In addition to threats, shame, and intimidation, one of the many hurdles faced by survivors, including the women Holtzclaw assaulted, is how quick the public or the defense may resort to accusations of false testimony or mischaracterized evidence.

25 In December 2017, Holtzclaw's attorneys applied for an appeal on the basis of insufficient evidence and improper procedure by grouping all thirty-six charges

together. The appeal was denied on August 1, 2019, in a unanimous opinion by the Oklahoma Court of Criminal Appeals.

26 For more on racial ambiguity in the context of Asian America, see Ho, *Racial Ambiguity*.

27 See Taylor, "Cop Used Whiteness"; and Schmitz, "Daniel Holtzclaw Used Race."

28 Harris, "Whiteness as Property," 1719.

29 C. Kim, *Asian Americans in an Anti-Black World*, 11.

30 Leroy, "Insurgency and Asian American Studies."

31 Sulkowicz, *Ceci N'est Pas Un Viol*.

32 Sulkowicz, *Ceci N'est Pas Un Viol*.

33 Saketopoulou, *Sexuality Beyond Consent*, 2.

34 Saketopoulou, *Sexuality Beyond Consent*, 3.

35 Sulkowicz, *Ceci N'est Pas Un Viol*; emphasis in original.

36 Armus, "Sulkowicz Films Herself."

37 Alptraum, "There Is Life After Campus Infamy."

38 Tarana Burke founded the Me Too movement when she first used the phrase "Me too" in 2006. The hashtag began to circulate virally in October 2017 following the sexual assault allegations against Weinstein.

39 V. Huang, *Surface Relations*, 70.

40 V. Huang, *Surface Relations*, 70.

41 Lye, *America's Asia*.

42 Holtzclaw Trial, "Daniel Holtzclaw Interrogation," 1:03:19–1:03:39.

43 Rivera, *Model Minority Masochism*.

44 Hong, *Death Beyond Disavowal*, 29.

45 Garcia-Navarro and Beltran, "Understanding Multiracial Whiteness."

46 For a sweeping portrayal of neoliberal multiculturalism, see Melamed, *Represent and Destroy*. On the neoliberal national imaginary, normativity, and the specific positioning of Asian Americans in suburbia, see Tongson, *Relocations*.

47 I must note that the cover of Miller's book references the art of kintsugi, which offers a meditation on the concept of *torn* that this book takes up. As written underneath Miller's author bio: "The gold veins on the cover represent the Japanese art of kintsugi, 'golden repair,' in which pieces of broken pottery are mended with powdered gold and lacquer, rather than treating the breaks as blemishes to conceal. The technique shows us that although an object cannot be returned to its original state, fragments can be made whole again."

48 A prominent example is Alek Minassian, the perpetrator of the 2018 Toronto van attack, who cited Rodger on a Facebook post shortly before the attack: "Private (Recruit) Minassian Infantry 00010, wishing to speak to Sgt 4chan please. C23249161. The Incel Rebellion has already begun! We will overthrow all the Chads and Stacys! All hail the Supreme Gentleman Elliot Rodger!"

49 Miller, *Know My Name*, 87.

50 Miller, *Know My Name*, 90.

51 Miller, *Know My Name*, 90–91; emphasis in original.

52 Miller, *Know My Name*, 91; emphasis in original.

53 Miller, *Know My Name*, 91.
54 Rodger, "Elliot Rodger's Retribution," 1:12–1:13, 0:45–0:50.
55 Rodger, "Elliot Rodger's Retribution," 1:28–2:03.
56 Rodger, "Elliot Rodger's Retribution," 0:37–0:39, 5:33–5:37.
57 Rodger, "Elliot Rodger's Retribution," 5:12–5:25.
58 Rodger, "Elliot Rodger's Retribution," 5:17–5:19.
59 Rodger, *My Twisted World*, 82; emphasis in original.
60 Rodger, *My Twisted World*, 117.
61 Doyle, *Campus Sex, Campus Security*.
62 Rodger, *My Twisted World*, 87.
63 Rodger, *My Twisted World*, 121; emphasis in original.
64 Rodger, *My Twisted World*, 90.
65 Rodger, *My Twisted World*, 84; emphasis in original.
66 Rodger, *My Twisted World*, 17.
67 See "Holden's Manifesto," *Law and Order: Special Victims Unit*, season 16, episode 4, aired October 15, 2014.
68 These descriptions appeared in news reporting. See "Rejected Brat," *Blacklisted*; Christien Kafton on *KTVU News* in May 2014; Kaplan, "Sheriff"; and Warren, "Elliot Rodger."
69 "The Secret Life of Elliot Rodger," ABC *20/20*.
70 "The Secret Life of Elliot Rodger," ABC *20/20*.
71 Here, I am referencing Chad Kultgen's 2007 novel *The Average American Male*.
72 See Allely and Faccini, "'Path to Intended Violence'"; Blake, "Global Mass Violence"; Blum and Jaworski, "From Suicide and Strain"; Brogaard, "Elliot Rodger's Narcissism"; Langman, "Elliot Rodger"; Murray, "Role of Sexual, Sadistic"; Vito, Admire, and Hughes, "Masculinity, Aggrieved Entitlement, and Violence."
73 Rodger, *My Twisted World*, 17.
74 Rodger, *My Twisted World*, 1, 99, 99; emphasis in original.
75 Rodger, *My Twisted World*, 137; emphasis in original.
76 I credit a PhD student for telling me about this performance after a talk I gave with the Duke/UNC Americanist series in October 2023.
77 Gansky, "In Performance."
78 Rodger, "Why Do Girls Hate Me So Much?"
79 Gansky, "In Performance."
80 Glass, "Jane Doe," 64:07–64:42.
81 When I presented about the Hapacalypse at the 2023 meeting of the Association of Asian American Studies, the room erupted in laughter upon hearing my description of the theory's premise.
82 Raymundo, "Monster Minority."
83 A. Liu, "MRAsians"; Tamai, "To Be Hybrid Anticipates the Future."
84 Bow, *Racist Love*, 200.
85 Bow, *Racist Love*, 158. As Bow unveils racist love as an anxiety transformed into pleasure, she invites speculation into the relationship between racialized desire, racial legibility, and racial abstraction, which, like abstraction in art, "refuses overt

references to material reality." In a footnote, Bow gives us a rundown of abstraction, pointing us toward Sianne Ngai's engagement with Leigh Claire Le Berge who suggests that abstraction is "a mode of nonfigurative representation." Then there is Phillip Brian Harper for whom abstraction denotes a "state of *withdrawal* from some originary point." But Bow is mostly aligned with Manthia Diawara's notion of transtextuality, which is about style. That is, as Bow writes, "abstracted through style, race is transportable as an associative sign system freed from the human body" (205n3).

86 One entry on Urban Dictionary defines the Hapacalypse as follows: "The post apocalyptic event that involves Eurasian kids who will gather up and rise up against their white supremacist fathers with Asian tiger mothers, who are also known as 'fetish couples' or WMAF's for short. . . . Mainly famous for the hapa forums on Reddit, sons and daughters of WMAF pairings will constantly bash and humiliate their hateful, racist, insecure, mentally ill, brainwashed, abusive parents online . . . but when given the chance they will band together and protest on the streets, annoying other WMAF fetish couples, who will eventually break up and fear the power of the Eurasian tigers."

87 A collection of his top videos on racism, white supremacy, and self-hate is available at https://www.reddit.com/r/hapas/comments/7xz8sv/collection_of_eurasian_tigers_top_youtube_videos/.

88 Red Pill Comics are available at https://imgur.com/a/odxAV and https://incels.wiki/w/Inceldom_comics.

89 There is speculation that he has left the United States because of the dating disparities, according to a comment on Reddit: "Asian guy on Eurasian Tiger's blog claims that he left USA because of seeing huge dating disparity. Is this the only solution left for other full Asian/Half Asian men to escape from emasculation/humiliation in the west???"

90 Bow, *Racist Love*, 34.

91 Bow, *Racist Love*, 67.

CHAPTER 4. RACIST INTIMACIES

A version of this chapter appears as "Racist Intimacies; or, The Femme Alter Ego and Her Retribution," *differences: A Journal of Feminist Cultural Studies* 35, no. 1 (2024): 97–133.

1 McGreal, "John Derbyshire Fired."

2 Kyle Chapman is the father of a mixed Asian son. His ex, Haley Ly, is an Asian woman. In July 2017, at Comic-Con, he was asked a question about his dating status and was quoted saying, "I'm single again. . . . We'll see what happens, Man. I'm new on the Market, so, we'll see what's crackin'. Definitely, uh, white Women, I think, are the most beautiful Women on Earth. So, that's most likely what's going to happen." See the page "Kyle Chapman" on *InfoMekka*. In 2022, Chapman was arrested for attacking health-care workers in Idaho. See Weill, "Former Proud Boy Leader."

3 For a study on Asian women who pursue Western men in order to fulfill what the global economy has long denied them, see M. Liu, *Seeking Western Men.*

4 Amy Chua, author of the controversial parenting memoir *Battle Hymn of the Tiger Mother* (2011), not only endorsed Donald Trump's Supreme Court nomination of Brett Kavanaugh even after allegations of sexual assault emerged against him but is also a mentor to J. D. Vance, who credited her influence on him in his memoir, *Hillbilly Elegy* (2016).

5 Lowe, *Intimacies of Four Continents.*

6 Bow, *Racist Love.*

7 Holland, *Erotic Life of Racism.*

8 Young, *Colonial Desire*, xii.

9 In the first chapter of *Colonial Desire*, Young offers a vignette on the prime meridian line in Greenwich Park, London, describing the area where the earth's longitude meets zero as "the centre of time itself" (1). For Young, the prime meridian separates the East from the West. To step with one foot on each side is to "become undecidably mixed with otherness: an Occidental and an Oriental at once" (1). Calling this geopolitical location the "cleavage of East and West," Young ties his study on colonial desire to the juncture where white meets other—that is, to the location where difference is made. That this London landmark defines time as we have come to understand it since the modern era suggests that time's coordinates are graphed onto the bodies who cross such lines delineating East from West.

10 See Marchetti, *Romance and the Yellow Peril*; Shimizu, *Hypersexuality of Race*; and Kang, *Compositional Subjects.*

11 Kang, *Compositional Subjects*, 71.

12 See Koshy, *Sexual Naturalization*, 3; and Nemoto, *Racing Romance*, 3–6.

13 See Gonzalez, *Empire's Mistress*; and Winkelmann, *Dangerous Intercourse.*

14 See Heinrich, *Race and Role*; Poulsen, "Writing Madame Butterfly's Child"; and Shaffer, "Choreographing Multiraciality."

15 See Lim, *Brown Boys and Rice Queens*; Han, *Racial Erotics*; and Marchetti, *Romance and the Yellow Peril.*

16 Govreau's alter ego is heavily influenced by Japanese music and MF Doom, one of the artist's favorite rappers who is known for embodying a slew of evil characters including King Ghidorah, a giant three-headed dragon hydra and famous kaiju (Japanese fictional monster) known as Godzilla's archenemy. Queen Gidrea is the queer and femme version of King Ghidorah, "a multi-headed golden dragon and merciless destroyer. She slants effortlessly through time slit constellations, blasting psychic/social ruptures into ancient and future civilizations. Rarely visible in the human spectrum, she is inherently evil." Govreau's Queen Gidrea is uninterested in a gentle redistribution of power. With a height of 150 meters and a wingspan of 175 meters, Queen Gidrea enacts revenge on those who hypersexualize her human form. Govreau fuses dark humor with femme opulence and often collaborates with martial artists, dancers, street artists, and photographers to create narratives of selfhood in photographic, video, and live installations. See Govreau, "Queen Gidrea."

17 See Halberstam, *Skin Shows*, 21; and Nakashima, "An Invisible Monster."
18 Chu, "Mixed Metaphor."
19 A shitagi is a kimono undergarment. To wear the shitagi alone is considered an illicit, inappropriate, and even culturally ignorant act, but it was precisely this forbidden quality that prompted Govreau to wear the undergarment during the performance. In their words, it is "plain, but intimate." Chanel Matsunami Govreau, "Permission to Use Image for Publication," email, September 23, 2023.
20 Govreau, *Requesting Access*, 0:06–0:28.
21 Govreau, *Requesting Access*, 0:34–1:04.
22 Govreau, personal interview.
23 These racialized and sexualized sentiments were not uncommon for Govreau to hear. In college, the artist had Japanese classmates who encouraged them to become an escort if they ever wanted to live in Japan. In their eyes, escorting would be a lucrative job for someone of mixed race. Their peers' reasoning was racist, believing that the artist could never be fully recognized in Japanese society because of their race. As Govreau explains, "Once again my value and money-making potential became directly linked to my mixed-race + sexual desirability." See Govreau, "Permission to Use Image for Publication."
24 Govreau, *Requesting Access*, 2:49.
25 Govreau, *Requesting Access*, 4:08–5:11.
26 Nishime, *Undercover Asians*.
27 Nishime, *Undercover Asians*, xv.
28 Nishime, *Undercover Asians*, xvii.
29 McKittrick, *Sylvia Wynter*, 3.
30 McKittrick, *Sylvia Wynter*, 3–4.
31 Benedicto, "Agents and Objects of Death," 275.
32 Benedicto, "Agents and Objects of Death," 276, 287.
33 Benedicto, "Agents and Objects of Death," 290.
34 Holland, *Erotic Life of Racism*, 7; Saketopoulou, "#Consentsowhite."
35 As of September 2023, Henry "Enrique" Tarrio, the former national chairman of the Proud Boys, was sentenced to twenty-two years in prison for charges related to the US Capitol breach on January 6, 2021, including seditious conspiracy. Other leaders of the Proud Boys, including Ethan Nordean, Joseph Biggs, Zachary Rehl, and Dominic Pezzola, were also sentenced. See "Proud Boys Leader." Upon returning to office in January 2025, President Trump pardoned all of the aforementioned Proud Boys.
36 Huynh, "Check Out Phung Huynh's Artwork."
37 See Ahmed's blog "Feminist Killjoys," www.feministkilljoys.com; and Ahmed, *Living a Feminist Life*.
38 Rivera, "Rocky's Revenge," 2018.
39 Chambers-Letson, *After the Party*, 5.
40 I borrow this phrasing from Vanita Reddy's presentation on "Feminist and Queer Afro-Asian Formations," University of Maryland, College Park.
41 Gómez-Barris, *Extractive Zone*, 9; Musser, *Sensual Excess*, 144.

42 Lorde, "The Uses of Anger."
43 J. Rodríguez, *Sexual Futures*, 7.
44 Butler, *Gender Trouble*, 200–201.
45 Musser, *Sensual Excess*, 4.
46 To be clear, feminist rage, though not at all novel, enjoyed a reawakening after the 2016 presidential inauguration of Donald Trump. In her 2018 book *Eloquent Rage*, academic and Crunk Feminist Collective cofounder Brittney Cooper articulates how contemporary Black women possess a powerful and "eloquent rage." In the same year, writer and activist Soraya Chemaly urged women to harness their anger as a means to enact transformative justice in her book *Rage Becomes Her*. In 2021, the feminist journal *Signs* published a special issue on "Rage," and Egyptian author Mona Eltahawy lists anger as one of the seven necessary sins women and girls ought to commit in order to survive in the twenty-first century. See Cooper, *Eloquent Rage*; Chemaly, *Rage Becomes Her*; Eltahawy, *Seven Necessary Sins*.
47 I credit an anonymous reviewer for directing my thinking to this point.
48 Muñoz, "Feeling Brown, Feeling Down," 676.
49 I credit another anonymous reviewer for directing my thinking to this point.
50 Chin and Chan, "Racist Love."
51 Chin et al., *Aiiieeeee!*
52 D. Kim, *Writing Manhood in Black and Yellow*.
53 Bow, *Racist Love*, 158.
54 Lowe, *Intimacies of Four Continents*, 19.
55 Bow, *Racist Love*, 173.
56 Mackrandilal, "How to Be a Monster."
57 Mackrandilal, "#NEWGLOBALMATRIARCHY."
58 This timing is relevant for another reason. Mackrandilal explained to me that she purchased the Confederate flag trunks on Amazon not too long before Bree Newsome climbed the South Carolina flagpole, angering and inciting white supremacists, which then drove Amazon to remove all items with the Confederate flag off its site. *How to Be a Monster* marks the end of an era when the public could purchase racist garb not yet considered threats by the corporate eye.
59 Stallings, *A Dirty South Manifesto*, 1.
60 Robinson, *Black Marxism*, 175.
61 See Lorde, "Uses of the Erotic"; Stallings, *Funk the Erotic*; Nash, *Black Body in Ecstasy*; and Miller-Young, *A Taste for Brown Sugar*.
62 McClintock, *Imperial Leather*, 139.
63 Amin, *Disturbing Attachments*, 80.
64 See A. Cruz, *The Color of Kink*; and Weiss, *Techniques of Pleasure*.
65 Holland, *Erotic Life of Racism*, 3; emphasis in original.
66 Holland, *Erotic Life of Racism*, 4; emphasis in original.
67 Holland, *Erotic Life of Racism*, 4; emphasis in original.
68 See Bow, *Partly Colored*; Day, *Alien Capital*; and C. Kim, "Racial Triangulation of Asian Americans."

69 Holland, *Erotic Life of Racism*, 6; emphasis in original.

70 Bow, *Racist Love*, 208n14.

71 Holland, *Erotic Life of Racism*, 9.

72 In an email exchange, Mackrandilal explains her interest in Phoolan Devi: "Female bandits were super rare, she might have been the only one at the time, I'm not sure. What occurred was that the leader of her bandit group, who was also her lover, was murdered and that group split along caste lines. The higher caste bandits in the group kidnapped her and brought her to the village where she was gangraped. The lower-caste members of her group (of similar caste to her) eventually rescued her. She then took that group, joined forces with another group, and they returned to the village—the bandits who had kidnapped her were not present, but all the men in the village were rounded up and shot by her group ostensibly as retribution for the rapes (she claims she did not give the order to kill them, but survivors of the massacre said that she did). I think the story holds a lot of resonance because caste-based sexual violence is so depressingly common in India, especially in rural areas, and the idea of a lower-caste woman exacting revenge for that violence was unheard of and I think captured a lot of people's imagination." See Mackrandilal, "Permission to Use Images for Publication."

73 Musser, *Sensual Excess*, 5, 9.

74 Muñoz, *Disidentifications*, 11.

75 Muñoz, *Sense of Brown*.

76 FEMelanin, *Bedtime Stories of White Supremacy*.

77 Mackrandilal, "Prologue."

78 Mackrandilal, "#NEWGLOBALMATRIARCHY: *Bedtime Stories of White Supremacy*."

79 Mackrandilal, "#NEWGLOBALMATRIARCHY: Performance and Poetry Circle."

80 Sharpe, *Monstrous Intimacies*.

81 Sharpe, *Monstrous Intimacies*, 3.

82 Sharpe, *Monstrous Intimacies*, 3.

83 Sharpe, *Monstrous Intimacies*, 3.

84 Sharpe, *Monstrous Intimacies*, 17, 4.

85 An exercise: Search Davis's quote in a web browser and scroll. Take note of the results. You will see that a range of entities—nonprofits, universities, community colleges, health departments, state departments, corporations, libraries, school districts, and more—have used this quote in their tool kits, statements of solidarity, and resource guides, showing (1) how compelling the phrase of anti-racism is and (2) how compatible the neoliberal interpretation of the quote (and not the radical politics of anti-racism) is with campaigns for diversity, equity, and inclusion. The quote, widely attributed to Davis, cannot be traced to a specific source, although it is said to have been spoken by her during a speech in the 1970s.

86 A Reddit post, "Updated: 2017 Full List of Neo-Nazis, Alt-Rights, Conservatives, White Supremacists Who Fetish/Marry/Date Asian Women," was uploaded in November 2016 by user eurasianlion.

87 hooks, "Eating the Other," 371.

1 See Arendt, *Origins of Totalitarianism*; Césaire, *Discourse on Colonialism*; and Foucault, "Society Must Be Defended."

2 Nye, "Torn Map."

3 See Lowe, *Intimacies of Four Continents*, 40–41, 163, 175.

4 On defection, think of Alfred Hitchcock's 1966 film *Torn Curtain*, a spy thriller set in the Cold War where an American physicist and double agent defects behind the Iron Curtain to East Berlin.

5 Nye, "No Explosions."

6 See Mullan, "What Is Decolonizing Therapy?"

7 Anzaldúa, *Borderlands/La Frontera*, 100.

8 Engels, "Letter to F. Mehring," 451; Berlant, *Cruel Optimism*, 1.

9 Muñoz, "Feeling Brown, Feeling Down."

10 Sedgwick, "Paranoid Reading and Reparative Reading."

11 Root, "Bill of Rights."

12 Ito, "Bill of Responsibilities."

13 Williams-León, "Off-White"; Seneviratne, *Wild Cinnamon and Winter Skin*.

14 See Jung, *Menace to Empire*, 25, 12.

15 To stay thinking of popular music in the millennial moment for just a second, we would recall that from the late 1990s to early 2000s, a number of songs were released with the title "Torn," suggesting that this project's concerns with the affliction and feeling of torn is tacked onto the very cultural moment in which it studies, the transition from the American century to the Asian century. See Natalie Imbruglia's 1997 electropop breakup hit "Torn," Creed's angsty 1997 metal rock track "Torn," and LeToya's 2006 R&B love song "Torn."

16 Vimalassery et al., "Colonial Unknowing," 1051.

17 See Vimalassery et al., "Colonial Unknowing," 1042, 1044; Bayoumi, "Our Work," 8; Chuh, *Difference Aesthetics Makes*, 129; and Lowe and Manjapra, "Comparative Global Humanities After Man."

18 Nozaki-Nasser, "Thresholds."

19 V. T. Nguyen, *Nothing Ever Dies*, 4.

20 Stepansky, "Israel's War on Gaza Updates."

21 See Said, *Question of Palestine*.

22 Srikanth, "Asian American Studies and Palestine," 146.

Bibliography

Abu-Lughod, Lila, Rema Hammami, and Nadera Shalhoub-Kevorkian, eds. *The Cunning of Gender Violence: Geopolitics and Feminism*. Durham, NC: Duke University Press, 2023.

Ahmed, Sara. *The Cultural Politics of Emotion*. London: Routledge, 2004.

Ahmed, Sara. *Living a Feminist Life*. Durham, NC: Duke University Press, 2017.

Ahmed, Sara. "A Phenomenology of Whiteness." *Feminist Theory* 8, no. 2 (2007): 149–68.

Ahmed, Sara. *The Promise of Happiness*. Durham, NC: Duke University Press, 2010.

Allely, Clare Sarah, and Lino Faccini. "'Path to Intended Violence' Model to Understand Mass Violence in the Case of Elliot Rodger." *Aggression and Violent Behavior* 37 (2017): 201–9.

"All Mixed Up: Half Asian, Half Caucasian, and 100% Cool. Why Eurasians Are the New Face of Asia." *Time* 157, no. 16 (2001).

Alptraum, Lux. "There Is Life After Campus Infamy." *New York Times*, July 21, 2018.

Althusser, Louis. "Ideology and Ideological State Apparatuses: Notes Towards an Investigation." In *Lenin and Philosophy and Other Essays*. New York: Monthly Review, 1972.

Altshuler, Bruce. "Introduction: On Gardens and Landscapes." In *Isamu Noguchi: Essays and Conversations*, edited by Diane Apostolos-Cappadona and Bruce Altshuler. New York: Abrams, 1994.

Amin, Kadji. *Disturbing Attachments: Genet, Modern Pederasty, and Queer History*. Durham, NC: Duke University Press, 2017.

Amin, Kadji, Amber Musser, and Roy Pérez. "Queer Form: Aesthetics, Race, and the Violences of the Social." *ASAP/Journal* 2, no. 2 (2017): 227–39.

Anderson, Carol. *White Rage: The Unspoken Truth of Our Racial Divide*. New York: Bloomsbury, 2016.

Anderson, Elijah. "The White Space." *Sociology of Race and Ethnicity* 1, no. 1 (2015): 10–21.

Anderson, Patrick. *So Much Wasted: Hunger, Performance, and the Morbidity of Resistance*. Durham, NC: Duke University Press, 2010.

Andrews, Kimberly Quiogue. *A Brief History of Fruit*. Akron, OH: University of Akron Press, 2020.

Anzaldúa, Gloria. *Borderlands/La Frontera: The New Mestiza*. San Francisco: Aunt Lute Press, 1987.

Appadurai, Arjun. "Grassroots Globalization and the Research Imagination." *Public Culture* 12, no. 1 (2000): 1–19.

Arendt, Hannah. *The Origins of Totalitarianism*. New York: Harcourt, Brace, Jovanovich, 1973.
Armus, Teo. "Sulkowicz Films Herself in a Violent Sex Scene for Newest Art Project." *Columbia Spectator*, June 5, 2015.
Arnold, Jeff. "Who Is Daniel Holtzclaw?" *SB Nation*, February 17, 2016.
Arrizón, Alicia. *Queering Mestizaje: Transculturation and Performance*. Ann Arbor: University of Michigan Press, 2006.
Arvin, Maile. *Possessing Polynesians: The Science of Settler Colonial Whiteness in Hawai'i and Oceania*. Durham, NC: Duke University Press, 2019.
Ashton, Dore. *Noguchi: East and West*. Berkeley: University of California Press, 1992.
Baik, Crystal Mun-hye. *Reencounters: On the Korean War and Diasporic Memory Critique*. Philadelphia: Temple University Press, 2020.
Bailey, Marlon. "Gender/Racial Realness: Theorizing the Gender System in Ballroom Culture." *Feminist Studies* 37, no. 2 (2011): 365–86.
Bailey, Moya. *Misogynoir Transformed: Black Women's Digital Resistance*. New York: New York University Press, 2021.
Bailey, Moya. "They Aren't Talking About Me . . ." *Crunk Feminist Collection*, March 4, 2010.
Balance, Christine Bacareza. "Notorious Kin: Filipino America Re-Imagines Andrew Cunanan." *Journal of Asian American Studies* 11, no. 1 (2008): 87–106.
Balance, Christine Bacareza. *Tropical Renditions: Making Musical Scenes in Filipino America*. Durham, NC: Duke University Press, 2016.
Balce, Nerissa. *Body Parts of Empire: Visual Abjection, Filipino Images, and the American Archive*. Ann Arbor: University of Michigan Press, 2016.
Barthes, Roland. *Camera Lucida: Reflections on Photography*. New York: Hill and Wang, 1982.
Barthes, Roland. *Mythologies*. Translated by Annette Lavers. New York: Noonday Press, 1957.
Bascara, Victor. *Model-Minority Imperialism*. Minneapolis: University of Minnesota Press, 2006.
Bayoumi, Moustafa. "Our Work Is of This World." *Amerasia* 31, no. 1 (2005): 6–9.
Belew, Kathleen. *Bring the War Home: The White Power Movement and Paramilitary America*. Cambridge, MA: Harvard University Press, 2018.
Benedicto, Bobby. "Agents and Objects of Death: Gay Murder, Boyfriend Twins, and Queer of Color Negativity." *GLQ: A Journal of Lesbian and Gay Studies* 25, no. 2 (2019): 273–96.
Bennett, Jane. *Vibrant Matter: A Political Ecology of Things*. Durham, NC: Duke University Press, 2010.
Berlant, Lauren. *Cruel Optimism*. Durham, NC: Duke University Press, 2011.
Berlant, Lauren. *The Female Complaint: The Unfinished Business of Sentimentality in American Culture*. Durham, NC: Duke University Press, 2008.
Berlant, Lauren. "Intimacy: A Special Issue." *Critical Inquiry* 24, no. 2 (1998): 281–88.
Berlant, Lauren, and Michael Warner. "Sex in Public." *Critical Inquiry* 24, no. 2 (1998): 547–66.

Beyer, Tamiko. *We Come Elemental*. Farmington, ME: Alice James Books, 2013.
Bhabha, Homi. "The Other Question: Stereotype, Discrimination, and the Discourse of Colonialism." In *The Location of Culture*. London: Routledge, 1994.
Blake, Felice. "Global Mass Violence: Examining Racial and Gendered Violence in the Twilight of Multiculturalism." *Ethnic and Racial Studies* 40, no. 14 (2017): 2615–33.
Blanco Borelli, Melissa. *She Is Cuba: A Genealogy of the Mulata Body*. New York: Oxford University Press, 2016.
Blum, Dinur, and Christian Gonzalez Jaworski. "From Suicide and Strain to Mass Murder." *Society* 53 (2016): 408–13.
Bost, Suzanne. *Mulattas and Mestizas: Representing Mixed Identities in the Americas, 1850–2000*. Athens: University of Georgia Press, 2005.
Bow, Leslie, ed. *Asian American Feminisms*. New York: Routledge, 2012.
Bow, Leslie. *Betrayal and Other Acts of Subversion: Feminism, Sexual Politics, Asian American Women's Literature*. Princeton, NJ: Princeton University Press, 2001.
Bow, Leslie. *Partly Colored: Asian Americans and Racial Anomaly in the Segregated South*. New York: New York University Press, 2010.
Bow, Leslie. *Racist Love: Asian Abstraction and the Pleasures of Fantasy*. Durham, NC: Duke University Press, 2022.
Brara, Noor. "Finding a Place for Third-Culture Kids in the Culture." *New York Times Style Magazine*, September 11, 2020.
Brina, Elizabeth Miki. *Speak, Okinawa*. New York: Knopf, 2021.
Brogaard, Berit. "Elliot Rodger's Narcissism." *Psychology Today*, June 4, 2014.
Brooks, Daphne. *Bodies in Dissent: Spectacular Performances of Race and Freedom, 1850–1910*. Durham, NC: Duke University Press, 2006.
Brown, Bill. *The Sense of Things: The Object Matter of American Literature*. Chicago: University of Chicago Press, 2003.
Brown, Bill. "Thing Theory." *Critical Inquiry* 28, no. 1 (2001): 1–22.
Brown, Kimberly Juanita. *Mortevivum: Photography and the Politics of the Visual*. Cambridge, MA: MIT Press, 2024.
Brown, Ruth Murray. *For a "Christian America": A History of the Religious Right*. New York: Prometheus Books, 2002.
Bruce, La Marr Jurelle. *How to Go Mad Without Losing Your Mind: Madness and Black Radical Creativity*. Durham, NC: Duke University Press, 2021.
Brydon, Diana. "The White Inuit Speaks: Contamination as Literary Strategy." In *Unhomely States: Theorizing English-Canadian Postcolonialism*, edited by Cynthia Sugars. Toronto: Broadview Press, 2004.
Buggs, Shantel Gabrieal, and Trevor Hoppe, eds. *Unsafe Words: Queering Consent in the #MeToo Era*. New Brunswick, NJ: Rutgers University Press, 2023.
Bui, Keva X. "Eugenic Ecologies of Herbicidal Warfare in the Vietnam War." *Journal of Asian American Studies* 26, no. 3 (2023): 315–37.
Bui, Keva X. "Objects of Warfare: Infrastructures of Race and Napalm in the Vietnam War." *Amerasia Journal* 47, no. 2 (2021): 299–313.
Butler, Judith. *Bodies that Matter: On the Discursive Limits of Sex*. New York: Routledge, 2011.

Butler, Judith. *The Force of Nonviolence: An Ethico-Political Bind*. New York: Verso, 2020.

Butler, Judith. *Gender Trouble: Feminism and the Subversion of Identity*. London: Routledge, 1990.

Cabico, Regie. "Love Letter from Andrew Cunanan." In *Take Out: Queer Writing from Asian Pacific America*, edited by Quang Bao and Hanya Yanagihara. New York: Asian American Writers Workshop and Temple University Press, 2000.

Calador, Jesa Marie. "Gwen Stefani: 'I Said, "My God, I'm Japanese."'" *Allure*, January 10, 2023.

Campt, Tina M. *Listening to Images*. Durham, NC: Duke University Press, 2017.

Carrigan, William D. *The Making of a Lynching Culture: Violence and Vigilantism in Central Texas, 1836–1916*. Champaign: University of Illinois Press, 2006.

Carter, Greg. *The United States of the United Races: A Utopian History of Racial Mixing*. New York: New York University Press, 2013.

Ceizyk, Denny, and Kurt Adams. "Fixer-Upper Loans: Best Options." *Lending Tree*, April 20, 2023.

Césaire, Aimé. *Discourse on Colonialism*. New York: Monthly Review Press, 2000.

Chambers-Letson, Joshua. *After the Party: A Manifesto for Queer of Color Life*. New York: New York University Press, 2018.

Chambers-Letson, Joshua Takano, and Elizabeth W. Son. "Performed Otherwise: The Political and Social Possibilities of Asian/American Performance." *Theater Survey* 54, no. 1 (2013): 131–39.

Chaney, Michael A. "Touring the Spectacle of Slavery at Magnolia Gardens Plantation." *Southern Quarterly* 40, no. 4 (2002): 126–40.

Chang, Sharon H. *Hapa Tales and Other Lies: A Mixed Race Memoir About the Hawai'i I Never Knew*. Seattle: Rising Song Press, 2018.

Chang, Sharon H. *Raising Mixed Race: Multiracial Asian Children in a Post-Racial World*. New York: Routledge, 2016.

Chee, Alexander. *How to Write an Autobiographical Novel*. Boston: Mariner Books, 2018.

Chemaly, Soraya. *Rage Becomes Her: The Power of Women's Anger*. New York: Atria Books, 2018.

Chen, Ching-In, Jai Dulani, and Leah Lakshmi Piepzna-Samarasinha, eds. *The Revolution Starts at Home: Confronting Intimate Violence Within Activist Communities*. New York: South End Press: 2011.

Chen, Jian Neo. *Trans Exploits: Trans of Color Cultures and Technologies in Movement*. Durham, NC: Duke University Press, 2019.

Chen, Mel. *Animacies: Biopolitics, Racial Mattering, and Queer Affect*. Durham, NC: Duke University Press, 2012.

Chen, Mel. *Intoxicated: Race, Disability, and Chemical Intimacy Across Empire*. Durham, NC: Duke University Press, 2023.

Cheng, Anne Anlin. *Ornamentalism*. New York: Oxford University Press, 2019.

Cheung-Miaw, Calvin. "The Fate of 'Shared Interests Among People of Color': Asian American Intellectuals and Access to Education in the Post-Bakke Era." *Journal of American History* 111, no. 1 (2024): 91–114.

Chin, Frank, and Jeffery Paul Chan, "Racist Love." In *Seeing Through Shuck*, edited by Richard Kostelanetz. New York: Ballantine, 1972.
Chin, Frank, Jeffery Paul Chan, Lawson Fusao Inada, and Shawn Hsu Wong, eds. *Aiiieeeee! An Anthology of Asian-American Writers*. Washington, DC: Howard University Press, 1974.
Cho, Grace M. *Haunting the Korean Diaspora: Shame, Secrecy, and the Forgotten War*. Minneapolis: University of Minnesota Press, 2008.
Cho, Grace M. *Tastes like War: A Memoir*. New York: Feminist Press, 2021.
Chong, Sylvia Shin Huey. *The Oriental Obscene: Violence and Racial Fantasies in the Vietnam Era*. Durham, NC: Duke University Press, 2011.
Chou, Elaine Hsieh. *Disorientation: A Novel*. New York: Penguin, 2022.
Choudhury, Athia N. "The Making of the American Calorie and the Metabolic Metrics of Empire." *Journal of Transnational American Studies* 13, no. 1 (2022): 15–44.
Choy, Catherine Ceniza. *Empire of Care: Nursing and Migration in Filipino American History*. Durham, NC: Duke University Press, 2003.
Chu, Andrea Long. "The Mixed Metaphor: Why Does the Half-Asian, Half-White Protagonist Make Us So Anxious?" *Vulture*, September 27, 2022.
Chuh, Kandace. *The Difference Aesthetics Makes: On the Humanities "After Man."* Durham, NC: Duke University Press, 2019.
Chuh, Kandace. *Imagine Otherwise: On Asian Americanist Critique*. Durham, NC: Duke University Press, 2003.
Chung, Kelly I. "The Defiant Still Worker: Ramiro Gomez and the Expressionism of Abstract Labor." *Women and Performance: a journal of feminist theory* 29, no. 1 (2019): 62–76.
Clough, Patricia Ticineto, and Jean Halley, eds. *The Affective Turn: Theorizing the Social*. Durham, NC: Duke University Press, 2007.
Collins, Patricia Hill. "Some Group Matters: Intersectionality, Situated Standpoints, and Black Feminist Thought." In *A Companion to African-American Philosophy*, edited by Tommy Lee Lott and John P. Pittman. Malden, MA: Wiley-Blackwell, 2003.
Cooper, Brittney. *Eloquent Rage: A Black Feminist Discovers Her Superpower*. New York: St. Martin's, 2018.
Coráñez Bolton, Sony. *Crip Colony: Mestizaje, US Imperialism, and the Queer Politics of Disability in the Philippines*. Durham, NC: Duke University Press, 2023.
"Cottonland Castle." Clio. Accessed May 20, 2024. https://theclio.com/entry/17237.
Cox, Aimee. *Shapeshifters: Black Girls and the Choreography of Citizenship*. Durham, NC: Duke University Press, 2015.
Crosby, Christina. *A Body Undone: Living on After Great Pain*. New York: New York University Press, 2015.
Cross, Robert Christopher. "Daniel Holtzclaw: Guilty Until Proven Innocent Part I." *Medium*, December 2017.
Cruz, Ariane. *The Color of Kink: Black Women, BDSM, and Pornography*. New York: New York University Press, 2016.
Cruz, Denise. *Transpacific Femininities: The Making of the Modern Filipina*. Durham, NC: Duke University Press, 2012.

Cuéllar, Jorge E. "Waterproofing the State: Migration, River-Borders, and Ecologies of Control." *Comparative American Studies: An International Journal* 18, no. 1 (2021): 59–74.

Cummins, Eleanor. "Fast Furniture Is an Environmental Fiasco." *New Republic*, January 14, 2020.

Cvetkovich, Ann. *An Archive of Feelings: Trauma, Sexuality, and Lesbian Public Cultures*. Durham, NC: Duke University Press, 2003.

Cvetkovich, Ann. *Depression: A Public Feeling*. Durham, NC: Duke University Press, 2012.

DaCosta, Kimberly McClain. *Making Multiracials: State, Family, and Market in the Redrawing of the Color Line*. Stanford, CA: Stanford University Press, 2007.

Dalmage, Heather M., ed. *The Politics of Multiracialism: Challenging Racial Thinking*. Albany: State University of New York Press, 2004.

Daniher, Colleen Kim. "Yella Gal: Eartha Kitt's Racial Modulations." *Women and Performance: a journal of feminist theory* 28, no. 1 (2018): 16–33.

Dariotis, Wei Ming. "Hapa: The Word of Power." Mixed Heritage Center Information and Resources for People of Mixed Heritage, 2007.

Dariotis, Wei Ming. "To Be 'Hapa' or Not to Be 'Hapa'": What to Name Mixed Asian Americans?" In *At 40 Asian American Studies @ San Francisco State*. San Francisco: College of Ethnic Studies, San Francisco State University, 2009.

David, Emmanuel. "The Sexual Fields of Empire: On the Ethnosexual Frontiers of Global Outsourcing." *Radical History Review* 2015, no. 123 (2015): 115–43.

Davis, Angela Y., Gina Dent, Erica R. Meiners, and Beth E. Richie. *Abolition. Feminism. Now.* Chicago: Haymarket Books, 2022.

Day, Iyko. *Alien Capital: Asian Racialization and the Logic of Settler Colonial Capitalism*. Durham, NC: Duke University Press, 2016.

de Lauretis, Teresa. *Alice Doesn't: Feminism, Semiotics, Cinema*. Bloomington: Indiana University Press, 1984.

De Rango-Adem, Adebe. *Other Tongues: Mixed Race Women Speak Out*. Toronto: Inanna Publications, 2010.

DiAngelo, Robin. *White Fragility: Why It's So Hard for White People to Talk About Racism*. Boston: Beacon, 2018.

Diaz, Josen Masangkay. *Postcolonial Configurations: Dictatorship, the Racial Cold War, and Filipino America*. Durham, NC: Duke University Press, 2023.

Diaz, Joseph, Eric M. Strauss, Susan Welsh, Lauren Effron, and Alexa Valiente. "Ex-Oklahoma City Cop Spending 263 Years in Prison for Rape and His Accusers Share Their Stories." *ABC News*, April 21, 2016.

Diggs, Taye, and Shane W. Evans. *Mixed Me!* New York: Feiwel and Friends, 2015.

Dixon, Ejeris, and Leah Lakshmi Piepzna-Samarasinha. *Beyond Survival: Strategies and Stories from the Transformative Justice Movement*. Chico, CA: AK Press, 2020.

Dolan, Jill. *Utopia in Performance: Finding Hope at the Theater*. Ann Arbor: University of Michigan Press, 2005.

Doolan, Yuri. "The Cold War Construction of the Amerasian, 1950–1982." *Diplomatic History* 46, no. 4 (2022): 782–807.

Doolan, Yuri. *The First Amerasians: Mixed Race Koreans from Camptowns to America.* New York: Oxford University Press, 2024.

Doyle, Jennifer. *Campus Sex, Campus Security.* Cambridge, MA: MIT Press, 2015.

Duggan, Lisa. *The Twilight of Equality? Neoliberalism, Cultural Politics, and the Attack on Democracy.* Boston: Beacon, 2003.

Edwards, Erica R. *The Other Side of Terror: Black Women and the Culture of US Empire.* New York: New York University Press, 2021.

Ehlers, Nadine, and Shiloh Krupar. *Deadly Biocultures: The Ethics of Life-Making.* Minneapolis: University of Minnesota Press, 2019.

Elam, Michele. *The Souls of Mixed Folk: Race, Politics, and Aesthetics in the New Millennium.* Stanford, CA: Stanford University Press, 2011.

Eltahawy, Mona. *The Seven Necessary Sins for Women and Girls.* Boston: Beacon, 2019.

Eng, David. "Colonial Object Relations." *Social Text* 34, no. 1 (2016): 1–19.

Eng, David. *The Feeling of Kinship: Queer Liberalism and the Racialization of Intimacy.* Durham, NC: Duke University Press, 2010.

Eng, David. *Racial Castration: Managing Masculinity in Asian America.* Durham, NC: Duke University Press, 2001.

Eng, David. "Reparations and the Human." *Columbia Journal of Gender and Law* 21, no. 2 (2011): 561–83.

Eng, David, and Shinhee Han. *Racial Melancholia, Racial Dissociation: On the Social and Psychic Lives of Asian Americans.* Durham, NC: Duke University Press, 2019.

Engels, Friedrich. "Letter to F. Mehring." In *Karl Marx and Friedrich Engels: Selected Works in Two Volumes, Volume II.* Moscow: Foreign Languages Publishing House, 1949.

Espiritu, Yen Le. *Body Counts: The Vietnam War and Militarized Refugees.* Berkeley: University of California Press, 2014.

Fanon, Frantz. *The Wretched of the Earth.* New York: Grove, 1961.

FBI. "Andrew Phillip Cunanan." Accessed December 17, 2024. https://vault.fbi.gov/andrew-phillip-cunanan/andrew-phillip-cunanan-part-01-of-01/view.

FEMelanin. *Bedtime Stories of White Supremacy*, February 10, 2016. https://issuu.com/mayamackrandilal/docs/bsws-publication.

Ferguson, Roderick. *Aberrations in Black: Toward a Queer of Color Critique.* Minneapolis: University of Minnesota Press, 2004.

Fern, Alan. Foreword to *Isamu Noguchi: Portrait Sculpture*, edited by Nancy Grove. Washington, DC: National Portrait Gallery, Smithsonian Institution, 1989.

Fleetwood, Nicole. "The Case of Rihanna: Erotic Violence and Black Female Desire." *African American Review* 45, no. 3 (2012): 419–35.

Fleetwood, Nicole. *Troubling Vision: Performance, Visuality, and Blackness.* Chicago: University of Chicago Press, 2011.

Foucault, Michel. "Society Must Be Defended." In *Security, Territory, Population: Lectures at the Collège de France 1977–1978.* London: Palgrave Macmillan, 2004.

Frances, Terri. "Review of 'Shiplap.'" *Journal of Videographic Film and Moving Image Studies* 9, no. 2 (2022).

Freeman, Elizabeth, ed. "Queer Temporalities." *GLQ* 13, no. 2–3 (2007).

Freeman, Elizabeth. *Time Binds: Queer Temporalities, Queer Histories*. Durham, NC: Duke University Press, 2010.

Fukaya, Michiyo. "The Stone House." In *A Fire Is Burning, It Is in Me: The Life and Writing of Michiyo Fukaya*, edited by Gwendolyn L. Shervington. Norwich, VT: New Victoria Publishers, 1996.

Fulbeck, Kip. *Part Asian, 100% Hapa*. San Francisco: Chronicle Books, 2006.

Funderburg, Lise. "The Changing Face of America." *National Geographic*, October 2013.

Fung, Richard. "Looking for My Penis: The Eroticized Asian in Gay Video Porn." In *How Do I Look? Queer Film and Video*, edited by *Bad Object-Choices*. Seattle: Bay Press, 1991.

Gaines, Chip, and Joanna Gaines. *Fixer Upper*. Season 1, episode 6, "Family Craves Urban Appeal." Aired May 22, 2014.

Gaines, Chip, and Joanna Gaines. *Fixer Upper*. Season 1, episode 8, "Single Mom Starts New Life with Fixer Upper." Aired June 5, 2014.

Gaines, Chip, and Joanna Gaines. *Fixer Upper*. Season 1, episode 9, "Missionaries' Retreat in Waco, Texas." Aired June 12, 2014.

Gaines, Chip, and Joanna Gaines. *Fixer Upper*. Season 1, episode 10, "Family Returning to Waco Craves Cowboy Charm for Fixer Upper." Aired May 29, 2014.

Gaines, Chip, and Joanna Gaines. *Fixer Upper: The Castle*. Season 1, episode 3, "Story of Color." Aired October 28, 2022.

Gaines, Chip, Joanna Gaines, and Mark Dagostino. *The Magnolia Story*. Nashville: W Publishing, 2016.

Gaines, Joanna. "The Castle: A Restoration Story." *Magnolia Blog*, July 15, 2022.

Gaines, Joanna. "From the Journal: Coming Home Again." *Magnolia Blog*, February 12, 2024.

Gaines, Joanna. *Magnolia Table, Volume 3*. New York: HarperCollins, 2023.

Gaines, Joanna. *The Stories We Tell: Every Piece of Your Story Matters*. New York: Harper Select, 2022.

Gansky, Ben. "In Performance: Royal Osiris Karaoke Ensemble's the Art of Luv (Part 1) at Under the Radar Festival's Incoming! Series." *Contemporary Performance*, January 12, 2015.

Garcia-Navarro, Lulu, and Cristina Beltran. "Understanding Multiracial Whiteness and Trump Supporters." NPR, January 24, 2021.

Garza, Cristina Rivera. *The Restless Dead: Necrowriting and Disappropriation*. Translated by Robin Myers. Nashville: Vanderbilt University Press, 2020.

General, Ryan. "Growing Makeup Trend Transforms Asian Faces to Appear 'Mixed Race.'" *NextShark*, October 19, 2023.

Ghanayem, Eman. "Proactive Grief: Palestinian Reflections on Death." *Meridians* 21, no. 2 (2022): 397–412.

Giacomazzo, Bernadette. "Who Is Joanna Gaines' Father? New Details on Jerry Stevens and His Role in an Alleged Prostitution Ring." *Your Tango*, May 3, 2019.

Gilmore, Ruth Wilson. *Golden Gulag: Prisons, Surplus, Crisis, and Opposition in Globalizing California*. Berkeley: University of California Press, 2007.

Giovanetti, Erika. "How to Finance a Fixer-Upper Home." *U.S. News*, April 17, 2024.
Glass, Ira. "Jane Doe." *This American Life*, May 26, 2023.
Gómez-Barris, Macarena. *The Extractive Zone: Social Ecologies and Decolonial Perspectives*. Durham, NC: Duke University Press, 2017.
Gonzalez, Vernadette Vicuña. *Empire's Mistress, Starring Isabel Rosario Cooper*. Durham, NC: Duke University Press, 2021.
Gonzalez, Vernadette Vicuña. *Securing Paradise: Tourism and Militarism in Hawai'i and the Philippines*. Durham, NC: Duke University Press, 2013.
Gopinath, Gayatri. *Impossible Desires: Queer Diasporas and South Asian Public Cultures*. Durham, NC: Duke University Press, 2005.
Gordon, Avery. *Ghostly Matters: Haunting and the Sociological Imagination*. Minneapolis: University of Minnesota Press, 1997.
Govreau, Chanel Matsunami. "Permission to Use Image for Publication." Email. September 23, 2023.
Govreau, Chanel Matsunami. Personal interview. April 30, 2019. Brooklyn, NY.
Govreau, Chanel Matsunami. "Queen Gidrea." Accessed April 30, 2019. https://queengidrea.com/about.php.
Govreau, Chanel Matsunami. *Requesting Access*. Video recording. Arts Lofts, Madison, WI, 2010.
Gramsci, Antonio. *Selections from the Prison Notebooks*. Edited by Quintin Hoare and Geoffrey Nowell Smith. New York: International Publications, 1997.
Griffiths, Gareth. "The Myth of Authenticity." In *The Post-Colonial Studies Reader*, edited by Bill Ashcroft, Gareth Griffiths, and Helen Tiffin. London: Routledge, 1995.
Grosz, Elizabeth. *Volatile Bodies: Toward a Corporeal Feminism*. Bloomington: Indiana University Press, 1994.
Grove, Nancy. *Isamu Noguchi: Portrait Sculpture*. Washington, DC: National Portrait Gallery, Smithsonian Institution, 1989.
Guevarra, Rudy P., Jr. *Becoming Mexipino: Multiethnic Identities and Communities in San Diego*. New Brunswick, NJ: Rutgers University Press, 2012.
Guillermo, Kawika. *Nimrods: A Fake-Punk Self-Hurt Anti-Memoir*. Durham, NC: Duke University Press, 2023.
Hageman, Eva C. "Creator's Statement—Shiplap." *Journal of Videographic Film and Moving Image Studies* 9, no. 2 (2022).
Hageman, Eva C. "Debt by Design: Race and Home Valorization on Reality TV." In *Racism Postrace*, edited by Roopali Mukherjee, Sarah Banet-Weiser, and Herman Gray. Durham, NC: Duke University Press, 2019.
Hageman, Eva C. "Shiplap." *Journal of Videographic Film and Moving Image Studies* 9, no. 2 (2022).
Halberstam, Jack. *In a Queer Time and Place: Transgender Bodies, Subcultural Lives*. New York: New York University Press, 2005.
Halberstam, Jack. *Skin Shows: Gothic Horror and the Technology of Monsters*. Durham, NC: Duke University Press, 1995.
Haley, Sarah. *No Mercy Here: Gender, Punishment, and the Making of Jim Crow Modernity*. Chapel Hill: University of North Carolina Press, 2016.

Hall, Lisa Kahaleole Chang. “Eating Salt.” In *Names We Call Home*, edited by Becky Thompson and Sangeeta Tyagi. New York: Routledge, 1996.
Hamad, Ruby. *White Tears/Brown Scars: How White Feminism Betrays Women of Color*. New York: Catapult, 2020.
Han, C. Winter. *Racial Erotics: Gay Men of Color, Sexual Racism, and the Politics of Desire*. Seattle: University of Washington Press, 2021.
“Hapa Issues Forum Records.” Online Archive of California. Accessed December 17, 2024. https://oac.cdlib.org/findaid/ark:/13030/c8sq93rd/.
Haraway, Donna. “Situated Knowledges: The Science Question in Feminism and the Privilege of Partial Perspective.” *Feminist Studies* 14, no. 3 (1988): 575–99.
Haritaworn, Jinthana. *The Biopolitics of Mixing: Thai Multiracialities and Haunted Ascendancies*. New York: Routledge, 2012.
Harris, Cheryl. “Whiteness as Property.” *Harvard Law Review* 106, no. 8 (1993): 1707–91.
Hart, Dakin, and Karen Lemmey, curators. *Isamu Noguchi, Archaic/Modern*. Washington, DC: Smithsonian American Art Museum, exhibited November 11, 2016–March 19, 2017.
Hartman, Saidiya. “Venus in Two Acts.” *Small Axe* 12, no. 2 (2008): 1–14.
Hartsock, Nancy C. M. “The Feminist Standpoint: Developing the Ground for a Specifically Feminist Historical Materialism.” In *Discovering Reality: Feminist Perspectives on Epistemology, Metaphysics, Methodology, and Philosophy of Science*, edited by Sandra Harding and Merrill B. Hintikka. Dordrecht: Springer, 1983.
Hasso, Frances. *Buried in the Red Dirt: Race, Reproduction, and Death in Modern Palestine*. Cambridge: Cambridge University Press, 2021.
Heinrich, Rena M. *Race and Role: The Mixed-Race Asian Experience in American Drama*. New Brunswick, NJ: Rutgers University Press, 2023.
Hemmings, Clare. *Why Stories Matter: The Political Grammar of Feminist Theory*. Durham, NC: Duke University Press, 2011.
Heneghan, Bridget T. *Whitewashing America: Material Culture and Race in the Antebellum Imagination*. Jackson: University Press of Mississippi, 2008.
Hennessy, Rosemary. *Profit and Pleasure: Sexual Identities in Late Capitalism*. New York: Routledge, 2000.
Herrera, Hayden. *Listening to Stone: The Art and Life of Isamu Noguchi*. New York: Farrar, Straus and Giroux, 2015.
Hirsch, Afua. “‘We Are All Mixed’: Henry Louis Gates Jr. on Race, Being Arrested and Working Towards America’s Redemption.” *Guardian*, March 10, 2024.
Ho, Jennifer Ann. *Racial Ambiguity in Asian American Culture*. New Brunswick, NJ: Rutgers University Press, 2015.
Hobart, Hi’ilei Julia Kawehipuaakahaopulani. *Cooling the Tropics: Ice, Indigeneity, and Hawaiian Refreshment*. Durham, NC: Duke University Press, 2022.
Hochberg, Gil Z. *Becoming Palestine: Toward an Archival Imagination of the Future*. Durham, NC: Duke University Press, 2021.
Hochberg, Gil Z. *Visual Occupations: Violence and Visibility in a Conflict Zone*. Durham, NC: Duke University Press, 2015.

Holland, Sharon Patricia. *The Erotic Life of Racism*. Durham, NC: Duke University Press, 2012.

Holtzclaw Trial. "Former Oklahoma City Police Officer Daniel Holtzclaw Interrogation Video (Complete)." YouTube, uploaded January 28, 2017.

Honey, Vanilla. "The Architect." Intimate Theaters. Accessed May 27, 2024. https://www.intimatetheaters.com/about.

Honey, Vanilla. "The Work." Intimate Theaters. Accessed May 27, 2024. https://www.intimatetheaters.com/work.

Hong, Grace Kyungwon. *Death Beyond Disavowal: The Impossible Politics of Difference*. Minneapolis: University of Minnesota Press, 2015.

Hong, Grace Kyungwon, and Roderick Ferguson. *Strange Affinities: The Gender and Racial Politics of Comparative Racialization*. Durham, NC: Duke University Press, 2011.

hooks, bell. "Eating the Other: Desire and Resistance." In *Black Looks: Race and Representation*. Boston: South End Press, 1992.

hooks, bell. "Homeplace (a Site of Resistance)." In *Yearning: Race, Gender, and Cultural Politics*. Boston: South End Press, 1990.

Horton, Maggie. "Do Chip and Joanna Gaines Still Own the 'Fixer Upper' Castle?" *Country Living*, April 6, 2024.

Huang, Mingwei. *Reconfiguring Racial Capitalism: South Africa in the Chinese Century*. Durham, NC: Duke University Press, 2024.

Huang, Vivian. *Surface Relations: Queer Forms of Inscrutability*. Durham, NC: Duke University Press, 2022.

Huang, Vivian L., and Summer Kim Lee. "Contingency Plans." *Women and Performance: a journal of feminist theory* 30, no. 1 (2020): 1–19.

Hu Pegues, Juliana. *Space-Time Colonialism: Alaska's Indigenous and Asian Entanglements*. Chapel Hill: University of North Carolina Press, 2021.

Huynh, Phung. "Check Out Phung Huynh's Artwork." *Voyage LA*, October 24, 2018.

Hyphen, no. 13 (2007).

Ifekwunigwe, Jayne O. *"Mixed Race" Studies: A Reader*. New York: Routledge, 2004.

INCITE! Women of Color Against Violence, ed. *Color of Violence: The INCITE! Anthology*. Durham, NC: Duke University Press, 2006.

Isaac, Allan Punzalan. *American Tropics: Articulating Filipino America*. Minneapolis: University of Minnesota Press, 2006.

Ito, Emi. "Bill of Responsibilities for Multiracial People of Color with Light Skin and White Passing Privilege." 2019.

Iyamah, Jacquelyn Ogorchukwu. "Interior Race Theory: Using Interior Objects to Resist Harmful Racial Conditioning." *Journal of Interior Design* 49, no. 1 (2024): 12–16.

Jaleel, Rana M. *The Work of Rape*. Durham, NC: Duke University Press, 2021.

Johnson, Akemi. "Who Gets to Be 'Hapa'?" *Code Switch: Race and Identity, Remixed*. NPR, August 8, 2016.

Jung, Moon-Ho. "Loyalty to Empire." *Journal of Asian American Studies* 26, no. 1 (2023): 1–9.

Jung, Moon-Ho. *Menace to Empire: Anticolonial Solidarities and the Transpacific Origins of the US Security State*. Berkeley: University of California Press, 2023.
Kaba, Mariame, and Shira Hassan, eds. *Fumbling Towards Repair: A Workbook for Community Accountability Facilitators*. Chico, CA: AK Press, 2019.
Kaeser, Gigi, and Peggy Gillespie. *Of Many Colors: Portraits of Multiracial Families*. Amherst: University of Massachusetts Press, 1997.
Kalman, Robert. *No Difference Between Them: The Black and White Portraits*. Self-published, 2009.
Kaminer, Ariel. "Accusers and the Accused, Crossing Paths at Columbia University." *New York Times*, December 21, 2014.
Kanesaka, Erica. "The Mixed-Race Fantasy Behind Kawaii Aesthetics." *Catapult*, January 17, 2023.
Kang, Laura Hyun Yi. *Compositional Subjects: Enfiguring Asian/American Women*. Durham, NC: Duke University Press, 2002.
Kang, Laura Hyun Yi. *Traffic in Asian Women*. Durham, NC: Duke University Press, 2020.
Kapadia, Ronak K. *Insurgent Aesthetics: Security and the Queer Life of the Forever War*. Durham, NC: Duke University Press, 2019.
Kaplan, Rebecca. "Sheriff: Elliot Rodger Long Concealed Mental Health Issues." *CBS News*, May 25, 2014.
Karuka, Manu. *Empire's Tracks: Indigenous Nations, Chinese Workers, and the Transcontinental Railroad*. Berkeley: University of California Press, 2019.
Kelly, Jennifer Lynn. *Invited to Witness: Solidarity Tourism Across Occupied Palestine*. Durham, NC: Duke University Press, 2023.
Kendi, Ibram X. *How to Be an Antiracist*. New York: One World, 2019.
Khokha, Sasha, and Marisa Lagos. "Writer and Activist Cherríe Moraga on Her 'Mixed Blood' Chicana Heritage, Skin Privilege and Embracing Discomfort." *KQED*, April 13, 2023.
Khubchandani, Kareem. *Decolonize Drag*. New York: OR Books, 2023.
Khubchandani, Kareem. *Ishtyle: Accenting Gay Indian Nightlife*. Ann Arbor: University of Michigan Press, 2006.
Kim, Claire Jean. *Asian Americans in an Anti-Black World*. New York: Cambridge University Press, 2023.
Kim, Claire Jean. "The Racial Triangulation of Asian Americans." *Politics and Society* 27, no. 1 (1999): 105–38.
Kim, Daniel Y. *Writing Manhood in Black and Yellow: Ralph Ellison, Frank Chin, and the Literary Politics of Identity*. Stanford, CA: Stanford University Press, 2005.
Kim, Helen Jin. *Race for Revival: How Cold War South Korea Shaped the American Evangelical Empire*. Oxford: Oxford University Press, 2022.
Kim, Jinah. *Postcolonial Grief: The Afterlives of the Pacific Wars in the Americas*. Durham, NC: Duke University Press, 2019.
Kim, Jodi. *Settler Garrison: Debt Imperialism, Militarism, and Transpacific Imaginaries*. Durham, NC: Duke University Press, 2022.
Kim, Ju Yon. *The Racial Mundane: Asian American Performance and the Embodied Everyday*. New York: New York University Press, 2015.

Kina, Laura, and Jan Christian Bernabe. *Queering Contemporary Asian American Art.* Seattle: University of Washington Press, 2017.

Kina, Laura, and Wei Ming Dariotis. *War Baby/Love Child: Mixed Race Asian American Art.* Seattle: University of Washington Press, 2013.

King, Nia. *Queer and Trans Artists of Color: Stories of Some of Our Lives.* Edited by Jessica Glennon-Zukoff and Terra Mikalson. Charleston, SC: CreateSpace, 2014.

King, Tiffany Lethabo. *The Black Shoals: Offshore Formations of Black and Native Studies.* Durham, NC: Duke University Press, 2019.

King-O'Riain, Rebecca Chiyoko. "Model Majority? The Struggle for Identity Among Multiracial Japanese Americans." In *The Politics of Multiracialism: Challenging Racial Thinking*, edited by Heather M. Dalmage. Albany: State University of New York Press, 2004.

King-O'Riain, Rebecca Chiyoko. "#Wasian Check: Remixing 'Asian + White' Multiraciality on TikTok." *Genealogy* 6, no. 2 (2022): 55.

King-O'Riain, Rebecca Chiyoko, Stephen Small, Minelle Mahtani, Miri Song, and Paul Spickard, eds. *Global Mixed Race.* New York: New York University Press, 2014.

Kondo, Dorinne. *Worldmaking: Race, Performance, and the Work of Creativity.* Durham, NC: Duke University Press, 2018.

Koshy, Susan. *Sexual Naturalization: Asian Americans and Miscegenation.* Stanford, CA: Stanford University Press, 2004.

Kristeva, Julia. *Powers of Horror: An Essay on Abjection.* New York: Columbia University Press, 1982.

Kuang, R. F. *Yellowface.* New York: William Morrow, 2023.

Kultgen, Chad. *The Average American Male: A Novel.* New York: Harper Perennial, 2007.

Langman, Peter. "Elliot Rodger: An Analysis." *Journal of Campus Behavioral Intervention* 2 (2014): 5–19.

Lee, Rachel. *The Exquisite Corpse of Asian America: Biopolitics, Biosociality, and Posthuman Ecologies.* New York: New York University Press, 2014.

Lee, Seulghee. *Other Lovings: An AfroAsian American Theory of Life.* Columbus: Ohio State University Press, 2025.

Lee, Summer Kim. "Staying In: Mitski, Ocean Vuong, and Asian American Asociality." *Social Text* 37, no. 1 (2019): 27–50.

León, Christina. "Forms of Opacity: Roaches, Blood, and Being Stuck in Xandra Ibarra's Corpus." *ASAP/Journal* 2, no. 2 (2017): 369–94.

Leroy, Justin. "Insurgency and Asian American Studies in the Time of Black Lives Matter." *Journal of Asian American Studies* 20, no. 2 (2017): 279–81.

Lim, Eng-Beng. *Brown Boys and Rice Queens: Spellbinding Performance in the Asias.* New York: New York University Press, 2006.

Liu, Angela. "MRAsians: A Convergence Between Asian American Hypermasculine Ethnonationalism and the Manosphere." *Journal of Asian American Studies* 24, no. 1 (2021): 93–112.

Liu, Monica. *Seeking Western Men: Email-Order Brides Under China's Global Rise.* Stanford, CA: Stanford University Press, 2022.

Lorde, Audre. "Age, Race, Class and Sex: Women Redefining Difference." In *Sister Outsider: Essays and Speeches*. Freedom, CA: Crossing Press, 1984.

Lorde, Audre. "The Uses of Anger: Women Responding to Racism." Keynote at *National Women's Studies Association Conference*, Storrs, CT, 1981.

Lorde, Audre. "Uses of the Erotic: The Erotic as Power." *Fourth Berkshire Conference on the History of Women*, Mount Holyoke College, August 25, 1978. Published as a pamphlet by Out & Out Books. Reprinted in Lorde, Audre. *Sister Outsider: Essays and Speeches*. Freedom, CA: Crossing Press, 1984.

Lothian, Alexis. *Old Futures: Speculative Fiction and Queer Possibility*. New York: New York University Press, 2018.

Love, Heather. *Feeling Backward: Loss and the Politics of Queer History*. Cambridge, MA: Harvard University Press, 2009.

Lowe, Lisa. *Immigrant Acts: On Asian American Cultural Politics*. Durham, NC: Duke University Press, 1996.

Lowe, Lisa. *The Intimacies of Four Continents*. Durham, NC: Duke University Press, 2015.

Lowe, Lisa, and Kris Manjapra. "Comparative Global Humanities After Man: Alternatives to the Coloniality of Knowledge." *Theory, Culture and Society* 36, no. 5 (2019): 23–48.

Lye, Colleen. *America's Asia: Racial Form and American Literature*. Princeton, NJ: Princeton University Press, 2005.

Mackinder, Halford. "The Geographical Pivot of History." In *Democratic Ideals and Reality*. Washington, DC: National Defense University Press, 1996.

Mackrandilal, Maya. "How to Be a Monster." Dangerous Women Project, September 6, 2016. https://dangerouswomenproject.org/2016/09/06/how-to-be-a-monster/.

Mackrandilal, Maya. "#NEWGLOBALMATRIARCHY." Accessed December 17, 2024. https://mayamackrandilal.com/section/456314-NEWGLOBALMATRIARCHY.html.

Mackrandilal, Maya. "#NEWGLOBALMATRIARCHY: *Bedtime Stories of White Supremacy*." 2015. https://mayamackrandilal.com/section/436470-Bedtime-Stories-of-White-Supremacy.html.

Mackrandilal, Maya. "#NEWGLOBALMATRIARCHY: Performance and Poetry Circle." Accessed December 17, 2024. https://mayamackrandilal.com/section/483714-NGM-Performance-and-Poetry-Circle.html.

Mackrandilal, Maya. "Permission to Use Images for Publication." Email, October 9, 2023.

Mackrandilal, Maya. "Prologue: #NEWGLOBALMATRIARCHY; *Bedtime Stories of White Supremacy*." 2015. https://mayamackrandilal.com/artwork/4015026-Production%20Photo-%20Devis%20at%20the%20door.html.

Madison, D. Soyini. *Acts of Activism: Human Rights as Radical Performance*. New York: Cambridge University Press, 2010.

Magnolia. "The History of the Old Church." *Magnolia Blog*, September 21, 2020.

Mahtani, Minelle. *Mixed Race Amnesia: Resisting the Romanticization of Multiraciality*. Vancouver: University of British Columbia Press, 2014.

Maira, Sunaina Marr. *Missing: Youth, Citizenship, and Empire After 9/11*. Durham, NC: Duke University Press, 2009.

Manalansan, Martin F., IV. *Global Divas: Filipino Gay Men in the Diaspora*. Durham, NC: Duke University Press, 2003.

Mani, Lata. "Multiple Mediations: Feminist Scholarship in the Age of Multinational Reception." *Feminist Review* 35 (1990): 24–41.

Mannur, Anita. "Matter Out of Place: The Legacy of Strange Encounters in Asian American Studies." *Journal of Interculture Studies* 42, no. 1 (2021): 114–26.

Marchetti, Gina. *Romance and the Yellow Peril: Race, Sex, and Discursive Strategies in Hollywood*. Berkeley: University of California Press, 1994.

Matias, Cheryl E. *Feeling White: Whiteness, Emotionality, and Education*. Leiden: Sense, 2016.

Matthews, Lyndsey. "These 'Fixer Upper' Features Can Make Your Home More Valuable." *House Beautiful*, May 4, 2018.

Maurer, Anaïs. *The Ocean on Fire: Pacific Stories from Nuclear Survivors and Climate Activists*. Durham, NC: Duke University Press, 2024.

Mayberry, Kate. "Third Culture Kids: Citizens of Everywhere and Nowhere." BBC, November 18, 2016.

McClintock, Anne. *Imperial Leather: Race, Gender and Sexuality in the Colonial Contest*. London: Routledge, 1995.

McCormack, Donna. *Queer Postcolonial Narratives and the Ethics of Witnessing*. New York: Bloomsbury, 2014.

McGreal, Chris. "John Derbyshire Fired for Article Urging Children to Avoid African Americans." *Guardian*, April 8, 2012.

McKittrick, Katherine, ed. *Sylvia Wynter: On Being Human as Praxis*. Durham, NC: Duke University Press, 2015.

McMaster, James. "Revolting Self-Care: Mark Aguhar's Virtual Separatism." *American Quarterly* 72, no. 1 (2020): 181–205.

McMillan, Uri. *Embodied Avatars: Genealogies of Black Feminist Art and Performance*. New York: New York University Press, 2015.

McSorley, Kevin. *War and the Body: Militarisation, Practice and Experience*. New York: Routledge, 2015.

Mehta, Samira K. *The Racism of People Who Love You: Essays on Mixed Race Belonging*. Boston: Beacon, 2023.

Meillier, Alex. "History of the Noguchi Museum." Produced by Ager Meillier Films Inc. Narration by Brett Littman. Footage from *Isamu Noguchi*, directed by Michael Blackwood, 1972.

Melamed, Jodi. *Represent and Destroy: Rationalizing Violence in the New Racial Capitalism*. Minneapolis: University of Minnesota Press, 2011.

Mendoza, Victor Román. *Metroimperial Intimacies: Fantasy, Racial-Sexual Governance, and the Philippines in U.S. Imperialism, 1899–1913*. Durham, NC: Duke University Press, 2015.

Mengesha, Lilian G., and Lakshmi Padmanabhan. "Performing Refusal/Refusing to Perform." *Women and Performance: a journal of feminist theory* 29, no. 1 (2019): 1–8.

Miller, Chanel. *Know My Name: A Memoir*. New York: Viking, 2019.

Miller-Young, Mireille. *A Taste for Brown Sugar: Black Women in Pornography*. Durham, NC: Duke University Press, 2014.

Min, Susette. *Unnamable: The Ends of Asian American Art*. New York: New York University Press, 2018.

Mitchell, Jasmine. *Imagining the Mulatta: Blackness in U.S. and Brazilian Media*. Urbana: University of Illinois Press, 2020.

Mockett, Marie Mutsuki. *American Harvest: God, Country, and Farming in the Heartland*. Minneapolis: Graywolf, 2020.

Moraga, Cherríe. "The Breakdown of the Bicultural Mind." In *Names We Call Home*, edited by Becky Thompson and Sangeeta Tyagi. New York: Routledge, 1996.

Mullan, Jennifer. *Decolonizing Therapy: Oppression, Historical Trauma, and Politicizing Your Practice*. New York: Norton, 2023.

Mullan, Jennifer. "What Is Decolonizing Therapy?" *Decolonizing Therapy*. Accessed June 8, 2024. https://www.decolonizingtherapy.com/what-is-dt.

Muñoz, José Esteban. *Cruising Utopia: The Then and There of Queer Futurity*. New York: New York University Press, 2009.

Muñoz, José Esteban. *Disidentifications: Queers of Color and the Performance of Politics*. Minneapolis: University of Minnesota Press, 1999.

Muñoz, José Esteban. "Feeling Brown, Feeling Down: Latina Affect, the Performativity of Race, and the Depressive Position." *Signs: Journal of Women in Culture and Society* 31, no. 3 (2006): 675–88.

Muñoz, José Esteban. *The Sense of Brown*. Edited by Joshua Chambers-Letson and Tavia Nyong'o. Durham, NC: Duke University Press, 2020.

Murphy-Shigematsu, Stephen, ed. *When Half Is Whole: Multiethnic Asian American Identities*. Stanford, CA: Stanford University Press, 2012.

Murray, Jennifer L. "The Role of Sexual, Sadistic, and Misogynistic Fantasy in Mass and Serial Killing." *Deviant Behavior* 38, no. 7 (2017): 735–43.

Musser, Amber Jamilla. *Sensational Flesh: Race, Power, and Masochism*. New York: New York University Press, 2014.

Musser, Amber Jamilla. *Sensual Excess: Queer Femininity and Brown Jouissance*. New York: New York University Press, 2018.

Nakashima, Cynthia. "An Invisible Monster: The Creation and Denial of Mixed-Race People in America." In *Racially Mixed People in America*, edited by Maria P. P. Root. Thousand Oaks, CA: Sage, 1992.

Nakashima, Cynthia. "Servants of Culture: The Symbolic Role of Mixed-Race Asians in American Discourse." In *Mixed-Race Studies: A Reader*, edited by Jayne O. Ifekwunigwe. New York: Routledge, 2004.

Nash, Jennifer C. *The Black Body in Ecstasy: Reading Race, Reading Pornography*. Durham, NC: Duke University Press, 2014.

Nemoto, Kumiko. *Racing Romance: Love, Power, and Desire Among Asian American/White Couples*. New Brunswick, NJ: Rutgers University Press, 2009.

"The New Face of America: How Immigrants Are Shaping the World's First Multicultural Society." *Time* 142, no. 21 (1993).

Ngô, Fiona I. B. *Imperial Blues: Geographies of Race and Sex in Jazz Age New York.* Durham, NC: Duke University Press, 2014.

Nguyen, Tan Hoang. *A View from the Bottom: Asian American Masculinity and Sexual Representation.* Durham, NC: Duke University Press, 2014.

Nguyen, Viet Thanh. *Nothing Ever Dies: Vietnam and the Memory of War.* Cambridge, MA: Harvard University Press, 2016.

Nguyen, Viet Thanh. *The Sympathizer.* New York: Grove, 2015.

Ninh, erin Khuê, and Shireen Roshanravan, eds. "#WeToo." *Journal of Asian American Studies* 24, no. 1 (2021).

Nishime, LeiLani. *Undercover Asians: Multiracial Asian Americans in Visual Culture.* Urbana: University of Illinois Press, 2014.

Noguchi, Isamu. "Guggenheim Proposal." In *Isamu Noguchi: Essays and Conversations,* edited by Diane Apostolos-Cappadona and Bruce Altshuler. New York: Abrams, 1994.

Noguchi, Isamu. *The Isamu Noguchi Garden Museum.* New York: Abrams, 1987.

Nopper, Tamara K., and Eve Zelickson. "Wellness Capitalism." *Data and Society* (2023).

Nozaki-Nasser, Bianca. "Thresholds." In *In These Times.* Exhibition. LA Art Core, September 9–23, 2022.

Nye, Naomi Shihab. "No Explosions." In *The Tiny Journalist: Poems.* Rochester, NY: BOA Editions, 2019.

Nye, Naomi Shihab. "Torn Map." In *Come with Me: Poems for a Journey.* New York: Greenwillow Books, 2000.

Nyong'o, Tavia. *The Amalgamation Waltz: Race, Performance, and the Ruses of Memory.* Minneapolis: University of Minnesota Press, 2009.

O'Hearn, Claudine Chiawei, ed. *Half and Half: Writers on Growing Up Biracial and Bicultural.* New York: Pantheon Books, 1998.

Omi, Michael, and Howard Winant. *Racial Formation in the United States: From the 1960s to the 1990s.* 2nd ed. New York: Routledge, 1994.

Orth, Maureen. "The Killer's Trail." *Vanity Fair,* September 1997.

Orth, Maureen. *Vulgar Favors: The Assassination of Gianni Versace.* New York: Bantam, 1999.

Overdeep, Meghan. "Chip and Joanna's $10.4 Million Magnolia Market Expansion Includes Relocating a Historic Church." AOL, June 21, 2019.

Oz, Shola, and Shifa Annisa. *I Am Whole: A Multi-Racial Children's Book Celebrating Diversity, Language, Race and Culture.* New York: Nielsen, 2020.

Palumbo-Lio, David. *Asian/American: Historical Crossings of a Racial Frontier.* Stanford, CA: Stanford University Press, 1999.

Pascoe, Peggy. *What Comes Naturally: Miscegenation Law and the Making of Race in America.* New York: Oxford University Press, 2009.

Patterson, Brandon E. "Oklahoma Cop Convicted of Raping Four Black Women and Assaulting Four Others." *Mother Jones,* December 11, 2015.

Pauline Gumbs, Alexis. Foreword to *Beyond Survival: Strategies and Stories from the Transformative Justice Movement,* edited by Leah Lakshmi Piepzna-Samarasinha and Ejeris Dixon. Chico, CA: AK Press, 2020.

Pérez, Hiram. *A Taste for Brown Bodies: Gay Modernity and Cosmopolitan Desire*. New York: New York University Press, 2015.

Pérez, Laura E. *Chicana Art: The Politics of Spiritual and Aesthetic Altarities*. Durham, NC: Duke University Press, 2007.

Pérez, Roy. "Proximity: On the Work of Mark Aguhar." In *Trap Door: Trans Cultural Production and the Politics of Visibility*, edited by Johanna Burton, Reina Gossett, and Eric Stanley. Cambridge, MA: MIT Press, 2017.

Perry, Tony, and Judy Pasternak. "Cunanan Doesn't Fit Serial Killer Mold." *Los Angeles Times*, July 20, 1997.

Pfluger, Ryan. *Holding Space: Life and Love Through a Queer Lens*. New York: Princeton Architectural Press, 2022.

Piepzna-Samarasinha, Leah Lakshmi. *Dirty River: A Queer Femme of Color Dreaming Her Way Home*. Vancouver: Arsenal Pulp Press, 2015.

Pollock, David C., and Ruth E. Van Reken. *Third Culture Kids: Growing Up Among Worlds*. Rev. ed. Boston: Nicholas Brealey America, 2009.

Ponce, Martin. *Beyond the Nation: Diaspora Filipino Literature and Queer Reading*. New York: New York University Press, 2012.

Ponce De León, Jennifer. *Another Aesthetics Is Possible: Arts of Rebellion in the Fourth World War*. Durham, NC: Duke University Press, 2021.

Porzuki, Nina. "How the Hawaiian Word 'Hapa' Came to Be Used by People of Mixed Heritage." *The World*, September 15, 2015.

Poulsen, Melissa Eriko. "Writing Madame Butterfly's Child: Japonisme and Mixed Race in Winnifred Eaton's 'A Half Caste.'" *Amerasia Journal* 43, no. 2 (2017): 158–75.

Prins, Harald E. L. "Coming to Light: Edward S. Curtis and the North American Indians." *American Anthropologist* 102, no. 4 (2000).

"Proud Boys Leader Sentenced to Twenty-Two Years in Prison for Seditious Conspiracy and Other Charges Related to U.S. Capitol Breach." Office of Public Affairs, US Department of Justice, September 5, 2023.

Puar, Jasbir K. *The Right to Maim: Debility, Capacity, Disability*. Durham, NC: Duke University Press, 2017.

Puar, Jasbir K. *Terrorist Assemblages: Homonationalism in Queer Times*. Durham, NC: Duke University Press, 2007.

Rabin, Nicole Myoshi. "Excursus on 'Hapa'; or the Fate of Identity." *Asian American Literature: Discourses and Pedagogies* 3 (2012): 119–29.

Rafael, Vicente L. *White Love and Other Events in Filipino History*. Durham, NC: Duke University Press, 2000.

Ramos, Iván A. *Unbelonging: Inauthentic Sounds in Mexican and Latinx Aesthetics*. New York: New York University Press, 2023.

Raymundo, Emily. "The Monster Minority: John Yoo's Multicultural Instruction and the 'Torture Memos.'" *Review of International American Studies* 15, no. 1 (2022): 31–49.

Reddy, Chandan. *Freedom with Violence: Race, Sexuality, and the US State*. Durham, NC: Duke University Press, 2011.

Reddy, Vanita. "Feminist and Queer Afro-Asian Formations." Presentation in *Reimagining Everything: Women of Color Feminisms, Art, Culture, and the Humanities Symposium*, University of Maryland, College Park, September 16, 2016.

Reed, T. V. *The Art of Protest: Culture and Activism from the Civil Rights Movement to the Streets of Seattle*. Minneapolis: University of Minnesota Press, 2005.

"Rejected Brat Goes on Killing Spree Because Girls Didn't Like Him." *Blacklisted News*, May 24, 2014.

Rekdal, Paisley. *Appropriate: A Provocation*. New York: Norton, 2021.

Rekdal, Paisley. "Intimacy." In *Animal Eye*. Pittsburgh: University of Pittsburgh Press, 2012.

Rekdal, Paisley. *Intimate: An American Family Photo Album*. North Adams, MA: Tupelo Press, 2011.

Rice, Karen Gonzalez. *Long Suffering: American Endurance Art as Prophetic Witness*. Ann Arbor: University of Michigan Press, 2016.

Rico, Brittany, Paul Jacobs, and Alli Coritz. "2020 Census Shows Increase in Multiracial Population in All Age Categories." United States Census Bureau, June 1, 2023.

Ritchie, Andrea J. *Invisible No More: Police Violence Against Black Women and Women of Color*. Boston: Beacon, 2017.

Ritchie, Andrea J. "Law Enforcement Violence Against Women of Color." In *Color of Violence: The INCITE! Anthology*, edited by INCITE! Women of Color Against Violence. Durham, NC: Duke University Press, 2016.

Ritchie, Beth E. *Arrested Justice: Black Women, Violence, and America's Prison Nation*. New York: New York University Press, 2012.

Rivera, Takeo. *Model Minority Masochism: Performing the Cultural Politics of Asian American Masculinity*. New York: Oxford University Press, 2022.

Robinson, Cedric J. *Black Marxism: The Making of the Black Radical Tradition*. Chapel Hill: University of North Carolina Press, 1983.

Rodger, Elliot. "Elliot Rodger's Retribution." YouTube, uploaded May 23, 2014.

Rodger, Elliot. *My Twisted World*. Accessed August 15, 2019. https://www.documentcloud.org/documents/1173808-elliot-rodger-manifesto/.

Rodger, Elliot. "Why Do Girls Hate Me So Much?" YouTube, uploaded May 22, 2014.

Rodríguez, Dylan. *Suspended Apocalypse: White Supremacy, Genocide, and the Filipino Condition*. Minneapolis: University of Minnesota Press, 2010.

Rodríguez, Juana María. "Pornographic Encounters and Interpretive Interventions: *Vanessa del Rio: Fifty Years of Slightly Slutty Behavior*." *Women and Performance: a journal of feminist theory* 25, no. 3 (2015): 315–35.

Rodríguez, Juana María. *Sexual Futures, Queer Gestures, and Other Latina Longings*. New York: New York University Press, 2014.

Roh, David S., Betsy Huang, and Greta A. Niu, eds. *Techno-Orientalism: Imagining Asia in Speculative Fiction, History, and Media*. New Brunswick, NJ: Rutgers University Press, 2015.

Rondilla, Joanne L., Rudy P. Guevarra, and Paul Spickard, eds. *Red and Yellow, Black and Brown: Decentering Whiteness in Mixed Race Studies*. New Brunswick, NJ: Rutgers University Press, 2017.

Root, Maria P. P. "Bill of Rights for People of Mixed Heritage." In *The Multiracial Experience: Racial Borders as the New Frontier*. Thousand Oaks, CA: Sage, 1995.

Root, Maria P. P. *Racially Mixed People in America*. Thousand Oaks, CA: Sage, 1992.

Ross, Elliot. "Colonialism in the Décor: We Can't Keep Sweeping the Past Under the Leopard Skin Rug." *Correspondent*, November 14, 2019.

Ruiz, Sandra. "El Caribe on the Horizon: José Esteban Muñoz and the Commitment to Futurity." *Small Axe: A Caribbean Journal of Criticism* 19, no. 2. (2015): 94–103.

Ruiz, Sandra. *Ricanness: Enduring Time in Anticolonial Performance*. New York: New York University Press, 2019.

Ruiz, Sandra. "Waiting in the Seat of Sensation: The Brown Existentialism of Ryan Rivera." *Women and Performance: a journal of feminist theory* 25, no. 3 (2015): 336–52.

Rundstrom, Robert. "Heartland." In *The American Midwest: An Interpretive Encyclopedia*, edited by Richard Sisson, Christian Zacher, and Andrew Cayton. Bloomington: Indiana University Press, 2006.

Saegert, Rhiannon. "Magnolia 'Deconstruction' of Historic Church Draws Preservationist Criticism." *Waco Tribune-Herald*, March 3, 2020.

Said, Edward. *Orientalism*. New York: Pantheon, 1978.

Said, Edward. *The Question of Palestine*. New York: Times Books, 1979.

Saketopoulou, Avgi. "#Consentsowhite: On the Erotics of Slave Play in 'Slave Play.'" *Los Angeles Review of Books*, January 10, 2020.

Saketopoulou, Avgi. *Sexuality Beyond Consent: Risk, Race, and Traumatophilia*. New York: New York University Press, 2023.

Saldaña-Portillo, María Josefina. *The Revolutionary Imagination in the Americas and the Age of Development*. Durham, NC: Duke University Press, 2003.

Saldanha, Arun. "Reontologising Race: The Machinic Geography of Phenotype." *Environment and Planning D: Society and Space* 24, no. 1 (2006): 9–24.

Saranillio, Dean Itsuji. *Unsustainable Empire: Alternative Histories of Hawai'i Statehood*. Durham, NC: Duke University Press, 2018.

Saraswati, L. Ayu. *Scarred: A Feminist Journey Through Pain*. New York: New York University Press, 2023.

Schalk, Sami. *Bodyminds Reimagined: (Dis)ability, Race, and Gender in Black Women's Speculative Fiction*. Durham, NC: Duke University Press, 2018.

Schmitz, Melanie. "Daniel Holtzclaw Used Race to Bully His Victims into Submission and His Victims Know Exactly Why." *Bustle*, December 11, 2015.

Scott, Joan W. "The Evidence of Experience." *Critical Inquiry* 17, no. 4 (1991): 773–97.

Scrimgeour, Guthrie. "Inside Mark Zuckerberg's Top-Secret Hawaii Compound." *Wired*, December 14, 2023.

"The Secret Life of Elliot Rodger." ABC *20/20*, June 27, 2014.

Sedgwick, Eve Kosofsky. "Paranoid Reading and Reparative Reading, or, You're So Paranoid You Probably Think This Essay Is About You." In *Touching Feeling: Affect, Pedagogy, Performativity*. Durham, NC: Duke University Press, 2002.

Sedgwick, Eve Kosofsky. *Touching Feeling: Affect, Pedagogy, Performativity*. Durham, NC: Duke University Press, 2002.

Seneviratne, Seni. *Wild Cinnamon and Winter Skin*. Leeds: Peepal Tress Press, 2007.

Sexton, Jared. *Amalgamation Schemes: Antiblackness and the Critique of Multiracialism.* Minneapolis: University of Minnesota Press, 2008.

Sexton, Jared. "People-of-Color-Blindness: Notes on the Afterlife of Slavery." *Social Text* 28, no. 2 (2010): 31–56.

Shaffer, Miya. "Choreographing Multiraciality: Mixed-Race Methods in North American Contemporary Dance." *Arts* 13, no. 1 (2024): 1–6.

Shah, Nayan. *Stranger Intimacy: Contesting Race, Sexuality and the Law in the North American West.* Oakland: University of California Press, 2011.

Shalson, Lara. *Performing Endurance: Art and Politics Since 1960.* New York: Cambridge University Press, 2018.

Sharma, Nitasha. *Hawai'i Is My Haven: Race and Indigeneity in the Black Pacific.* Durham, NC: Duke University Press, 2021.

Sharpe, Christina. *In the Wake: On Blackness and Being.* Durham, NC: Duke University Press, 2016.

Sharpe, Christina. *Monstrous Intimacies: Making Post-Slavery Subjects.* Durham, NC: Duke University Press, 2010.

Shiao, Jiannbin Lee. "The Meaning of Honorary Whiteness for Asian Americans: Boundary Expansion or Something Else?" *Comparative Sociology* 16 (2017): 788–813.

Shimakawa, Karen. *National Abjection: The Asian American Body Onstage.* Durham, NC: Duke University Press, 2002.

Shimizu, Celine Parreñas. *The Hypersexuality of Race: Performing Asian/American Women on Screen and Scene.* Durham, NC: Duke University Press, 2007.

Shohat, Ella, and Robert Sham. *Unthinking Eurocentrism: Multiculturalism and the Media.* London: Routledge, 1994.

Shomali, Medjulene Bernard. *Between Banat: Queer Arab Critique and Transnational Arab Archives.* Durham, NC: Duke University Press, 2023.

Singh, Julietta. *No Archive Will Restore You.* New York: Punctum Books, 2018.

Singh, Julietta. *Unthinking Mastery: Dehumanism and Decolonial Entanglements.* Durham, NC: Duke University Press, 2018.

Somerville, Siobhan. *Queering the Color Line: Race and the Invention of Homosexuality in American Culture.* Durham, NC: Duke University Press, 2000.

Son, Elizabeth. *Embodied Reckonings: "Comfort Women," Performance, and Transpacific Redress.* Ann Arbor: University of Michigan Press, 2018.

Sontag, Susan. *On Photography.* New York: Farrar, Straus and Giroux, 1977.

Spade, Dean. *Normal Life: Administrative Violence, Critical Trans Politics, and the Limits of Law.* Durham, NC: Duke University Press, 2011.

Spargo, Chris. "Pastor Who Heads Church of Fixer Upper Stars Chip and Joanna Gaines Doubles Down on Anti-Gay Beliefs While Saying He Is Being Vilified for Being Against Same-Sex Marriage." *Daily Mail,* December 7, 2016.

Spickard, Paul. Afterword to *Part Asian, 100% Hapa.* San Francisco: Chronicle Books, 2006.

Spillers, Hortense. "Mama's Baby, Papa's Maybe: An American Grammar Book." *Diacritics* 17, no. 2 (1987): 65–81.

Srikanth, Rajini. “Asian American Studies and Palestine: The Accidental and Reluctant Pioneer.” In *Flashpoints for Asian American Studies*, edited by Cathy Schlund-Vials. New York: Fordham University Press, 2017.

Stallings, L. H. *A Dirty South Manifesto: Sexual Resistance and Imagination in the New South.* Berkeley: University of California Press, 2020.

Stallings, L. H. *Funk the Erotic: Transaesthetics and Black Sexual Cultures.* Urbana: University of Illinois Press, 2015.

Stein, Megan. “Joanna Gaines Reveals the One Thing She Can’t Live Without (and It’s Not What You Think).” *Yahoo! Entertainment*, May 5, 2017.

Stepansky, Joseph. “Israel’s War on Gaza Updates: Israeli Attacks Kill 25 Overnight in Gaza.” *Al Jazeera*, January 15, 2024.

Stoler, Ann Laura. *Duress: Imperial Durabilities in Our Times.* Durham, NC: Duke University Press, 2016.

Stoler, Ann Laura. *Haunted by Empire: Geographies of Intimacy in North American History.* Durham, NC: Duke University Press, 2006.

Stoler, Ann Laura, ed. *Imperial Debris: On Ruins and Ruination.* Durham, NC: Duke University Press, 2013.

Stoll, Emma. “Queertopias: Spaces of Belonging, Simulated Control, + Inclusive Pleasure.” BArch thesis, Syracuse University, 2018.

Storti, Anna M. Moncada. “A Case for the Two-Dimensional: Balinese Dance, Colonial Shadows, and Feeling Otherwise with Zavé Martohardjono.” *Asian Diasporic Visual Cultures and the Americas* 7 (2021): 267–92.

Storti, Anna M. Moncada. “Half and Both: On Color and Subject/Object Tactility.” *Women and Performance: a journal of feminist theory* 30, no. 1 (2020): 104–12.

Storti, Anna M. Moncada. “Racist Intimacies; or, The Femme Alter Ego and Her Retribution,” *differences: A Journal of Feminist Cultural Studies* 35, no. 1 (2024): 97–133.

Storti, Anna M. Moncada. “Scenes of Hope, Acts of Despair: Deidealizing Hybridity in Saya Woolfalk’s World of the Empathics.” *Frontiers: A Journal of Women Studies* 41, no. 3 (2020): 147–77.

Stuelke, Patricia. *The Ruse of Repair: US Neoliberal Empire and the Turn from Critique.* Durham, NC: Duke University Press, 2021.

Sueyoshi, Amy. *Queer Compulsions: Race, Nation, and Sexuality in the Affairs of Yone Noguchi.* Honolulu: University of Hawaiʻi Press, 2012.

Sulkowicz, Emma. *Ceci N’est Pas Un Viol.* June 3, 2015.

Sundstrom, Ronald R. *The Browning of America and the Evasion of Social Justice.* Albany: State University of New York Press, 2008.

Tadiar, Neferti X. M. *Remaindered Life.* Durham, NC: Duke University Press, 2022.

Tamai, Lily Anne Welty. “To Be Hybrid Anticipates the Future: Multiracial and Multiethnic Community and Activism.” *Journal of Asian American Studies* 25, no. 2 (2022): 229–46.

Tauber, Mike, and Pamela Singh. *Blended Nation: Portraits and Interviews of Mixed-Race America.* New York: Channel Photographics, 2009.

Taylor, Goldie. “Cop Used Whiteness as His Weapon to Rape Black Women.” *Daily Beast*, December 11, 2015.

Taylor, Goldie. "White Cop Convicted of Serial Rape of Black Women." *Daily Beast*, December 10, 2015.
Teng, Emma Jinhua. *Eurasian: Mixed Identities in the United States, China, and Hong Kong, 1842–1943*. Berkeley: University of California Press, 2013.
Thomas, Evan. "Facing Death." *Newsweek*, July 27, 1997.
"Tiger Woods on Being a Black Golfer on the PGA Tour." *Oprah Winfrey Show*, April 24, 1997.
Tompkins, Kyla Wazana. *Racial Indigestion: Eating Bodies in the 19th Century*. New York: New York University Press, 2012.
Tongson, Karen. *Normporn: Queer Viewers and the TV that Soothes Us*. New York: New York University Press, 2023.
Tongson, Karen. *Relocations: Queer Suburban Imaginaries*. New York: New York University Press, 2011.
Trask, Haunani Kay. "The Color of Violence." *Social Justice* 31, no. 4 (2004): 8–16.
Troeung, Y-Dang. *Landbridge: Life in Fragments*. Durham, NC: Duke University Press, 2024.
Tsing, Anna, Heather Swanson, Elaine Gan, and Nils Bubandt, eds. *Arts of Living on a Damaged Planet*. Minneapolis: University of Minnesota Press, 2017.
Vasconcelos, José. *The Cosmic Race/La raza cósmica*. Baltimore: Johns Hopkins University Press, 1997.
Villanueva, Alma. "Photographing Mixed-Raced Bodies: An Artistic and Scientific Visual Culture." PhD diss., Texas A&M University, 2023.
Vimalassery, Manu, Juliana Hu Pegues, and Alyosha Goldstein. "Colonial Unknowing and Relations of Study." *Theory and Event* 20, no. 4 (2017): 1042–54.
Vito, Christopher, Amanda Admire, and Elizabeth Hughes. "Masculinity, Aggrieved Entitlement, and Violence: Considering the Isla Vista Mass Shooting." *NORMA: International Journal for Masculinity Studies* 13, no. 2 (2018): 86–102.
Vuong, Ocean. *On Earth We're Briefly Gorgeous*. New York: Penguin, 2019.
Waldman, Katy. "The White Poet Who Used an Asian Pseudonym to Get Published Is a Cheater, Not a Crusader." *Slate*, September 7, 2015.
Warden, Peter. "6 Fixer-Upper Loans: How to Buy a Fixer-Upper Home in 2024." *Mortgage Reports*, January 2, 2024.
Warner, Michael. "Introduction: Fear of a Queer Planet." *Social Text* 29 (1991): 3–17.
Warren, Christina. "Elliot Rodger: Portrait of a Lonely Outcast Obsessed with Status." *Mashable*, May 25, 2014.
Washington, Jesse. "The Waco Horror." Andscape. Accessed May 20, 2024. https://andscape.com/features/the-waco-horror/.
Washington, Myra S. *Blasian Invasion: Racial Mixing in the Celebrity Industrial Complex*. Jackson: University Press of Mississippi, 2017.
Weheliye, Alexander G. *Habeas Viscus: Racializing Assemblages, Biopolitics, and Black Feminist Theories of the Human*. Durham, NC: Duke University Press, 2014.
Weill, Kelly. "Former Proud Boy Leader 'Based Stickman' Arrested for Attacking Health Care Workers." *Daily Beast*, January 12, 2022.

Weiss, Margot. *Techniques of Pleasure: BDSM and the Circuits of Sexuality.* Durham, NC: Duke University Press, 2011.

"What the Dash Cam Never Saw." ABC *20/20*, May 6, 2016.

Wiegman, Robyn. *Object Lessons.* Durham, NC: Duke University Press, 2012.

Wiegman, Robyn. "The Times We're In: Queer Feminist Criticism and the Reparative 'Turn.'" *Feminist Theory* 15, no. 1 (2014): 4–25.

Williams, Patricia. *The Alchemy of Race and Rights.* Cambridge, MA: Harvard University Press, 1992.

Williams, Raymond. *Marxism and Literature.* New York: Oxford University Press, 2009.

Williams-León, Teresa. "Off-White." In *Intersecting Circles: The Voices of Hapa Women in Poetry and Prose,* edited by Marie Hara and Nora Okja Keller. Honolulu: Bamboo Ridge Press, 1999.

Williams-León, Teresa, and Cynthia L. Nakashima, eds. *The Sum of Our Parts: Mixed-Heritage Asian Americans.* Philadelphia: Temple University Press, 2001.

Winfrey, Oprah. "Chip and Joanna Gaines." *Super Soul Sunday,* November 14, 2021.

Winkelmann, Tessa. *Dangerous Intercourse: Gender and Interracial Relations in the American Colonial Philippines, 1898–1946.* Ithaca, NY: Cornell University Press, 2023.

Wolf, Brotha. "Daniel Holtzclaw: Rapist Cop, Black Victims, and White Jury." *Intersection of Madness and Reality,* November 7, 2015.

Wolfson, Roberta. "'A Man of Two Faces and Two Minds': Just Memory and Metatextuality in *The Sympathizer*'s Rewriting of the Vietnam War." *College Literature* 50, no. 1 (2023): 57–86.

Wood, Kate. "Fixer-Upper Houses: What Home Shoppers Should Know." *Nerd Wallet,* February 13, 2024.

Yao, Xine. *Disaffected: The Cultural Politics of Unfeeling in Nineteenth-Century America.* Durham, NC: Duke University Press, 2021.

Yip, Randall. "Biracial Asians Viewed More Favorable, Study Concludes." *AsAmNews,* April 10, 2024.

Young, Robert. *Colonial Desire: Hybridity in Theory, Culture and Race.* London: Routledge, 1995.

Zauner, Michelle. *Crying in H Mart: A Memoir.* New York: Knopf, 2021.

Zimmern, Kirsteen. *The Eurasian Face.* Hong Kong: Blacksmith Books, 2011.

Index

Page numbers in italics refer to figures.